CW01024814

Metropolitan World Atlas

Metropolitan World Atlas

Arjen van Susteren

010 Publishers, Rotterdam 2007

Metropolitan World Atlas *7*
Arjen van Susteren

101 Metropolitan areas

World comparison of metropolitan data

Metropolitan World Atlas

What is a metropolis or more specifically a metropolitan area? Everyone has some spatial idea of the term, just as they do with the term 'architecture'. Since these individual spatial interpretations are often highly diverse as well as difficult to compare, the term 'metropolitan area' is hard to define objectively, let alone put in a spatial context.

The term 'metropolitan area' does seem to express a clearly urban concept for everyone: the superlative of the city. However, it leaves a few questions unanswered, such as: What does a metropolitan area look like? How big is a metropolitan area? What kind of spatial configuration does it have? And what are its physical characteristics? Some sources in the literature define a metropolitan area as a city with more than a million inhabitants. However, given the thousands of cities which now satisfy this criterion, this definition is unworkable. Apparently the term 'metropolitan area' implies a certain rare quality.

A metropolitan area can be considered as an urban region or conurbation with a global range of influence. In other words, a metropolitan area is a city with a global impact, an area where global relationships dominate over local ones. A metropolitan area is sensitive to world developments and also contributes to them.

When the world (the globe) and a metropolitan area are closely interrelated, global connections are needed to help metropolitan areas influence the world and each other. We have therefore chosen to define the term in the following way: Metropolitan areas are regions where global relationships dominate over local ones and which are characterised spatially by a high concentration of global connections and a high concentration of people.

A historical review of the populations of metropolitan areas over the centuries reveals that metropolitan areas have flourished and declined at various points in history and have thereby come to typify different eras and civilisations. It is nonetheless remarkable to find that 'the metropolitan area' seems to be a temporary spatial concept, and on the broad scale of time and space it is for this very reason that it seems to typify the various historical periods.

The beginning of what was to become today's global network of metropolitan areas came at the end of the fifteenth century with the arrival of the first intercontinental trade routes. Among other things, this 'innovation' resulted in the development of a global network of international navigation routes, stimulating the growth of the first worldwide trade flows in the course of the sixteenth century. On 20 March 1602, for example, the Dutch East India Company, a joint venture by several urban Dutch trading companies dealing in exotic products all over the world, was founded in the Netherlands. Some cities experienced rapid growth as a result of the worldwide connections offered by these new commercial opportunities.

Since the trade and transport networks of the time consisted primarily of water-based infrastructures, delta landscapes were attractive regions for settlement and trade. A delta area is defined as a low-lying, flat, sometimes triangular landscape where a river branches out before joining the sea. This junction of salt and fresh water connects the global network of seas and oceans (salt water) with the trade and transport network of canals and rivers (fresh water) – a physical configuration that has made a major contribution to the historical development of trade and transport.

These networks were not significantly expanded until the nineteenth century, as a result of various technological innovations. The first of these was the introduction of the telegraph. Until then, people, commodities, capital and information were all transported at the same speed. A message, for example, would be carried by a courier and the answer came back the same way, perhaps with a different courier. The introduction of the telegraph meant that the speed at which information (and later capital) was transported no longer depended on how fast a person could travel. A difference now arose between the speeds of transporting mass (people and goods) and data (capital and information), which had previously been the same.

The advent of the telegraph had far-reaching consequences for world communications and trade. One of them was the need for a global time system, in the interests of world commerce. The US-led International Meridian Conference was therefore convened in October 1884, and Greenwich Mean Time was established by delegates from 25 different countries by a majority of 22 to 1 (San Domingo voted against, and France and Brazil abstained). From that moment on, the world was divided into the 24 time zones which together form our 24-hour day, and the 'prime meridian' was defined as passing through the English borough of Greenwich.

Halfway through the nineteenth century, the telegraph network was growing slowly but surely into a full-fledged worldwide network, thanks among other things to the laying of the first transatlantic telegraph cable by Cyrus Field. This cable, financed by British private investors, created a worldwide telegraph and telephone network alongside the 300-year-old global network of water routes, that would eventually evolve into today's network of telecommunications, TV, the Internet, e-mail and so on.

In the same period, a new network was being introduced at a more local level – the railway network. Among other things, this considerably increased accessibility both within regions and between cities and the countryside. Cities that introduced an underground railway system during this period soon began to be known as 'metropolises'. In Paris, this was clearly reflected in Hector Guimard's 1899 design for the station entrances ('*Le Métropolitain*').

In the early twentieth century, two more technical innovations in transport were introduced within a short period: the car and the aeroplane. Both of these soon became accessible to a large portion of the population, with tremendous consequences for spatial development at both local and global level. In particular, the introduction of the 'Model T' Ford in 1908 brought great social, infrastructural and economic change. Ford's strategy was to achieve a lower price for the consumer through mass production. The idea worked, and by 1910 Ford assembly lines were turning out more than 25,000 Model T's every month. Its low price quickly brought the Model T within the reach of the American middle classes, increasing the mobility of much of the population. A parallel development occurred a few years later across the Atlantic. During the years preceding the Second World War, Hitler's Germany developed the Volkswagen 'Beetle' and strategically brought it within the reach of the middle classes by means of a save-as-you-earn scheme. The apparent increase in middle-class purchasing power increased the individual mobility of the population.

In 1903 the aeroplane was introduced by the Wright brothers, and less than twenty-five years after their first successful flight Charles Lindbergh flew the Spirit of St. Louis from New York to Paris, making transatlantic flight a reality. The advent of the car and the aeroplane added two more networks to the world's trade and transport system, with hubs concentrated in existing economic centres, confirming and reinforcing their position as metropolitan areas.

In the second half of the twentieth century, two more important networks became available to world trade and transport: the network of oil and gas pipelines and the satellite system. The worldwide pipeline network was the outcome of a great many local and private initiatives in the nineteenth century. During the twentieth century greater car and air traffic and a sharp rise in demand for oil and kerosene enabled the network to grow to global proportions.

What is for the time being the latest network was introduced in 1957, when the Soviet Union launched the first satellite. The satellite system has also greatly increased opportunities for studying the earth and land use. Opportunities for using this network were extended to much of the world's population during the second half of the twentieth century. The Internet, GIS and GPS systems and route planners now provide an immediate picture of the world in which we live and how we move about in it.

The choice of the 101 metropolitan areas in this atlas is based on the definition mentioned earlier, in which population and the existence of global hubs are determining factors. The selection was made from six rankings based on population size and the interaction of global air transport, shipping and telecommunication networks. Each selected metropolitan area is either one of the fifty largest cities in the world in terms of population, one of the world's twenty-five largest seaports, one of the world's thirty largest airports in terms of passenger numbers, cargo transport or air movements and/or one of the world's thirty largest telecommunication hubs. Another twelve cities were added to this initial selection of 89 metropolitan areas because of their political, cultural or religious status. The idea behind this is that the characteristics of each metropolitan area can be compared with those of one hundred other metropolitan areas throughout the world.

To determine to what extent regional attractiveness is reflected in business/economic settlement patterns, this selection was compared with the locations of the headquarters of the world's 50 financially fittest companies in terms of market value. Nearly 80% of these headquarters turned out to be in one of the 101 selected metropolitan areas. Thirty-nine of the 50 headquarters of the world's most valuable companies proved to be located in nineteen of the 101 metropolitan areas documented in this atlas.

Producing this atlas involved two main activities: collecting data and making the maps. To avoid distortion due to the fact that different sources often use different working and measuring methods, it was decided to use only a limited number of sources per topic. As a result, the same data are not always available for every metropolitan area.

The 101 metropolitan areas were approached in a uniform manner. Starting from a geographically projected world map, we zoomed in on each metropolitan area at regional level, with a 162 x 130 km framework and a 1 : 750,000 scale. This means that 1 cm on the map corresponds to 7.5 kilometres on the ground. Each map had the same scale, grain, frame and legend. The legend indicates bodies of water, land area, land elevation, railways, motorways, built-up areas, airports and seaports.

The statistical data for each metropolitan area are displayed next to each map in two different ways: cartographically, and in figures. The cartographic display shows proportions in relation to the maximum value that a given characteristic of the region can reach: a small dot represents a relatively low value compared with the maximum value, and a large dot a relatively high value.

In the second section of this atlas the data for the metropolitan regions are displayed by topic in a global perspective. The various regional values are shown in relation to each other on simplified world maps. Here again, a small circle represents a relatively low value compared with the maximum possible value, and a large circle a relatively high value.

The Metropolitan World Atlas is a valuable cartographic and statistical reference work. Its uniform methodology makes it possible to clearly and objectively compare the differences and similarities between given regional urban configurations from several different angles and perspectives in pictures and figures with a single common denominator.

The world's 10 largest cities through the ages

Sources: Chandler,T.(1987) Four Thousand Years
of Urban Growth: An Historical Census
(Lewiston) St. David's University Press,
demographia.com

THE WORLD'S 10 LARGEST CITIES IN TERMS OF
INHABITANTS IN THE YEAR 100

No.	Metropolitan area	Inhabitants
01	Rome, Italy	450,000
02	Luoyang, China	420,000
03	Baghdad, Iraq	250,000
04	Alexandria, Egypt	250,000
05	Antioch, Turkey	150,000
06	Anuradhapura, Sri Lanka	130,000
07	Peshawar, Pakistan	120,000
08	Carthage, Tunisia	100,000
09	Suzhou, China	n/a
10	Smyrna, Turkey	90,000

100

THE WORLD'S 10 LARGEST CITIES IN TERMS OF
INHABITANTS IN THE YEAR 1000

No.	Metropolitan area	Inhabitants
01	Cordova, Spain	450,000
02	Kaifeng, China	400,000
03	Istanbul, Turkey	300,000
04	Angkor, Cambodia	200,000
05	Kyoto, Japan	175,000
06	Cairo, Egypt	135,000
07	Baghdad, Iraq	125,000
08	Neyshabur, Iran	125,000
09	Al-Hasa, Saudi Arabia	110,000
10	Patan, India	100,000

1000

THE WORLD'S 10 LARGEST CITIES IN TERMS OF
INHABITANTS IN THE YEAR 1500

No.	Metropolitan area	Inhabitants
01	Beijing, China	672,000
02	Vijayanagar, India	500,000
03	Cairo, Egypt	400,000
04	Hangzhou, China	250,000
05	Tabriz, Iran	250,000
06	Istanbul, Turkey	200,000
07	Gaur, Nepal	200,000
08	Paris, France	185,000
09	Guangzhou, China	150,000
10	Nanjing, China	147,000

1500

THE WORLD'S 10 LARGEST CITIES IN TERMS OF
INHABITANTS IN THE YEAR 1800

No.	Metropolitan area	Inhabitants
01	Beijing, China	1,100,000
02	London, United Kingdom	861,000
03	Guangzhou, China	800,000
04	Tokyo, Japan	685,000
05	Istanbul, Turkey	570,000
06	Paris, France	547,000
07	Naples, Italy	430,000
08	Hangzhou, China	387,000
09	Osaka, Japan	383,000
10	Kyoto, Japan	377,000

1800

THE WORLD'S 10 LARGEST CITIES IN TERMS OF
INHABITANTS IN THE YEAR 1900

No.	Metropolitan area	Inhabitants
01	London, United Kingdom	6,480,000
02	New York, United States	4,242,000
03	Paris, France	3,330,000
04	Berlin, Germany	2,707,000
05	Chicago, United States	1,717,000
06	Vienna, Austria	1,698,000
07	Tokyo, Japan	1,497,000
08	St.Petersburg, Russia	1,439,000
09	Manchester, United Kingdom	1,435,000
10	Philadelphia, United States	1,418,000

1900

THE WORLD'S 10 LARGEST CITIES IN TERMS OF
INHABITANTS IN THE YEAR 1950

No.	Metropolitan area	Inhabitants
01	New York, United States	12,463,000
02	London, United Kingdom	8,860,000
03	Tokyo, Japan	7,000,000
04	Paris, France	5,900,000
05	Shanghai, China	5,400,000
06	Moscow, Russia	5,100,000
07	Buenos Aires, Argentina	5,000,000
08	Chicago, United States	4,906,000
09	Rhine-Ruhr, Germany	4,900,000
10	Calcutta, India	4,800,000

1950

THE WORLD'S 10 LARGEST CITIES IN TERMS OF
INHABITANTS IN THE YEAR 2000

No.	Metropolitan area	Inhabitants
01	Tokyo-Yokohama, Japan	33,190,000
02	New York, United States	20,270,000
03	Seoul-Inchon, South Korea	19,920,000
04	Mexico City, Mexico	19,620,000
05	São Paulo, Brazil	17,720,000
06	Mumbai, India	17,580,000
07	Kobe-Osaka-Kyoto, Japan	16,930,000
08	Los Angeles, United States	16,200,000
09	Manila, Philipines	14,140,000
10	Cairo, Egypt	14,000,000

2000

The world's 50 largest cities

THE WORLD'S 50 LARGEST CITIES IN TERMS
OF INHABITANTS IN THE YEAR 2000
Sources: demographia.com, Eurostat,
citypopulation.de, Regio Randstad,
StatsCanada, US Census

No.	Metropolitan area	Inhabitants	No.	Metropolitan area	Inhabitants
01	Tokyo-Yokohama	33,190,000	26	Tianjin	9,920,000
02	Seoul-Incheon	22,877,000	27	Chicago	9,549,000
03	New York	21,767,000	28	Hong Kong	9,180,000
04	Mumbai	20,043,000	29	Nagoya	8,837,000
05	Mexico City	19,620,000	30	Dhaka	8,610,000
06	São Paulo	17,720,000	31	Washington-Baltimore	7,910,000
07	Kobe-Osaka-Kyoto	16,930,000	32	Lima	7,420,000
08	Los Angeles	16,200,000	33	Taipei	7,260,000
09	Manila	14,140,000	34	Bangkok	7,250,000
10	Cairo	14,000,000	35	San Francisco-Oakland	7,154,000
11	London	13,945,000	36	Bogotá	6,990,000
12	Calcutta	13,940,000	37	Chennai	6,700,000
13	New Delhi	13,730,000	38	Randstad Holland	6,600,000
14	Shanghai	13,580,000	39	Hyderabad	6,390,000
15	Buenos Aires	13,390,000	40	Santiago de Chile	6,061,000
16	Djakarta	13,330,000	41	Philadelphia	6,010,000
17	Beijing	13,160,000	42	Lahore	5,920,000
18	Moscow	13,100,000	43	Boston	5,815,000
19	Rhine-Ruhr	11,100,000	44	Dallas-Ft.Worth	5,785,000
20	Karachi	11,020,000	45	Kinshasa	5,750,000
21	Rio de Janeiro	10,810,000	46	Bangalore	5,687,000
22	Tehran	10,740,000	47	Johannesburg	5,530,000
23	Paris	10,600,000	48	Toronto	5,470,000
24	Istanbul	10,430,000	49	Detroit	5,415,000
25	Lagos	10,030,000	50	St.Petersburg	5,410,000

The world's 25 largest seaports

THE WORLD'S 25 LARGEST SEAPORTS IN TERMS OF CONTAINER CAPACITY IN THE YEAR 2000
Source: marad.gov

THE WORLD'S 25 LARGEST SEAPORTS IN TERMS OF OIL TANKER CAPACITY IN THE YEAR 2000
Source: marad.gov

THE WORLD'S 25 LARGEST SEAPORTS IN TERMS OF DRY-BULK CAPACITY IN THE YEAR 2000
Source: marad.gov

No.	Metropolitan area	Capacity*
01	Hong Kong	412,264
02	Singapore	354,686
03	Kaohsiung	199,284
04	Busan	164,795
05	Los Angeles-Long Beach	124,281
06	Kobe	116,447
07	Randstad Holland-Rotterdam	110,192
08	Kuala Lumpur	109,883
09	Yokohama	103,399
10	Tokyo	102,198
11	Taipee-Keelung	94,522
12	Nagoya	91,331
13	New York	87,463
14	San Francisco	82,958
15	Le Havre	82,329
16	Antwerp	76,312
17	Hamburg	74,067
18	Osaka	57,659
19	Bangkok-Laem Chabang	49,820
20	Shanghai	47,449
21	São Paulo-Santos	42,749
22	Taichung	33,604
23	Durban	29,088
24	Houston	19,799
25	New Orleans	10,853

* Capacity = Calls x Cargo load

No.	Metropolitan area	Capacity*
01	Singapore	436,844
02	Houston	134,809
03	Randstad Holland-Rotterdam	121,957
04	New Orleans	81,956
05	Los Angeles-Long Beach	66,045
06	New York	65,965
07	Le Havre	53,308
08	San Francisco	50,653
09	Kaohsiung	48,032
10	Yokohama	36,129
11	Antwerp	34,071
12	Nagoya	28,669
13	Hong Kong	26,774
14	Taichung	25,561
15	Durban	23,604
16	São Paulo-Santos	17,342
17	Bangkok-Laem Chabang	15,027
18	Hamburg	14,349
19	Kuala Lumpur	10,480
20	Taipei-Keelung	10,350
21	Kobe	9,012
22	Shanghai	6,208
23	Osaka	5,244
24	Busan	4,555
25	Tokyo	260

No.	Metropolitan area	Capacity*
01	Singapore	242,708,835
02	New Orleans	119,269,571
03	Randstad Holland-Rotterdam	73,729,965
04	Kaohsiung	69,756,449
05	Taichung	54,157,795
06	Nagoya	51,990,836
07	Busan	51,190,873
08	Antwerp	41,746,851
09	Hong Kong	34,261,861
10	Hamburg	32,753,024
11	São Paulo-Santos	31,261,763
12	Houston	28,342,021
13	Durban	27,353,729
14	San Francisco	22,619,164
15	Bangkok-Laem Chabang	20,056,938
16	Kuala Lumpur	18,796,533
17	Yokohama	17,725,119
18	Osaka	17,638,437
19	Kobe	14,049,098
20	Taipei-Keelung	13,544,786
21	New York	10,099,197
22	Le Havre	6,681,024
23	Shanghai	4,415,656
24	Los Angeles-Long Beach	3,756,811
25	Tokyo	769,992

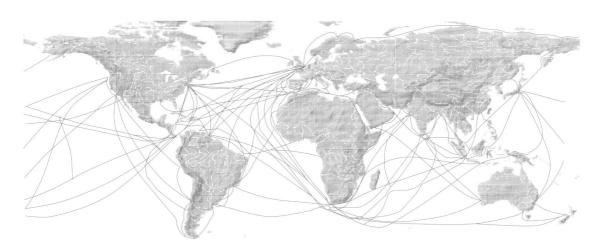

The world's 30 largest airports

THE WORLD'S 30 LARGEST AIRPORTS IN TERMS OF PASSENGERS TRANSPORTED IN THE YEAR 2000 (ARRIVALS, DEPARTURES AND TRANSFERS) Source: airports.org

THE WORLD'S 30 LARGEST AIRPORTS IN TERMS OF CARGO TRANSPORTED IN THE YEAR 2000 (TONNES OF CARGO AND MAIL) Source: airports.org

THE WORLD'S 30 LARGEST AIRPORTS IN TERMS OF FLIGHT MOVEMENTS IN THE YEAR 2000 (NUMBER OF TAKEOFFS AND LANDINGS) Source: airports.org

No.	Metropolitan area	Passengers	No.	Metropolitan area	Tonnes	No.	Metropolitan area	Flight movements
01	Atlanta [ATL]	75,858,500	01	Memphis [MEM]	2,631,131	01	Chicago [ORD]	911,917
02	Chicago [ORD]	67,448,064	02	Hong Kong [HKG]	2,100,276	02	Atlanta [ATL]	590,494
03	Los Angeles [LAX]	61,606,204	03	Anchorage [ANC]*	1,873,750	03	Dallas-Ft.Worth [DFW]	783,556
04	London [LHR]	60,743,084	04	Los Angeles[LAX]	1,774,402	04	Los Angeles [LAX]	738,114
05	Tokyo [HND]	58,692,688	05	Tokyo [NRT]	1,680,937	05	Phoenix [PHX]	553,310
06	Dallas-Ft.Worth [DFW]	55,150,693	06	Miami [MIA]	1,639,760	06	Paris [CDG]	523,400
07	Frankfurt [FRA]	48,559,980	07	Frankfurt [FRA]	1,613,179	07	Detroit [DTW]	552,132
08	Paris [CDG]	47,996,529	08	Paris [CDG]	1,591,310	08	Minneapolis-St.Paul [MSP]	501,465
09	Randstad-Amsterdam [AMS]	39,531,123	09	Singapore [SIN]	1,529,930	09	Las Vegas [LAS]	493,722
10	Denver [DEN]	36,092,806	10	Louisville [SDF]	1,468,837	10	Denver [DEN]	486,030
11	Phoenix [PHX]	35,439,031	11	New York [JFK]	1,430,727	11	St.Louis [STL]	474,161
12	Las Vegas [LAS]	34,180,960	12	Chicago [ORD]	1,299,628	12	Miami [MIA]	471,008
13	Houston [IAH]	34,803,580	13	London [LHR]	1,263,572	13	Houston [IAH]	470,916
14	San Francisco [SFO]	34,632,474	14	Randstad-Amsterdam [AMS]	1,234,161	14	Philadelphia [PHL]	466,985
15	Minneapolis-St.Paul [MSP]	34,308,389	15	Incheon [ICN]	1,196,843	15	London [LHR]	463,568
16	Madrid [MAD]	34,047,931	16	Taipei [TPE]	1,189,874	16	Charlotte [CLT]	461,264
17	Hong Kong [HKG]	32,546,029	17	Indianapolis [IND]	1,115,272	17	Frankfurt [FRA]	456,452
18	Detroit [DTW]	32,294,121	18	Kobe [KIX]	871,161	18	Boston [BOS]	454,625
19	Miami [MIA]	31,668,450	19	Bangkok [BKK]	841,150	19	Pittsburgh [PIT]	451,739
20	London [LGW]	31,182,364	20	New York-Newark [EWR]	795,584	20	New York-Newark [EWR]	436,420
21	Bangkok [BKK]	30,623,366	21	Dallas-Ft.Worth [DFW]	784,085	21	Randstad-Amsterdam [AMS]	432,101
22	New York-Newark [EWR]	30,558,000	22	Atlanta [ATL]	739,927	22	Toronto [YYZ]	406,360
23	New York [JFK]	29,349,000	23	Tokyo [HND]	725,124	23	Seattle [SEA]	400,635
24	Orlando [MCO]	28,253,248	24	San Francisco [SFO]	636,006	24	Orlando-Sanford [SFB]	397,557
25	Singapore [SIN]	28,093,759	25	Dubai [DXB]	632,224	25	Washington [IAD]	396,876
26	Toronto [YYZ]	28,042,692	26	Seoul [SEL]	598,620	26	San Francisco-Oakland [OAK]	395,635
27	Seattle [SEA]	27,036,073	27	San Francisco-Oakland [OAK]	593,634	27	Memphis [MEM]	394,826
28	St.Louis [STL]	26,695,019	28	Beijing [PEK]	591,195	28	San Francisco [SFO]	387,594
29	Rio de Janeiro [FCO]	25,565,727	29	Brussels [BRU]	583,685	29	Cincinnati [CVG]	387,462
30	Tokyo [NRT]	25,379,370	30	Philadelphia [PHL]	536,270	30	Los Angeles-Santa Ana [SNA]	378,903

* [ANC] Includes transfer freight

16

The world's 30 largest telecom ports

THE WORLD'S 30 LARGEST TELECOM PORTS
IN TERMS OF MEGABITS PER SECOND IN THE
YEAR 2000
Source: telegeography.com

No.	Metropolitan area	Mbps
01	New York	1,498,345
02	London	855,187
03	Randstad Holland-Amsterdam	244,796
04	Paris	225,518
05	San Francisco	208,136
06	Tokyo	167,456
07	Washington	132,612
08	Miami	119,124
09	Los Angeles	112,270
10	Copenhagen	104,170
11	Frankfurt	93,515
12	Seattle	58,917
13	Sydney	43,890
14	São Paulo	43,165
15	Taipei	37,384
16	Seoul	37,341
17	Hong Kong	26,948
18	Madrid	24,880
19	Buenos Aires	22,857
20	Mexico City	21,660
21	Dallas	15,460
22	Sacramento	14,090
23	Stockholm	13,970
24	Osaka	13,950
25	Milan	12,935
26	Singapore	12,760
27	Perth	10,920
28	Monterey	10,770
29	Auckland	10,200
30	Rio de Janeiro	9,810

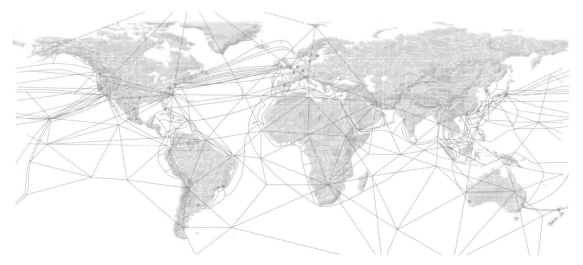

The 12 additional metropolitan areas

The lists of the world's 50 largest cities, 25 largest seaports, 30 largest airports and 30 largest telecom ports when combined give a total of 89 different metropolitan areas

12 METROPOLITAN AREAS ADDED TO PRODUCE A TOTAL OF 101 METROPOLITAN AREAS

Metropolitan area

Berlin
Oslo
Lisbon
Jerusalem-Tel Aviv
Baghdad
Tangier
Barcelona
Geneva
Athens
Vancouver
Montreal
Melbourne

The 101 metropolitan areas

METROPOLITAN AREAS SELECTED
FOR THE METROPOLITAN WORLD
ATLAS

Metropolitan area	Metropolitan area	Metropolitan area	Metropolitan area
Anchorage	Djakarta	Louisville	Rhine-Ruhr
Antwerp-Brussels	Dubai	Madrid	Rio de Janeiro
Athens	Durban	Manila	Rome
Atlanta	Frankfurt	Melbourne	Sacramento
Auckland	Geneva	Memphis	San Francisco-Oakland
Baghdad	Hamburg	Mexico City	Santiago de Chile
Bangalore	Hong Kong	Miami	São Paulo
Bangkok	Houston	Milan	Seattle
Barcelona	Hyderabad	Minneapolis-St.Paul	Seoul-Incheon
Beijing	Indianapolis	Monterey	Shanghai
Berlin	Istanbul	Montreal	Singapore
Bogotá	Jerusalem-Tel Aviv	Moscow	St.Louis
Boston	Johannesburg	Mumbai	St.Petersburg
Buenos Aires	Kaohsiung	Nagoya	Stockholm
Busan	Karachi	New Delhi	Sydney
Cairo	Kinshasa	New Orleans	Taichung
Calcutta	Kobe-Osaka-Kyoto	New York	Taipei
Charlotte	Kuala Lumpur	Orlando	Tangier
Chennai	Lagos	Oslo	Tehran
Chicago	Lahore	Paris	Tianjin
Cincinnati	Las Vegas	Perth	Tokyo-Yokohama
Copenhagen	Le Havre	Philadelphia	Toronto
Dallas-Ft.Worth	Lima	Phoenix	Vancouver
Denver	Lisbon	Pittsburgh	Washington-Baltimore
Detroit	London	Randstad Holland	
Dhaka	Los Angeles		

101 Metropolitan areas

Metropolitan area Country

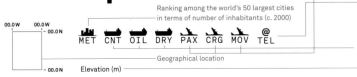

00.0W 00.0W
- 00.0 N

MET CNT OIL DRY PAX CRG MOV @ TEL

Ranking among the world's 50 largest cities in terms of number of inhabitants (c. 2000)

Ranking among the world's 25 largest seaports in terms of container capacity (CNT), oil tanker capacity (OIL) and dry-bulk capacity (DRY) in the year 2000
marad.gov

- 00.0 N

Geographical location

Elevation (m)

Average height above sea level of the region in which the metropolitan area is located, in metres in the year 2004
weatherbase.com

Population

Number of inhabitants

Inhabitants XXXX

Number of inhabitants in the metropolitan area in the year XXXX
demographia.com, citypopulation.de, Eurostat, Regio Randstad, StatsCanada, US Census

Metropolitan development

Increase or decrease in the number of inhabitants of the metropolitan core as opposed to the metropolitan periphery
demographia.com

Year

Years in which increase or decrease in number of inhabitants was registered

Total metropolitan inhabitants

Total number of inhabitants in the metropolitan core and periphery

Inhabitants in metropolitan core

Total number of inhabitants in the metropolitan core

Core share

Percentage of the total number of inhabitants in the metropolitan area living in the core

Inhabitants in metropolitan periphery

Total number of inhabitants in the metropolitan periphery

Periphery share

Percentage of the total number of inhabitants in the metropolitan area living in the periphery

Employment

Employment characteristics in the year 1990, 1998 or 2001
demographia.com

Area (km²)

Total built-up surface area of the metropolitan area and the central business district

Area share

Percentage of total built-up surface area taken up by the central business district

Employment

Total employment in the metropolitan area and central business district

Employment share

Percentage of metropolitan employment in the central business district

Employment density (employment/km²)

Average density of employment in the metropolitan area and the central business district

Economy

Economic characteristics in the year 1991, 1996 or 2000

Average per capita income of the metropolitan population in euros in the year 2000 or 2002
asiaweek.com, bestplaces.net

Average income per capita (€)

Gross regional product per capita (€)

Average gross regional product per capita of the metropolitan population in euros in the year 1991
demographia.com

Unemployment rate

Percentage of working-age population that is unemployed in the year 1996, 2000 or 2002
asiaweek.com, bestplaces.net, Eurostat

Health

Health and health care characteristics in the year 1996 or 2000
asiaweek.com, Eurostat

Hospital beds per 1,000 inhabitants

Hospital capacity in terms of average number of hospital beds available per 1,000 inhabitants in the year 1996 or 2000

Average life expectancy at birth

Average life expectancy for newborn babies in the year 1996 or 2000

Crime

Crimes per 100,000 inhabitants

Number of violent crimes and property crimes per 100,000 inhabitants in the year 1996, 2000 or 2002
asiaweek.com, bestplaces.net, Eurostat

Ranking among the world's 30 largest telecom ports in terms of megabits per second in the year 2000
telegeography.com

Ranking among the world's 30 largest airports in terms of numbers of passengers transported (PAX), cargo transported (CRG) and flight movements (MOV) in the year 2000
airports.org

Metropolitan density
Population density in terms of number of inhabitants per km² of built-up area
demographia.com

Inhabitants — Number of inhabitants
Built-up area (km²) — Total built-up surface area of the metropolitan area in km²
Population density (inhabitants/km²) — Population density in terms of number of inhabitants per km² of built-up area

Residential density
Population density in residential districts in terms of number of inhabitants per km² of residential area
demographia.com

Year — Years in which the density was measured
Inhabitants — Number of inhabitants in residential districts
Residential area (km²) — Built-up area of residential areas in km²
Residential density (inhabitants/km²) — Population density in residential districts in terms of number of inhabitants per km² of residential area

Change in density (1970–1990)
Increase or decrease in number of inhabitants in proportion to increase or decrease in built-up area between 1970 and 1990
demographia.com

Change in inhabitants — Increase or decrease in number of inhabitants
Change in area (km²) — Increase or decrease in built-up area
Change in density (inhabitants/km²) — Increase or decrease in number of inhabitants in proportion to increase or decrease in urban built-up area

Traffic and transport
Traffic and transportation characteristics

Public transport market share — Market share of public transport traffic in total metropolitan traffic and transportation in the year 1991
publicpurpose.com
Private vehicle market share — Market share of private vehicle traffic in total metropolitan traffic and transportation in the year 1991
publicpurpose.com
Average commuting time (minutes) — Average number of minutes an inhabitant needed to get to work in the year 1991, 1996, 2000 or 2002
asiaweek.com, bestplaces.net, demographia.com, Eurostat

Road use
Road use in the metropolitan area in the year 1995
publicpurpose.com

Average road speed (km/hour) — Average speed on the metropolitan road network in km/hour
Vehicle density (vehicle km/km²) — Average number of vehicle kilometres travelled per km² of metropolitan area

Railway use
Underground and light-rail use in the year 1990
demographia.com

Passenger density (passenger km/km) — Average number of passenger kilometres travelled per kilometre of underground and light-rail network
Rail vehicle density (vehicle km/km²) — Average number of rail vehicle kilometres travelled per km² of metropolitan area

Climate
Climatological characteristics of the region in which the metropolitan area is located
weatherbase.com

Average January temperature (°C) — Average temperature in January
Average July temperature (°C) — Average temperature in July

Pollution
Pollution and environmental characteristics of the metropolitan area in the year 1990
demographia.com

NOX (tonnes/km²) — Smog, average amount in tonnes of nitrogen oxide per km²
CO (tonnes/km²) — Toxic air, average amount in tonnes of carbon monoxide per km²
VOC (tonnes/km²) — Carbon particles and vapours, average amount in tonnes of volatile organic compounds per km²
Total pollution (tonnes/km²) — Total pollution in tonnes in the metropolitan area

Land elevation
Land cover and elevation pattern. The lines represent contours at 500 m intervals
earthetc.com, encarta.com, europa-tech.com, infomine.com, map24.com, map4travel.com, mapquest.com

Outlying towns
Towns and cities in the environs of the metropolitan area
earthetc.com, encarta.com, europa-tech.com, infomine.com, map24.com, map4travel.com, mapquest.com

Roads
National, international and regional paved roads
encarta.com, europa-tech.com, infomine.com, map24.com, map4travel.com, mapquest.com

Railways
National, international and regional railways. Underground and light-rail are excluded
encarta.com, europa-tech.com, infomine.com, map24.com, map4travel.com, mapquest.com

IATA airports
International civilian airports in the metropolitan area and environs as defined by the International Air Transport Association, with their international three-letter code and name
aircraft-charter-world.com, airports.org, encarta.com, europa-tech.com, fly.faa.gov, flyaow.com, fltplan.com, map24.com, map4travel.com, mapquest.com, Circle Mapper Flight Planning

Ports
Ports in the metropolitan area and environs
encarta.com, europa-tech.com, map24.com, map4travel.com, mapquest.com, marad.gov, Korea Container Terminal Authority

Political boundaries
International political boundaries
encarta.com, europa-tech.com, infomine.com, map24.com, mapquest.com, Times Atlas of the World 2000

Built-up development
Built-up areas in the region
earthetc.com, encarta.com,europa-tech.com, infomine.com, map24.com, mapquest.com

Bodies of water
Oceans, seas, rivers, lakes, glaciers, canals
earthetc.com, encarta.com, europa-tech.com, infomine.com, map24.com, map4travel.com, mapquest.com

Scale 1 : 750,000
1 cm on the map corresponds to 7.5 km on the ground

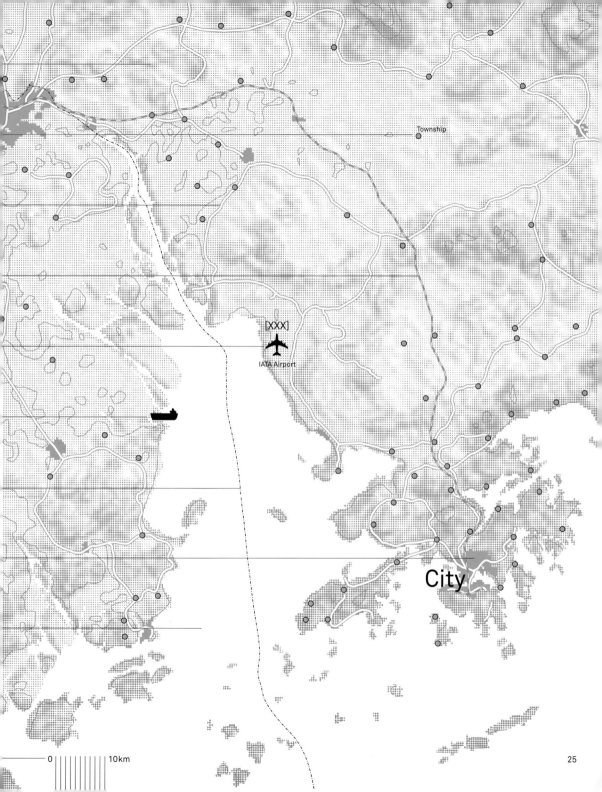

Township

[XXX]
✈
IATA Airport

City

0 |||||||||| 10km

25

Anchorage United States

151.0W 147.9W

61.9N

60.4N

Elevation (m)   35

CRG

3

Population

Inhabitants 2003   **339,286**
Inhabitants 1985   174,431
citypopulation.de

Traffic and transport

Average commuting time (minutes)   **20**
bestplaces.net, 1998

Economy
Average income per capita (€)   **22,750**
Unemployment rate   4.2%
bestplaces.net, 1998

Climate
Average January temperature (°C)   -13.3
Average July temperature (°C)   **18.3**
weatherbase.com

Crime
Crimes per 100,000 inhabitants   **5,024**
bestplaces.net, 1998

Antwerp-Brussels Belgium

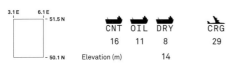

	CNT	OIL	DRY	CRG
3.1 E 6.1 E	16	11	8	29
51.5 N				
50.1 N				
Elevation (m)			14	

Population

Inhabitants 2000   **3,725,000**

Metropolitan density

Inhabitants	2,485,000
Built-up area (km²)	1,308
Population density (inhabitants/km²)	**1,900**

demographia.com, 1990

Metropolitan development (Brussels)

Year	1965	2000
Total metropolitan inhabitants	2,990,000	3,725,000
Inhabitants in metropolitan core	413,000	294,000
Core share	**13.8%**	**7.9%**
Inhabitants in metropolitan periphery	2,577,000	3,431,000
Periphery share	86.2%	92.1%

demographia.com

Employment (Brussels)

	Metr. Area	CBD
Area (km²)	1,308	3.1
Area share	100%	0.2%
Employment	602,408	144,906
Employment share	100%	24.1%
Employment density (employment/km²)	**461**	**46,744**

demographia.com, 1990

Traffic and transport (Brussels)

Average commuting time (minutes)	**22**

publicpurpose.com, 1990

Road use (Brussels)

Average road speed (km/hour)	37.8
Vehicle density (vehicle km/km²)	**110,913**

publicpurpose.com, 1990

Economy (Brussels)

Gross regional product per capita (€)	**27,803**
Unemployment rate	7.4%

Regio Randstad, 2002

Railway use (Brussels)

Passenger density (passenger km/km)	17,870
Rail vehicle density (vehicle km/km²)	**756,371**

publicpurpose.com, 1990

Health (Brussels)

Hospital beds per 1,000 inhabitants	**6**
Average life expectancy at birth	80

Eurostat, 1996

Climate (Brussels)

Average January temperature (°C)	0.6
Average July temperature (°C)	**21.7**

weatherbase.com

Crime (Brussels)

Crimes per 100,000 inhabitants	**9,890**

Eurostat, 1996

Pollution (Brussels)

NOX (tonnes/km²)	125.1
CO (tonnes/km²)	493.8
VOC (tonnes/km²)	77.2
Total pollution (tonnes/km²)	**696.1**

demographia.com, 1990

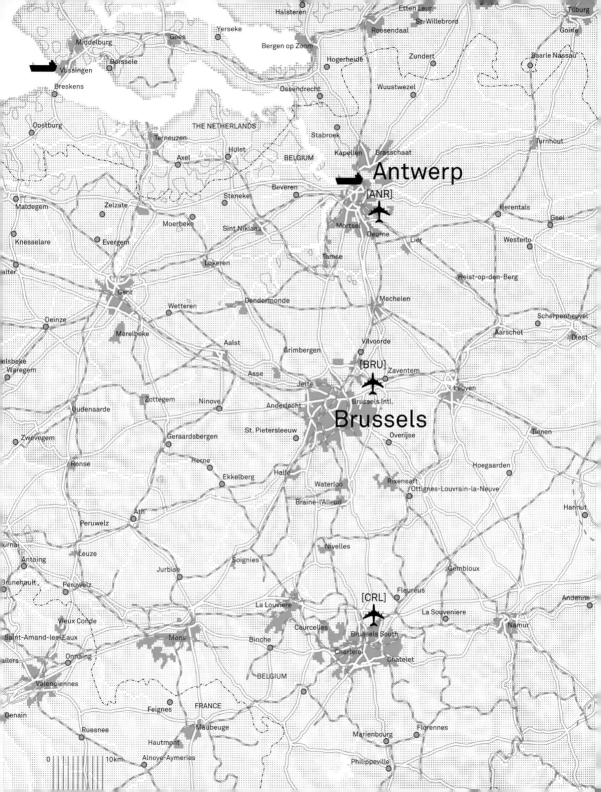

Athens Greece

22.2 E   25.2 E
— 38.8 N

— 37.4 N   Elevation (m)   21

Population

Inhabitants 2001   **3,188,000**
demographia.com

Metropolitan density

Inhabitants	3,188,000
Built-up area (km²)	466
Population density (inhabitants/km²)	**6,841**

demographia.com, 2001

Metropolitan development

Year	1965	2001
Total metropolitan inhabitants	1,950,000	3,188,000
Inhabitants in metropolitan core	650,000	745,000
Core share	**33.3%**	**23.4%**
Inhabitants in metropolitan periphery	1,300,000	2,443,000
Periphery share	66.7%	76.6%

demographia.com

Economy

Unemployment rate   4.3%
Eurostat, 1996

Health

Hospital beds per 1,000 inhabitants   **6**
Eurostat, 1996

Climate

Average January temperature (°C)	6.7
Average July temperature (°C)	**21.7**

weatherbase.com

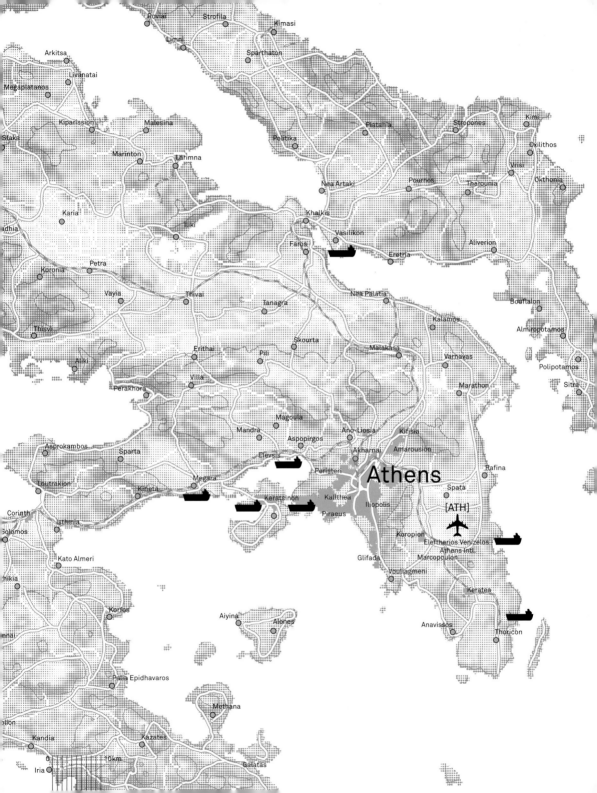

Atlanta United States

85.8 W 82.8 W
- 34.5 N
- 33.0 N

Elevation (m) 308

	PAX	CRG	MOV
	1	22	2

Population

Inhabitants 2000	**3,500,000**
Inhabitants 1985	1,613,000
Inhabitants 1970	1,172,000
US Census	

Metropolitan development

	1965	2000
Year		
Total metropolitan inhabitants	507,000	3,500,000
Inhabitants in metropolitan core	331,000	416,000
Core share	**65.3%**	**11.9%**
Inhabitants in metropolitan periphery	176,000	3,084,000
Periphery share	34.7%	88.1%
demographia.com		

Employment

	Metr. Area	CBD
Area (km²)	5,084	-
Area share	100%	-
Employment	1,469,298	181,711
Employment share	100%	12.4%
Employment density (employment/km²)	**289**	-
demographia.com, 2000		

Economy

Average income per capita (€)	**19,474**
Gross regional product per capita (€)	32,849
Unemployment rate	2.8%
bestplaces.net; demographia.com, 1998	

Crime

Crimes per 100,000 inhabitants	**13,490**
bestplaces.net, 1998	

Metropolitan density

Inhabitants	3,500,000
Built-up area (km²)	5,084
Population density (inhabitants/km²)	**688**
US Census, 2000	

Change in density (1970–1990)

Change in inhabitants	985,000
Change in area (km²)	2,307
Change in density (inhabitants/km²)	**427**
demographia.com	

Traffic and transport

Average commuting time (minutes)	**23**
bestplaces.net, 1998	

Road use

Vehicle density (vehicle km/km²)	**40,326**
publicpurpose.com, 1990	

Railway use

Passenger density (passenger km/km)	15,831
Rail vehicle density (vehicle km/km²)	**41,074**
publicpurpose.com, 1996	

Climate

Average January temperature (°C)	0.6
Average July temperature (°C)	**31.7**
weatherbase.com	

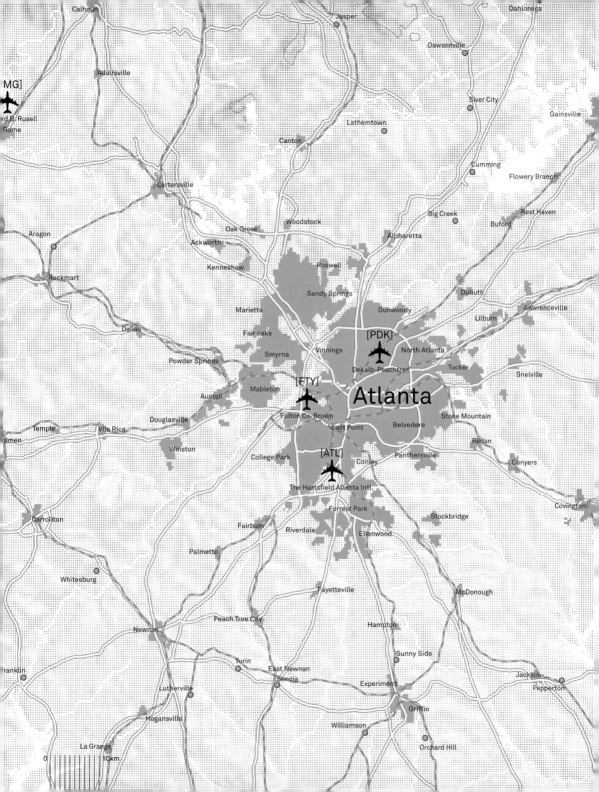

Auckland New Zealand

173.3 E   176.3 E
            36.1 S

            37.5 S   Elevation (m)   6

Population

Inhabitants 2001	**1,290,000**
Inhabitants 1985	873,905

demographia.com

Metropolitan development

Year	1965	2001
Total metropolitan inhabitants	500,000	1,290,000
Inhabitants in metropolitan core	148,000	406,000
Core share	**29.6%**	**31.5%**
Inhabitants in metropolitan periphery	352,000	884,000
Periphery share	70.4%	68.5%

demographia.com

@
TEL
29

Metropolitan density

Inhabitants	1,023,000
Built-up area (km²)	531
Population density (inhabitants/km²)	**1,927**

demographia.com, 1998

Climate

Average January temperature (°C)	16.7
Average July temperature (°C)	**13.3**

weatherbase.com

Baghdad Iraq

42.8 E   45.9 E
         ⌐ 34.0 N

         └ 32.6 N   Elevation (m)   34

Population

Inhabitants 1997   **5,400,000**
citypopulation.de

Residential density

Year	1985
Inhabitants	3,371,000
Residential area (km²)	251
Residential density (inhabitants/km²)	**13,430**

demographia.com

Climate

Average January temperature (°C)	3.3
Average July temperature (°C)	**43.3**

weatherbase.com

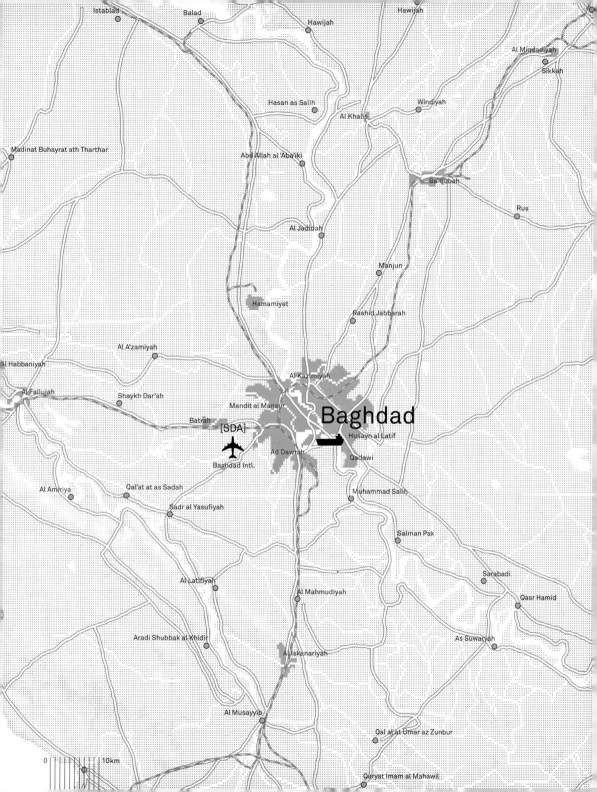

Bangalore India

MET
46

Elevation (m)	921

Population

Inhabitants 2001	**5,687,000**
Inhabitants 1985	2,921,751
demographia.com	

Metropolitan development

Year	1965	2001
Total metropolitan inhabitants	1,325,000	5,687,000
Inhabitants in metropolitan core	950,000	4,292,000
Core share	**71.7%**	**75.5%**
Inhabitants in metropolitan periphery	375,000	1,395,000
Periphery share	28.3%	24.5%
demographia.com		

Traffic and transport

Average commuting time (minutes)	**40**
asiaweek.com, 2000	

Economy

Average income per capita (€)	**954**
Unemployment rate	10.0%
asiaweek.com, 2000	

Health

Hospital beds per 1,000 inhabitants	**5**
Average life expectancy at birth	68
asiaweek.com, 2000	

Climate

Average January temperature (°C)	16.7
Average July temperature (°C)	**26.7**
weatherbase.com	

Crime

Crimes per 100,000 inhabitants	**200**
asiaweek.com, 2000	

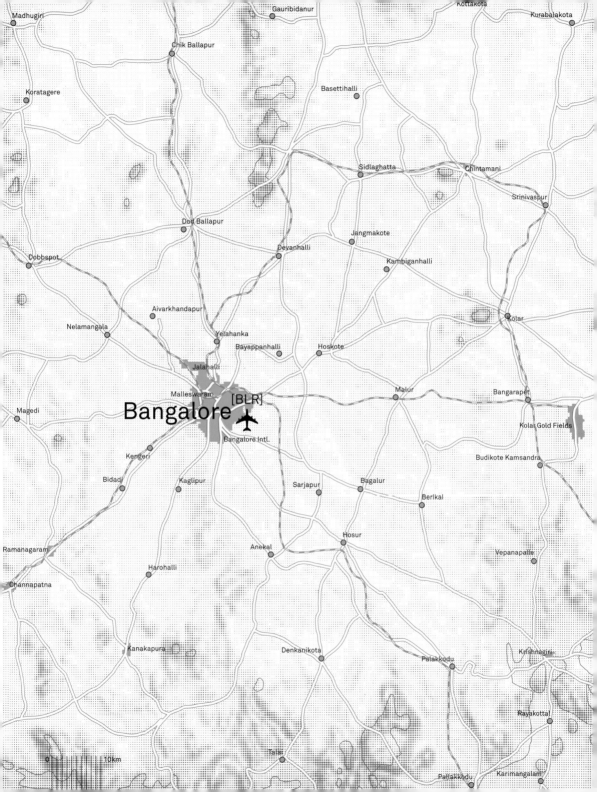

Bangkok Thailand

	MET	CNT	OIL	DRY	PAX	CRG
	34	19	17	15	21	19
Elevation (m)			20			

99.0 E 102.0 E
14.4 N
13.0 N

Population

Inhabitants 2000	**7,250,000**
Inhabitants 1985	5,018,327

demographia.com

Metropolitan development

Year	1965	2000
Total metropolitan inhabitants	2,100,000	7,250,000
Inhabitants in metropolitan core	1,500,000	6,320,000
Core share	**71.4%**	**87.2%**
Inhabitants in metropolitan periphery	600,000	930,000
Periphery share	28.6%	12.8%

demographia.com

Employment

	Metr. Area	CBD
Area (km²)	482	20.5
Area share	100%	4.2%
Employment	2,657,132	271,944
Employment share	100%	10.2%
Employment density (employment/km²)	**5,513**	**13,266**

demographia.com, 1995

Economy

Average income per capita (€)	**12,042**
Unemployment rate	2.2%

asiaweek.com, 2000

Health

Hospital beds per 1,000 inhabitants	**7**
Average life expectancy at birth	76

asiaweek.com, 2000

Crime

Crimes per 100,000 inhabitants	**3,050**

asiaweek.com, 2000

Metropolitan density

Inhabitants	6,685,000
Built-up area (km²)	482
Population density (inhabitants/km²)	**13,869**

demographia.com, 1995

Residential density

Year	1985
Inhabitants	4,998,000
Residential area (km²)	264
Residential density (inhabitants/km²)	**18,932**

demographia.com

Traffic and transport

Public transport market share	29.4%
Private vehicle market share	70.6%
Average commuting time (minutes)	**60**

publicpurpose.com, 1990; asiaweek.com, 2000

Road use

Average road speed (km/hour)	13.0
Vehicle density (vehicle km/km²)	**130,754**

publicpurpose.com, 1990

Railway use

Rail vehicle density (vehicle km/km²)	**2,652,288**

publicpurpose.com, 1990

Climate

Average January temperature (°C)	21.7
Average July temperature (°C)	**32.2**

weatherbase.com

Pollution

NOX (tonnes/km²)	53.7
CO (tonnes/km²)	1,264,1
VOC (tonnes/km²)	346.7
Total pollution (tonnes/km²)	**1,664.5**

demographia.com, 1990

Barcelona Spain

Elevation (m)   6

Population

Inhabitants 2001	**3,766,000**

demographia.com

Metropolitan density

Inhabitants	3,766,000
Built-up area (km²)	699
Population density (inhabitants/km²)	**5,388**

demographia.com, 2001

Metropolitan development

Year	1965	2001
Total metropolitan inhabitants	2,175,000	3,766,000
Inhabitants in metropolitan core	1,650,000	1,504,000
Core share	**75.9%**	**39.9%**
Inhabitants in metropolitan periphery	525,000	2,262,000
Periphery share	24.1%	60.1%

demographia.com

Traffic and transport

Public transport market share	48.8%
Private vehicle market share	51.2%
Average commuting time (minutes)	**24**

publicpurpose.com, 1990; Eurostat, 1996

Economy

Gross regional product per capita (€)	20,830
Unemployment rate	5.3%

Eurostat, 1996

Climate

Average January temperature (°C)	4.4
Average July temperature (°C)	**27.2**

weatherbase.com

Crime

Crimes per 100,000 inhabitants	**2,280**

Eurostat, 1996

Torello

Puigreig

Vich

Cardona

Sant Hilari Sacalm

Girona

[GRO]

Navas

Tona

Girona

Sona

Surla

Mola

Santa Coloma de Farnes

Casa de la Selva

Sallent

Centellas

Llagostera

Sant Fruitos de Bages

Arbucies

Videres

Manresa

Bigus

L'Ametlla de Valles

Lloret de Mar

Sant Vicenç de Castellet

Blanes

Palau de Plegamans

Linars de Valles

Sant Andreu

Iguatada

Terassa

Granollers

Arenys de Mar

Olesa de Montserrat

Sabadell

Montmelo

Mataro

Masquefa

Cerdanyola del Valles

Premia de Mar

Martorel

Rubi

El Masnou

La Palma

Sant Cugat del Valles

Molins de Rei

Santa Coloma de Gramenet

L'Hospitalet de Llobregat

Sant Adria de Besos

Villafranca del Panades

Viladecans

Barcelona

[BCN]

Les Corts

Sant Pere de Ribes

Gava

El Prat

Villanueva y Geltru

ndreit

0 |||||||||| 10km

Beijing China

114.9 E 117.9 E
40.7 N
39.7 N

MET
17

Elevation (m)   55

CRG
28

Population

Inhabitants 2000   **13,160,000**
demographia.com

Metropolitan density

Inhabitants	7,500,000
Built-up area (km²)	518
Population density (inhabitants/km²)	**14,479**

demographia.com, 1990

Residential density

Year	1985
Inhabitants	5,608,000
Residential area (km²)	391
Residential density (inhabitants/km²)	**14,343**

demographia.com

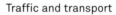

Traffic and transport

Average commuting time (minutes)   **45**
asiaweek.com, 2000

Economy

Average income per capita (€)	**3,729**
Unemployment rate	4.6%

asiaweek.com, 2000

Health

Hospital beds per 1,000 inhabitants	**6**
Average life expectancy at birth	71

asiaweek.com, 2000

Climate

Average January temperature (°C)	-8.3
Average July temperature (°C)	**30.0**

weatherbase.com

Crime

Crimes per 100,000 inhabitants   **520**
asiaweek.com, 2000

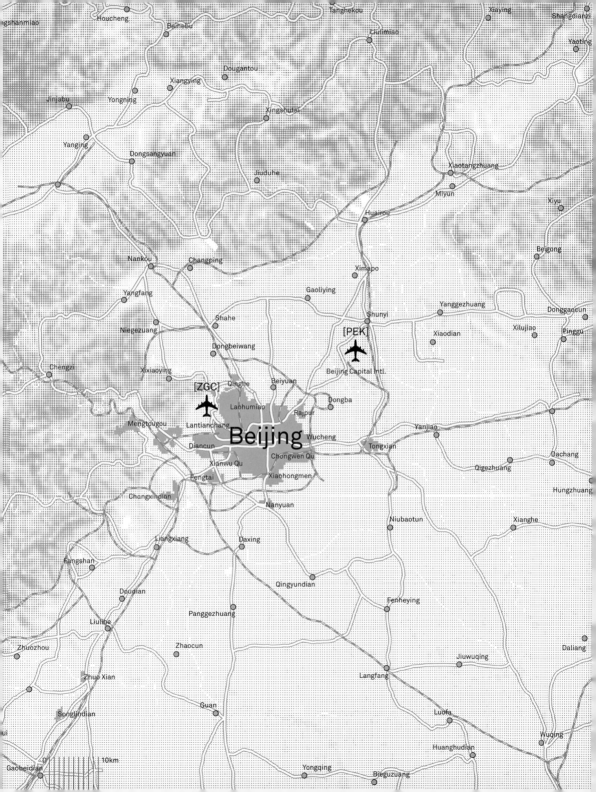

Berlin Germany

11.8E 14.9E
- 53.2 N
- 51.7 N

Elevation (m) 48

Population

Inhabitants 2002 **4,101,000**
demographia.com

Metropolitan development

Year	1965	2002
Total metropolitan inhabitants	4,025,000	4,101,000
Inhabitants in metropolitan core	3,241,000	3,388,000
Core share	**80.5%**	**82.6%**
Inhabitants in metropolitan periphery	784,000	713,000
Periphery share	19.5%	17.4%

demographia.com

Metropolitan density

Inhabitants	3,880,000
Built-up area (km²)	1,230
Population density (inhabitants/km²)	**3,154**

demographia.com, 2001

Residential density

Year	1985
Inhabitants	3,033,000
Residential area (km²)	709
Residential density (inhabitants/km²)	**4,278**

demographia.com

Traffic and transport

Public transport market share	46.0%
Private vehicle market share	54.0%
Average commuting time (minutes)	**30**

publicpurpose.com, 1990; Eurostat, 1996

Economy

Gross regional product per capita (€)	20,960
Unemployment rate	15.7%

Regio Randstad, 2002

Health

Hospital beds per 1,000 inhabitants	**6**
Average life expectancy at birth	76

Eurostat, 1996

Climate

Average January temperature (°C)	-3.3
Average July temperature (°C)	**22.8**

weatherbase.com

Crime

Crimes per 100,000 inhabitants	**17,190**

Eurostat, 1996

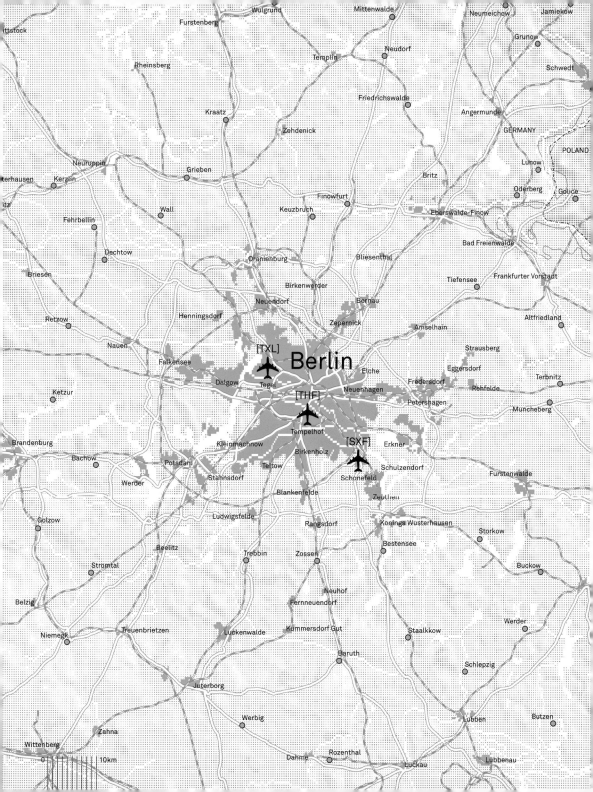

Bogotá Colombia

75.5 W 72.5 W
5.9 N

3.9 N

MET
36

Elevation (m) 2,547

Population

Inhabitants 2000	**6,990,000**

demographia.com

Metropolitan development

Year	1965
Total metropolitan inhabitants	1,350,000
Inhabitants in metropolitan core	1,150,000
Core share	**85.2%**
Inhabitants in metropolitan periphery	200,000
Periphery share	14.8%

demographia.com

Metropolitan density

Inhabitants	5,570,000
Built-up area (km²)	479
Population density (inhabitants/km²)	**11,628**

demographia.com, 1995

Residential density

Year	1985
Inhabitants	4,711,000
Residential area (km²)	205
Residential density (inhabitants/km²)	**22,980**

demographia.com

Climate

Average January temperature (°C)	6.1
Average July temperature (°C)	**17.8**

weatherbase.com

Caparrapi

Topaipi

Ubate

Andalucía

Choconta

Pacho

Guaduas

Vergara

Suspeta

Zipaquirá

Sesquile

Vileta

La Vega

Cajica

Guasca

Chila

Alban

Guavata

Facatativa

Anolaima

Sube el Prado

El Cedro

Madrid

[BOG]

La Calera

Funza

Ursaquen

Fontibon

Morato

La Mesa

El Dorado Intl.

La Providencia

San Antonio de Tena

San Bernardo

Bogotá

Bosa

Bravo Paez

Egipto

Colombia

Soacha

Tunjuello

San Isidro

Usme

Choachi

La Ruidosa

Formaque

Silvania

El Calvario

Fusagasuga

La Unión

Guayabetel

Melgar

Pandi

Iconozo

Villavicencio

Venecia

Cunday

San Juan

Cabrera

Acacias

0   10km

Boston United States

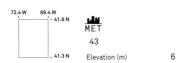

72.4 W	69.4 W		
	– 41.6 N	**MET**	
		43	
	– 41.3 N	Elevation (m)	6

MOV
18

Population

Inhabitants 2003	**5,815,000**
demographia.com	

Metropolitan development

Year	1965	2003
Total metropolitan inhabitants	3,540,000	5,815,000
Inhabitants in metropolitan core	670,000	582,000
Core share	**18.9%**	**10.0%**
Inhabitants in metropolitan periphery	2,870,000	5,233,000
Periphery share	81.1%	90.0%
demographia.com		

Metropolitan density

Inhabitants	5,690,000
Built-up area (km²)	5,144
Population density (inhabitants/km²)	**1,106**
demographia.com, 2000	

Residential density

Year	1985
Inhabitants	2,470,000
Residential area (km²)	784
Residential density (inhabitants/km²)	**3,151**
demographia.com, 1990	

Employment

	Metr. Area	CBD
Area (km²)	5,144	8.5
Area share	100%	0.2%
Employment	2,182,115	148,400
Employment share	100%	6.8%
Employment density (employment/km²)	**424**	**17,459**
demographia.com, 2000		

Economy

Average income per capita (€)	**18,333**
Gross regional product per capita (€)	32,241
Unemployment rate	2.2%
bestplaces.net, 1998; demographia.com, 1998	

Traffic and transport

Public transport market share	3.1%
Private vehicle market share	96.9%
Average commuting time (minutes)	**23**
publicpurpose.com, 1991; bestplaces.net, 1998	

Road use

Average road speed (km/hour)	52.3
Vehicle density (vehicle km/km²)	**35,397**
publicpurpose.com, 1990	

Railway use

Passenger density (passenger km/km)	19,816
Rail vehicle density (vehicle km/km²)	**79,089**
publicpurpose.com, 1990	

Climate

Average January temperature (°C)	-5.6
Average July temperature (°C)	**27.8**
weatherbase.com	

Crime

Crimes per 100,000 inhabitants	6,288
bestplaces.net, 1998	

Pollution

NOX (tonnes/km²)	30.5
CO (tonnes/km²)	267.6
VOC (tonnes/km²)	26.6
Total pollution (tonnes/km²)	**324.7**
demographia.com, 1990	

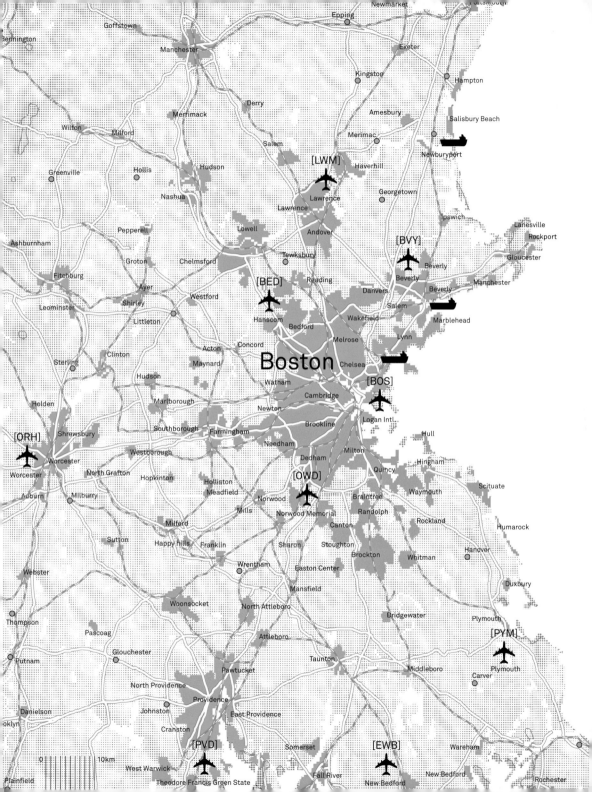

Buenos Aires Argentina

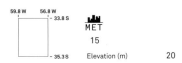

MET
15
Elevation (m) 20

TEL
19

Population

Inhabitants 2000   **13,390,000**
demographia.com

Metropolitan development

Year	1965
Total metropolitan inhabitants	7,700,000
Inhabitants in metropolitan core	2,950,000
Core share	**38.3%**
Inhabitants in metropolitan periphery	4,750,000
Periphery share	61.7%

demographia.com

Metropolitan density

Inhabitants	11,200,000
Built-up area (km²)	2,771
Population density (inhabitants/km²)	**4,042**

demographia.com, 1998

Residential density

Year	1985
Inhabitants	10,750,000
Residential area (km²)	1,385
Residential density (inhabitants/km²)	**7,762**

demographia.com

Climate

Average January temperature (°C)	17.8
Average July temperature (°C)	**14.4**

weatherbase.com

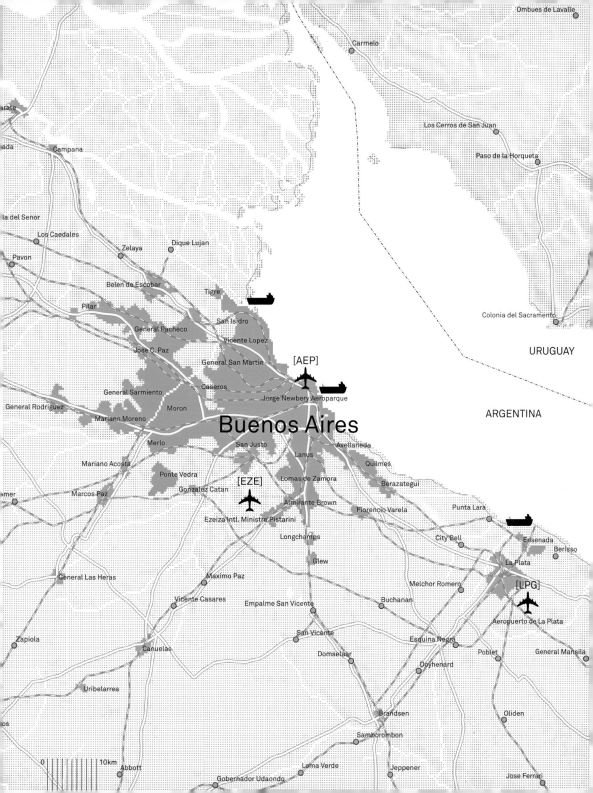

Busan South Korea

126.9 E   129.9 E
                    36.0 N

                    34.5 N

CNT OIL DRY
 4   24   7

Elevation (m)   71

Metropolitan density

Inhabitants	3,650,000
Built-up area (km²)	366
Population density (inhabitants/km²)	**9,973**

demographia.com, 2002

Population

Inhabitants 2002	**3,650,000**

demographia.com

Economy

Average income per capita (€)	**8,920**
Unemployment rate	9.1%

asiaweek.com, 2000

Health

Hospital beds per 1,000 inhabitants	**6**
Average life expectancy at birth	71

asiaweek.com, 2000

Climate

Average January temperature (°C)	-0.6
Average July temperature (°C)	**26.7**

weatherbase.com

Crime

Crimes per 100,000 inhabitants	**3,570**

asiaweek.com, 2000

Cairo Egypt

30.1 E 33.1 E
— 30.9 N

MET
10

— 29.5 N   Elevation (m)   74

Population

Inhabitants 2000   14,000,000
demographia.com

Metropolitan development

Year	1965	1999
Total metropolitan inhabitants	4,600,000	13,250,000
Inhabitants in metropolitan core	3,800,000	6,789,000
Core share	**82.6%**	**51.2%**
Inhabitants in metropolitan periphery	800,000	6,461,000
Periphery share	17.4%	48.8%

demographia.com

Metropolitan density

Inhabitants	13,250,000
Built-up area (km²)	482
Population density (inhabitants/km²)	**27,490**

demographia.com, 1999

Residential density

Year	1985
Inhabitants	8,595,000
Residential area (km²)	269
Residential density (inhabitants/km²)	**31,952**

demographia.com

Climate

Average January temperature (°C)	9.4
Average July temperature (°C)	**33.9**

weatherbase.com

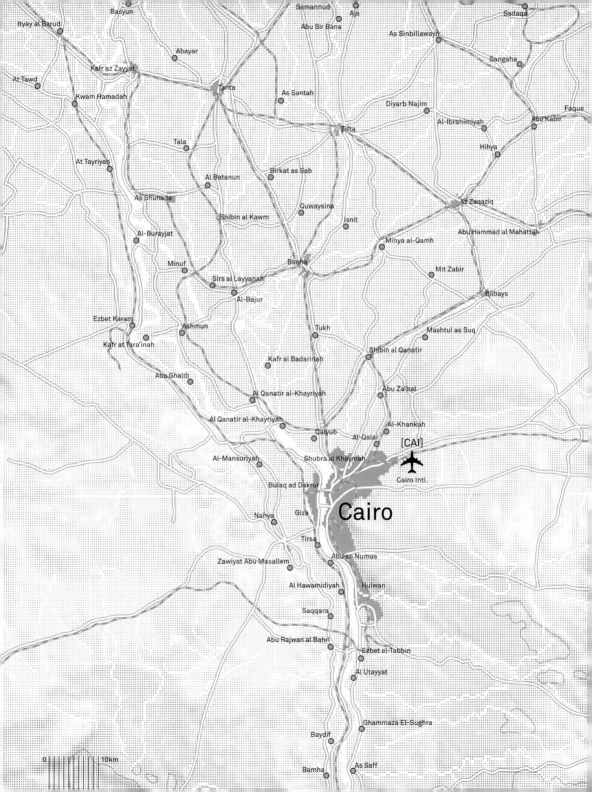

Basyun
Samannud
Aja
Sadaqa
Ityay al Barud
Abu Sir Bana
As Sinbillawayn
Sangaha
Abayar
Faqus
Kafr az Zayyat
At Tawd
Al-Ibrahimiyah
Abu Kabir
Tanta
Kwam Hamadah
Diyarb Najim
As Santah
Zifta
Hihya
Tala
At Tayriyah
Birkat as Sab
Al Batanun
As Shuhada
Az Zaqaziq
Shibin al Kawm
Quwaysina
Al-Burayjat
Isnit
Abu Hammad al Mahattah
Minya al-Qamh
Banha
Minuf
Mit Zabir
Sirs al Layyanah
Al-Bajur
Bilbays
Ezbet Karam
Ashmun
Tukh
Mashtul as Suq
Kafr at Tara'inah
Shibin al Qanatir
Kafr al Badarinah
Abu Ghalib
Abu Za'bal
Al Qanatir al-Khayriyah
Al-Khankah
Al Qanatir al-Khayriyah
Qalyub
[CAI]
Al-Qalai
Al-Mansuriyah
Shubra al Khaymah
Cairo Intl.
Bulaq ad Dakrur

Cairo

Nahya
Giza
Tirsa
Zawiyat Abu Masallem
Abu an Numus
Al Hawamidiyah
Hulwan
Saqqara
Abu Rajwan al Bahn
Ezbet el-Tabbin
Al Utayyat
Ghammaza El-Sughra
Baydif
Bamha
As Saff

0   10km

Calcutta India

86.8 E   89.8 E
- 23.3 N

MET

12

- 21.9 N   Elevation (m)   6

Population

Inhabitants 2000   **13,940,000**
demographia.com

Metropolitan density

Inhabitants	13,940,000
Built-up area (km²)	1,036
Population density (inhabitants/km²)	**13,456**

demographia.com, 2000

Residential density

Year	1985
Inhabitants	10,462,000
Residential area (km²)	541
Residential density (inhabitants/km²)	**19,338**

demographia.com

Climate

Average January temperature (°C)	13.9
Average July temperature (°C)	**31.7**

weatherbase.com

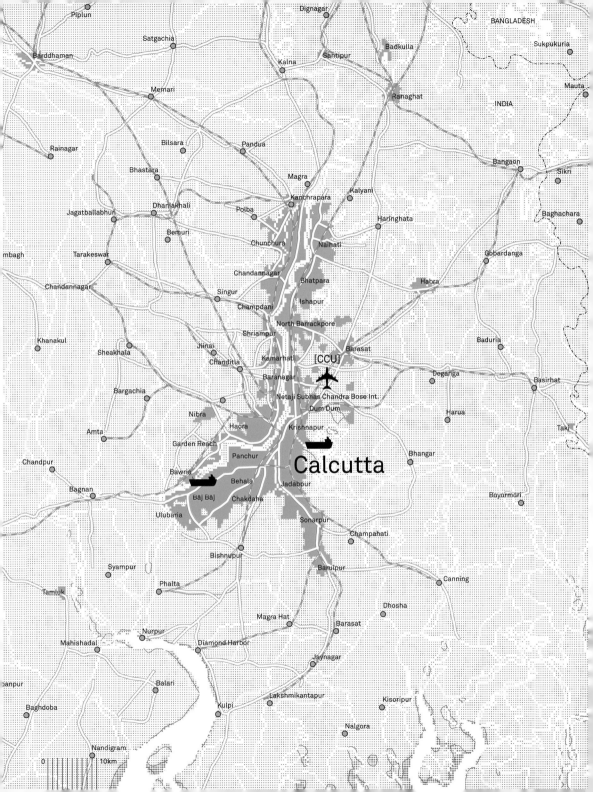

Charlotte United States

82.3 W 79.3 W
┌─ 35.9 N
│   │
│   │
└─ 34.5 N

Elevation (m)   213

Population

Inhabitants 2000	**759,000**
Inhabitants 1985	314,447

US Census

MOV
16

Metropolitan density

Inhabitants	759,000
Built-up area (km²)	1,126
Population density (inhabitants/km²)	**674**

US Census, 2000

Employment

	Metr. Area	CBD
Area (km²)	1,126	-
Area share	100%	-
Employment	634,924	46,782
Employment share	100%	7.4%
Employment density (employment/km²)	**564**	-

demographia.com, 2000

Traffic and transport

Average commuting time (minutes)	**21**

bestplaces.net, 1998

Economy

Average income per capita (€)	**20,465**
Unemployment rate	3.2%

bestplaces.net, 1998

Railway use

Rail vehicle density (vehicle km/km²)	**18,469**

publicpurpose.com, 1990

Climate

Average January temperature (°C)	-0.6
Average July temperature (°C)	**31.7**

weatherbase.com

Crime

Crimes per 100,000 inhabitants	**8,829**

bestplaces.net, 1998

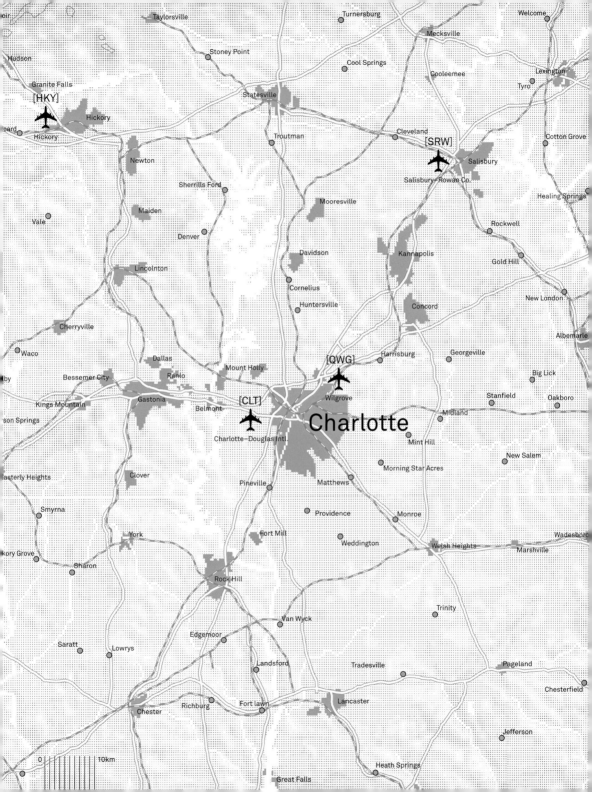

Chennai India

78.1 E　81.1 E

－13.7 N

MET

37

－12.3 N　Elevation (m)　16

Population

Inhabitants 2000	**6,700,000**
Inhabitants 1985	4,289,347

demographia.com

Metropolitan development

Year	1965	2000
Total metropolitan inhabitants	2,150,000	6,700,000
Inhabitants in metropolitan core	1,825,000	4,491,000
Core share	**84.9%**	**67,0%**
Inhabitants in metropolitan periphery	325,000	2,209,000
Periphery share	15.1%	33,0%

demographia.com

Metropolitan density

Inhabitants	6,083,000
Built-up area (km²)	456
Population density (inhabitants/km²)	**13,340**

demographia.com, 1995

Climate

Average January temperature (°C)	21.1
Average July temperature (°C)	**33.9**

weatherbase.com

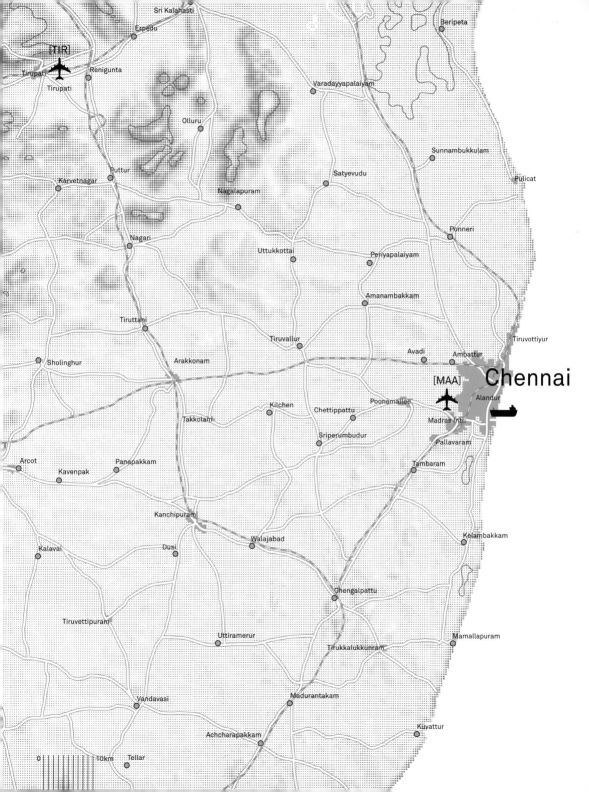

Chicago United States

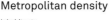

89.2 W	86.2 W		
	42.6 N		
		MET	PAX CRG MOV
		27	2 12 1
	41.1 N	Elevation (m) 205	

Population

Inhabitants 2003	**9,549,000**
demographia.com	

Metropolitan density

Inhabitants	8,960,000
Built-up area (km²)	5,499
Population density (inhabitants/km²)	**1,629**
demographia.com, 2000	

Residential density

Year	1985
Inhabitants	6,511,000
Residential area (km²)	1,973
Residential density (inhabitants/km²)	**3,300**
demographia.com	

Metropolitan development

Year	1965	2003
Total metropolitan inhabitants	7,090,000	9,549,000
Inhabitants in metropolitan core	3,575,000	3,869,000
Core share	**50.4%**	**40.5%**
Inhabitants in metropolitan periphery	3,515,000	5,680,000
Periphery share	49.6%	59.5%
demographia.com		

Employment

	Metr. Area	CBD
Area (km²)	5,499	18.6
Area share	100%	0.3%
Employment	3,870,378	977,700
Employment share	100%	25.3%
Employment density (employment/km²)	**704**	**52,565**
demographia.com, 2000		

Traffic and transport

Public transport market share	5.0%
Private vehicle market share	95.0%
Average commuting time (minutes)	**30**
bestplaces.net, 1998; publicpurpose.com, 1990	

Road use

Average road speed (km/hour)	45.1
Vehicle density (vehicle km/km²)	**44,997**
publicpurpose.com, 1990	

Economy

Average income per capita (€)	**14,533**
Gross regional product per capita (€)	31,507
Unemployment rate	4.1%
bestplaces.net, 1998	

Railway use

Passenger density (passenger km/km)	17,420
Rail vehicle density (vehicle km/km²)	**117,737**
publicpurpose.com, 1990	

Climate

Average January temperature (°C)	-10.6
Average July temperature (°C)	**28.9**
weatherbase.com	

Crime

Crimes per 100,000 inhabitants	**8,060**
bestplaces.net, 1998	

Pollution

NOX (tonnes/km²)	34.4
CO (tonnes/km²)	306.6
VOC (tonnes/km²)	33.2
Total pollution (tonnes/km²)	**374.1**
demographia.com, 1990	

Cincinnati United States

86.1 W 83.1 W

39.7 N

38.2 N

Elevation (m)   149

Population

Inhabitants 2000	**1,503,000**
Inhabitants 1985	1,123,000

US Census

MOV
29

Metropolitan density

Inhabitants	1,503,000
Built-up area (km²)	1,740
Population density (inhabitants/km²)	**864**

US Census, 2000

Metropolitan development

Year	1965	2000
Total metropolitan inhabitants	813,000	1,503,000
Inhabitants in metropolitan core	504,000	331,000
Core share	**62.0%**	**22.0%**
Inhabitants in metropolitan periphery	309,000	1,172,000
Periphery share	38.0%	78.0%

demographia.com

Change in density (1970–1990)

Change in inhabitants	101,000
Change in area (km²)	699
Change in density (inhabitants/km²)	**144**

demographia.com

Employment

	Metr. Area	CBD
Area (km²)	1,740	-
Area share	100%	-
Employment	828,139	77,198
Employment share	100%	9.3%
Employment density (employment/km²)	**476**	-

demographia.com, 2000

Traffic and transport

Average commuting time (minutes)	**20**

bestplaces.net, 1998

Road use

Vehicle density (vehicle km/km²)	30,472

publicpurpose.com, 1990

Economy

Average income per capita (€)	**13,862**
Unemployment rate	3.4%

bestplaces.net, 1998

Railway use

Rail vehicle density (vehicle km/km²)	**28,636**

publicpurpose.com, 1990

Climate

Average January temperature (°C)	-6.1
Average July temperature (°C)	**30.6**

weatherbase.com

Crime

Crimes per 100,000 inhabitants	**6,356**

bestplaces.net, 1998

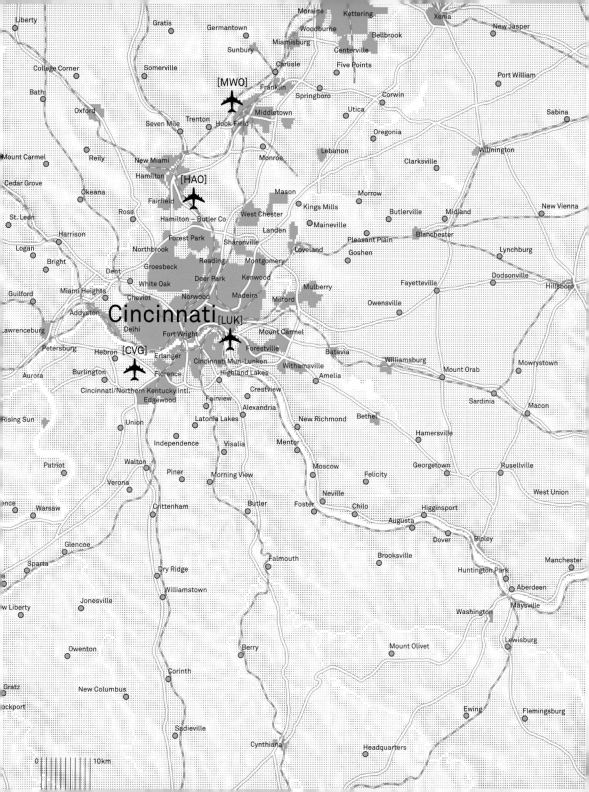

Copenhagen Denmark

11.0 E 14.0 E
- 56.5 N

- 55.0 N
Elevation (m)   5

Population

Inhabitants 2003	**1,524,000**
Inhabitants 1985	1,207,000
Inhabitants 1970	1,340,000
Inhabitants 1960	1,322,000

demographia.com

Metropolitan development

Year	1965	2003
Total metropolitan inhabitants	1,380,000	1,524,000
Inhabitants in metropolitan core	705,000	501,000
Core share	**51.1%**	**32.9%**
Inhabitants in metropolitan periphery	675,000	1,023,000
Periphery share	48.9%	67.1%

demographia.com

@
TEL
10

Metropolitan density

Inhabitants	1,524,000
Built-up area (km²)	816
Population density (inhabitants/km²)	**1,868**

demographia.com, 2003

Employment

	Metr. Area	CBD
Area (km²)	816	4.7
Area share	100%	0.6%
Employment	956,000	122,770
Employment share	100%	12.8%
Employment density (employment/km²)	**1,172**	**26,121**

demographia.com, 2003

Traffic and transport

Public transport market share	15.4%
Private vehicle market share	84.6%
Average commuting time (minutes)	**29**

publicpurpose.com, 1990

Road use

Average road speed (km/hour)	34.0
Vehicle density (vehicle km/km²)	**73,308**

publicpurpose.com, 1990

Economy

Gross regional product per capita (€)	41,944

Regio Randstad, 2002

Railway use

Rail vehicle density (vehicle km/km²)	**623,976**

publicpurpose.com, 1990

Health

Hospital beds per 1,000 inhabitants	**5**
Average life expectancy at birth	72

Eurostat, 1996

Climate

Average January temperature (°C)	-1.1
Average July temperature (°C)	**20.6**

weatherbase.com

Crime

Crimes per 100,000 inhabitants	**12,950**

Eurostat, 1996

Pollution

NOX (tonnes/km²)	38.2
CO (tonnes/km²)	314.7
VOC (tonnes/km²)	18.1
Total pollution (tonnes/km²)	**371.0**

demographia.com, 1990

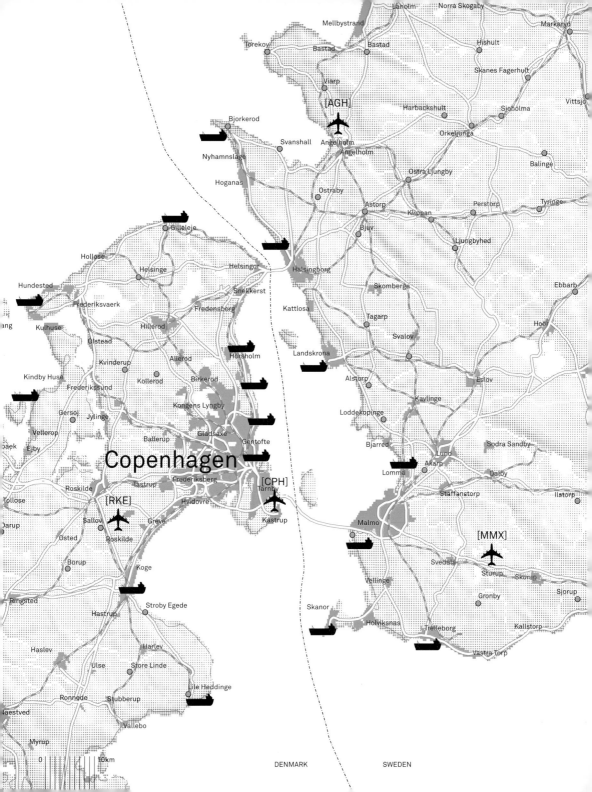

Laholm
Norra Skogaby
Mellbystrand
Markaryd
Torekov
Bastad
Bastad
Hishult
Skanes Fagerhult
Viarp
[AGH]
Harbackshult
Sjoholma
Bjorkerod
Angelholm
Vittsjo
Svanshall
Angelholm
Orkeljunga
Nyhamnslage
Balinge
Hoganas
Ostra Ljungby
Ostraby
Astorp
Perstorp
Tyringe
Klippan
Gilleleje
Bjuv
Ljungbyhed
Hollose
Helsingor
Halsingborg
Ebbarb
Helsinge
Skomberge
Snekkerst
Hundested
Frederiksvaerk
Kattlosa
Tagarp
Hool
Fredensborg
Landskrona
Svalov
ang
Kulhuse
Hillerod
Horsholm
Olstead
Allerod
Alstorp
Eslov
Kvinderup
Kindby Huse
Kollerod
Birkerod
Kavlinge
Frederikssund
Loddekopinge
Gersoj
Jylinge
Kongens Lyngby
Bjarred
Sodra Sandby
Vellerop
Ballerup
Lund
Dalby
aek
Ejby
Gladsaxe
Gentofte
Akarp

Copenhagen
Lomma
Ilstorp
Roskilde
Frederiksberg
Staffanstorp
Tastrup
[CPH]
Tarnby
[RKE]
Hvidovre
Malmo
[MMX]
Sallov
Greve
Kastrup
Osted
Roskilde
Svedala
Darup
Sturup
Skurup
Borup
Koge
Vellinge
Gronby
Sjorup
Tollose
Ringsted
Stroby Egede
Skanor
Hastrup
Holviksnas
Trelleborg
Kallstorp
Haslev
Harlev
Vastra Torp
Ulse
Store Linde
Ronnede
Stubberup
Lile Heddinge
aestved
Vallebo
Myrup

0   10km

DENMARK   SWEDEN

Dallas-Ft. Worth United States

98.4 W 95.4 W					

MET
44

Elevation (m)   168

PAX	CRG	MOV	@ TEL
6	21	2	21

Metropolitan density

Inhabitants	5,010,000
Built-up area (km²)	3,644
Population density (inhabitants/km²)	**1,375**

demographia.com, 2000

Population

Inhabitants 2003	**5,785,000**
Inhabitants 1985	2,451,000
Inhabitants 1970	2,016,000
Inhabitants 1960	1,435,000

demographia.com

Metropolitan development

Year	1965	2003
Total metropolitan inhabitants	1,820,000	5,785,000
Inhabitants in metropolitan core	1,150,000	1,794,000
Core share	**63.2%**	**31.0%**
Inhabitants in metropolitan periphery	670,000	3,991,000
Periphery share	36.8%	69.0%

demographia.com

Change in density (1970–1990)

Change in inhabitants	1,182,000
Change in area (km²)	1,354
Change in density (inhabitants/km²)	**873**

demographia.com

Employment

	Metr. Area	CBD
Area (km²)	3,644	-
Area share	100%	-
Employment	2,009,838	141,493
Employment share	100%	7.0%
Employment density (employment/km²)	**552**	-

demographia.com, 2000

Traffic and transport

Average commuting time (minutes)	**22**

bestplaces.net, 1998

Road use

Vehicle density (vehicle km/km²)	**36,343**

publicpurpose.com, 1990

Economy

Average income per capita (€)	**19,104**
Gross regional product per capita (€)	32,245
Unemployment rate	3.1%

demographia.com; bestplaces.net, 1998

Railway use

Passenger density (passenger km/km)	4,337
Rail vehicle density (vehicle km/km²)	**22,950**

publicpurpose.com, 1996

Climate

Average January temperature (°C)	1.1
Average July temperature (°C)	**35.6**

weatherbase.com

Crime

Crimes per 100,000 inhabitants	**9,615**

bestplaces.net, 1998

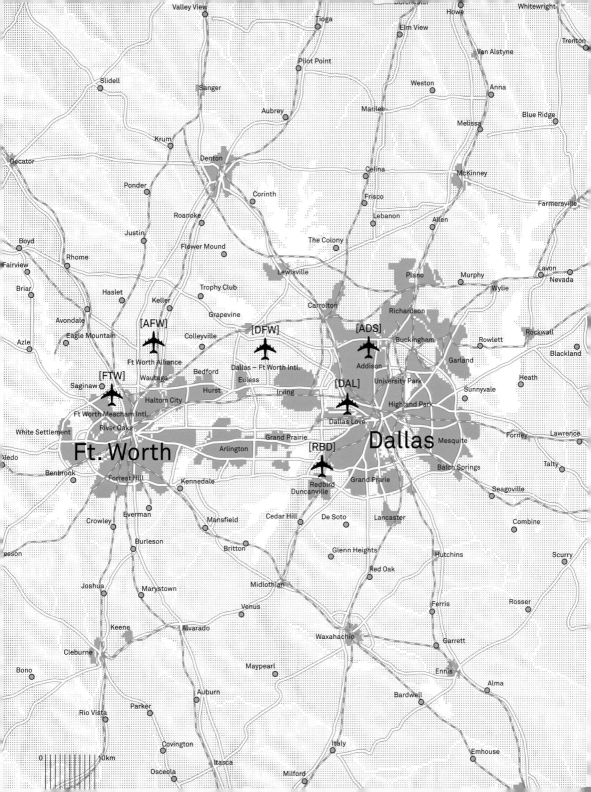

Denver United States

	PAX	MOV
	10	10

Elevation (m) 1611

Population

Inhabitants 2000	**1,984,000**
Inhabitants 1985	1,352,000
Inhabitants 1970	1,047,000

US Census

Metropolitan density

Inhabitants	1,984,000
Built-up area (km²)	1,292
Population density (inhabitants/km²)	**1,536**

US Census, 2000

Metropolitan development

	1965	2000
Year		
Total metropolitan inhabitants	499,000	1,984,000
Inhabitants in metropolitan core	416,000	555,000
Core share	**83.4%**	**28.0%**
Inhabitants in metropolitan periphery	83,000	1,429,000
Periphery share	16.6%	72.0%

demographia.com

Change in density (1970–1990)

Change in inhabitants	471,000
Change in area (km²)	756
Change in density (inhabitants/km²)	**623**

demographia.com

Employment

	Metr. Area	CBD
Area (km²)	1,292	22.0
Area share	100%	1.7%
Employment	982,659	166,722
Employment share	100%	17.0%
Employment density (employment/km²)	**761**	**7,578**

demographia.com, 2000

Traffic and transport

Public transport market share	1.4%
Private vehicle market share	98.6%
Average commuting time (minutes)	**20**

publicpurpose.com, 1990; bestplaces.net, 1998

Road use

Average road speed (km/hour)	58.1
Vehicle density (vehicle km/km²)	**36,166**

publicpurpose.com, 1990

Economy

Average income per capita (€)	**18,124**
Gross regional product per capita (€)	32,622
Unemployment rate	2.2%

demographia.com; bestplaces.net, 1998

Railway use

Passenger density (passenger km/km)	3,629
Rail vehicle density (vehicle km/km²)	**63,966**

publicpurpose.com, 1996

Climate

Average January temperature (°C)	-8.9
Average July temperature (°C)	**31.1**

weatherbase.com

Crime

Crimes per 100,000 inhabitants	**5,256**

bestplaces.net, 1998

Pollution

NOX (tonnes/km²)	24.7
CO (tonnes/km²)	302.3
VOC (tonnes/km²)	27.0
Total pollution (tonnes/km²)	**354.1**

demographia.com, 1990

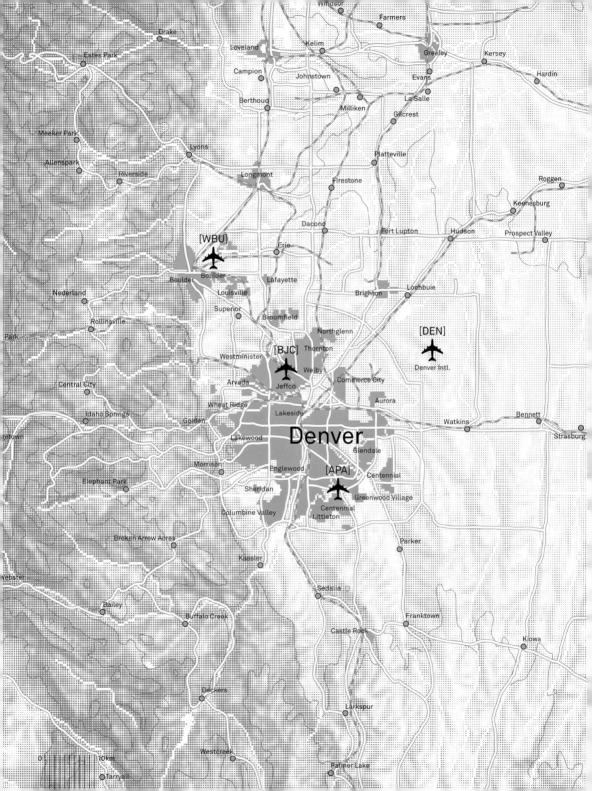

Detroit United States

MET
49

PAX
18

MOV
7

Elevation (m) 193

Population

Inhabitants 2003	**5,415,000**

demographia.com

Metropolitan development

Year	1965	2003
Total metropolitan inhabitants	4,370,000	5,415,000
Inhabitants in metropolitan core	1,600,000	911,000
Core share	**36.6%**	**16.8%**
Inhabitants in metropolitan periphery	2,770,000	4,504,000
Periphery share	63.4%	83.2%

demographia.com

Employment

	Metr. Area	CBD
Area (km²)	3,266	3.6
Area share	100%	0.1%
Employment	2,071,395	153.602
Employment share	100%	7.4%
Employment density (employment/km²)	**634**	**42,667**

demographia.com, 1990

Economy

Average income per capita (€)	**9,950**
Gross regional product per capita (€)	26,947
Unemployment rate	3.1%

demographia.com; bestplaces.net, 1998

Crime

Crimes per 100,000 inhabitants	**10,416**

bestplaces.net, 1998

Metropolitan density

Inhabitants	3,903,000
Built-up area (km²)	3,266
Population density (inhabitants/km²)	**1,195**

demographia.com, 1990

Residential density

Year	1985
Inhabitants	3,133,000
Residential area (km²)	1,212
Residential density (inhabitants/km²)	**2,585**

demographia.com

Change in density (1970–1990)

Change in inhabitants	-274,000
Change in area (km²)	1,002
Change in density (inhabitants/km²)	**-273**

demographia.com

Traffic and transport

Public transport market share	1.0%
Private vehicle market share	99.0%
Average commuting time (minutes)	**23**

publicpurpose.com, 1990; bestplaces.net, 1998

Road use

Average road speed (km/hour)	56.4
Vehicle density (vehicle km/km²)	**41,032**

publicpurpose.com, 1990

Railway use

Rail vehicle density (vehicle km/km²)	**32,246**

publicpurpose.com, 1990

Climate

Average January temperature (°C)	-8.9
Average July temperature (°C)	**28.3**

weatherbase.com

Pollution

NOX (tonnes/km²)	31.7
CO (tonnes/km²)	315.8
VOC (tonnes/km²)	31.7
Total pollution (tonnes/km²)	**379.2**

demographia.com, 1990

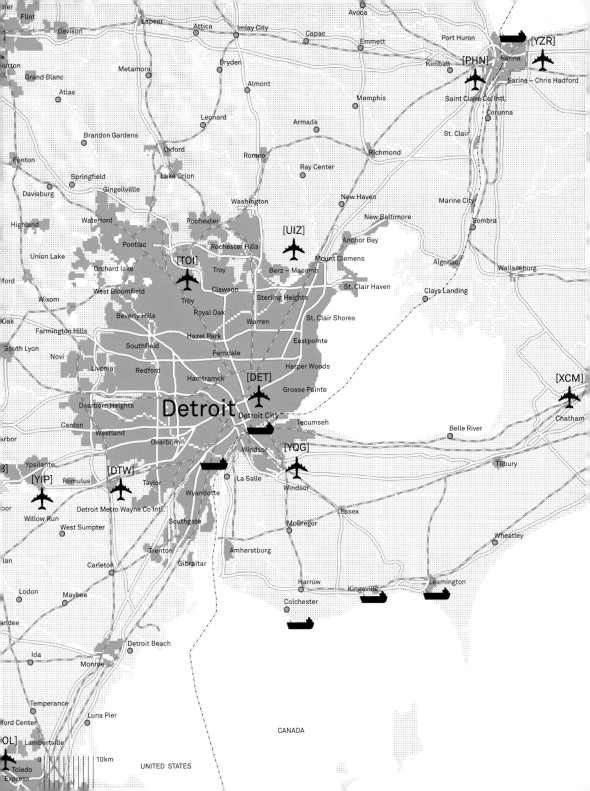

Dhaka Bangladesh

88.9 E   91.9 E   - 24.4 N

MET
30
Elevation (m)   9

- 22.9 N

Population

Inhabitants 2000	8,610,000

demographia.com

Metropolitan development

Year	1965
Total metropolitan inhabitants	750,000
Inhabitants in metropolitan core	362,000
Core share	**48.3%**
Inhabitants in metropolitan periphery	388,000
Periphery share	51.7%

demographia.com

Residential density

Year	1985
Inhabitants	3,283,000
Residential area (km²)	83
Residential density (inhabitants/km²)	**39,554**

demographia.com

Traffic and transport

Average commuting time (minutes)	**60**

asiaweek.com, 2000

Economy

Average income per capita (€)	**1,456**
Unemployment rate	40.1%

asiaweek.com, 2000

Health

Hospital beds per 1,000 inhabitants	1
Average life expectancy at birth	61

asiaweek.com, 2000

Climate

Average January temperature (°C)	14.4
Average July temperature (°C)	**30.6**

weatherbase.com

Crime

Crimes per 100,000 inhabitants	**200**

asiaweek.com, 2000

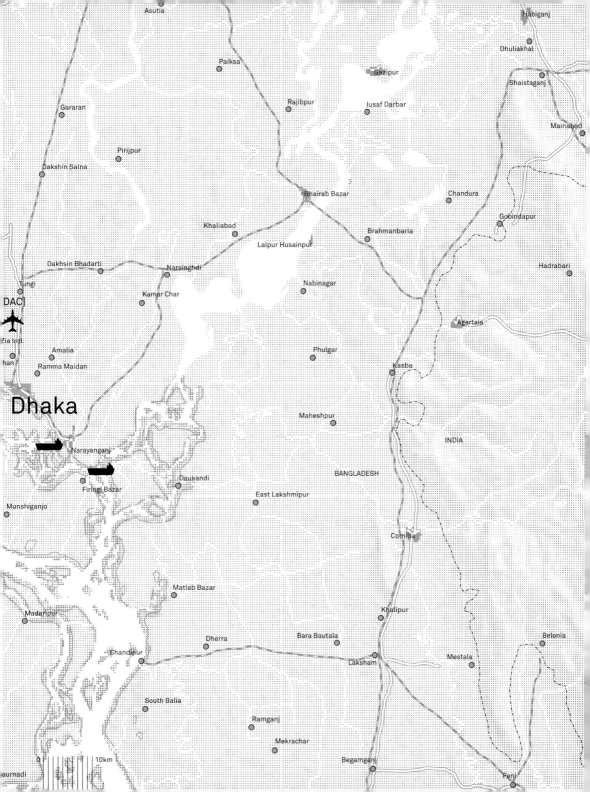

Djakarta Indonesia

105.3 E   108.3 E
-5.4 S

MET
16

-6.9 S   Elevation (m)   30

Population

Inhabitants 2000	**13,330,000**
Inhabitants 1970	4,761,000

demographia.com

Metropolitan density

Inhabitants	13,300,000
Built-up area (km²)	2,590
Population density (inhabitants/km²)	**5,135**

demographia.com, 2000

Residential density

Year	1985
Inhabitants	8,122,000
Residential area (km²)	197
Residential density (inhabitants/km²)	**41,228**

demographia.com

Change in density (1970–1990)

Change in inhabitants	3,461,000
Change in area (km²)	213
Change in density (inhabitants/km²)	**16,249**

demographia.com

Traffic and transport

Public transport market share	37.3%
Private vehicle market share	62.7%
Average commuting time (minutes)	**79**

publicpurpose.com, 1990; asiaweek.com, 2000

Road use

Average road speed (km/hour)	23.7
Vehicle density (vehicle km/km²)	**74.810**

publicpurpose.com, 1990

Economy

Average income per capita (€)	**5,815**
Unemployment rate	16.8%

asiaweek.com, 2000

Railway use

Rail vehicle density (vehicle km/km²)	**1,499,235**

publicpurpose.com, 1990

Health

Hospital beds per 1,000 inhabitants	**2**
Average life expectancy at birth	65

asiaweek.com, 2000

Climate

Average January temperature (°C)	23.9
Average July temperature (°C)	**31.1**

weatherbase.com

Crime

Crimes per 100,000 inhabitants	**220**
asiaweek.com, 2000	

Pollution

NOX (tonnes/km²)	276.8
CO (tonnes/km²)	986.1
VOC (tonnes/km²)	159.1
Total pollution (tonnes/km²)	**1,422.0**

demographia.com, 1990

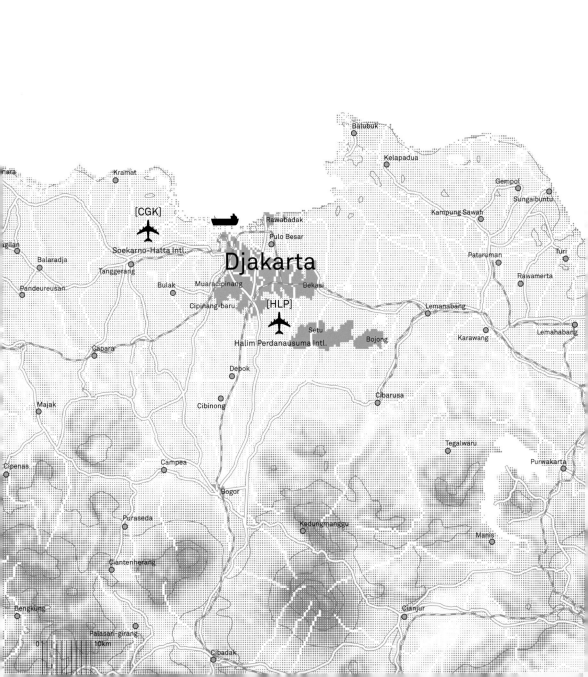

Batubuk

Kelapadua

Gempol

Sungaibuntu

Kampung Sawah

Kramat

Pataruman

Turi

[CGK]

Rawabadak

Rawamerta

Pulo Besar

Soekarno-Hatta Intl.

Djakarta

Balaradja

Tanggerang

Bulak

Muaracipinang

Bekasi

Lemanabang

Lemahabang

Pandeureusan

Cipinang-baru

[HLP]

Karawang

Capara

Halim Perdanausuma Intl.

Setu

Bojong

Depok

Cibarusa

Majak

Cibinong

Tegalwaru

Purwakarta

Cipenas

Campea

Bogor

Kedungmanggu

Manis

Puraseda

Ciantenherang

Bengkung

Cianjur

Patasan-gurang

10km

0

Cibadak

Dubai United Arab Emirates

54.5 E 57.5 E
— 27.2 N

— 24.7 N   Elevation (m)   5

CRG
25

Population

Inhabitants 2003   1,171,000
citypopulation.de

Climate

Average January temperature (°C)   14.4
Average July temperature (°C)   **39.4**
weatherbase.com

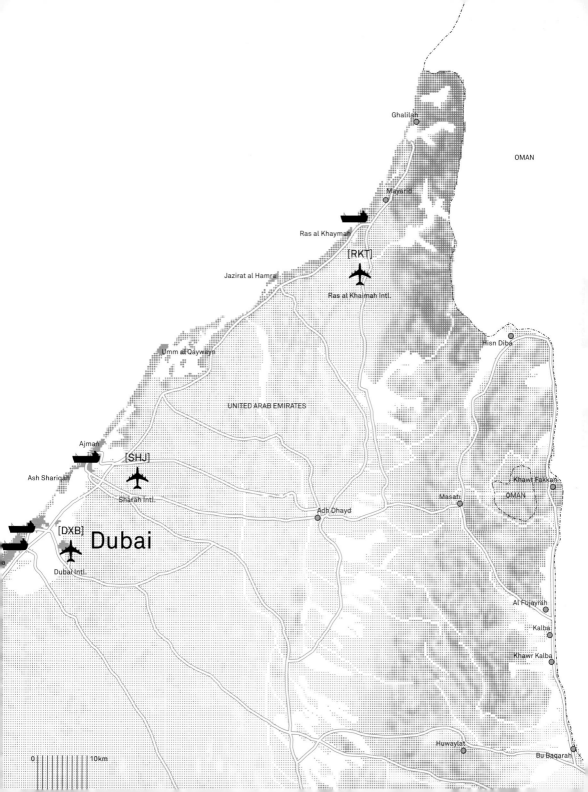

Durban South Africa

CNT OIL DRY
23   15   13

Elevation (m)   8

Population

Inhabitants 1996   2,117,650

citypopulation.de

Climate

| Average January temperature (°C) | 22.2 |
| **Average July temperature (°C)** | **22.2** |

weatherbase.com

Frankfurt Germany

	7.3 E	10.3 E
		50.7 N
		49.3 N

Elevation (m) 113

PAX	CRG	MOV	@ TEL
7	7	17	11

Metropolitan density

Inhabitants	2,600,000
Built-up area (km²)	984
Population density (inhabitants/km²)	**2,703**

demographia.com, 2001

Population

Inhabitants 2001	**2,600,000**

demographia.com

Metropolitan development

Year	1965	2001
Total metropolitan inhabitants	1,450,000	2,600,000
Inhabitants in metropolitan core	695,000	641,000
Core share	**47.9%**	**24.7%**
Inhabitants in metropolitan periphery	755,000	1,959,000
Periphery share	52.1%	75.3%

demographia.com

Employment

	Metr. Area	CBD
Area (km²)	984	2.3
Area share	100%	0.2%
Employment	119,735	-
Employment share	100%	-

demographia.com, 2001

Traffic and transport

Public transport market share	35.0%
Private vehicle market share	65.0%
Average commuting time (minutes)	**28**

publicpurpose.com, 1990

Road use

Average road speed (km/hour)	29.9
Vehicle density (vehicle km/km²)	**84,744**

publicpurpose.com, 1990

Economy

Gross regional product per capita (€)	35,268
Unemployment rate	5.5%

Regio Randstad, 2002

Railway use

Passenger density (passenger km/km)	10,429
Rail vehicle density (vehicle km/km²)	**359,506**

publicpurpose.com, 1990

Health

Hospital beds per 1,000 inhabitants	**6**
Average life expectancy at birth	75

Eurostat, 1996

Climate

Average January temperature (°C)	-1.1
Average July temperature (°C)	**23.9**

weatherbase.com

Crime

Crimes per 100,000 inhabitants	**19,530**

Eurostat, 1996

Pollution

NOX (tonnes/km²)	93.8
CO (tonnes/km²)	318.1
VOC (tonnes/km²)	56.4
Total pollution (tonnes/km²)	**468.3**

demographia.com, 1990

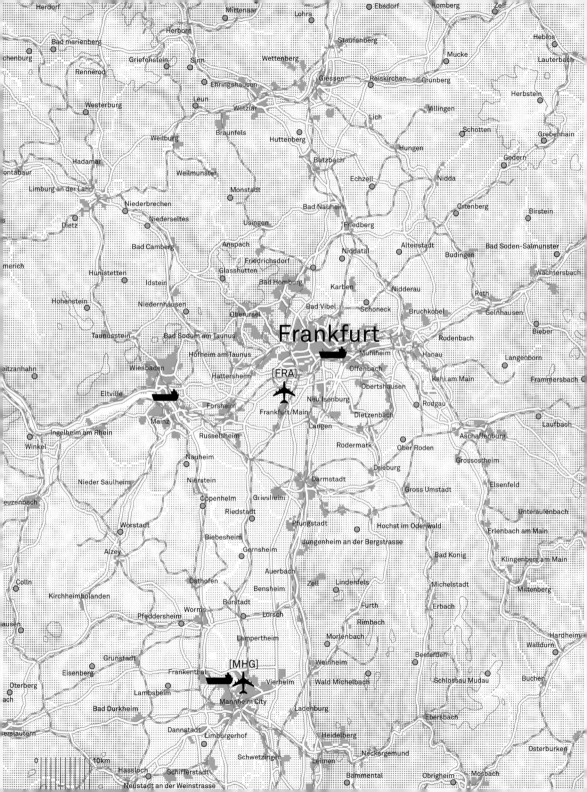

Geneva Switzerland

5.0 E   8.0 E
— 47.1 N

— 45.7N   Elevation (m)   416

Population

Inhabitants 2003	**399,000**
Inhabitants 1985	283,854

demographia.com

Metropolitan density

Inhabitants	399,000
Built-up area (km²)	114
Population density (inhabitants/km²)	**3,500**

demographia.com, 2003

Climate

Average January temperature (°C)	-1.7
Average July temperature (°C)	**25.0**

weatherbase.com

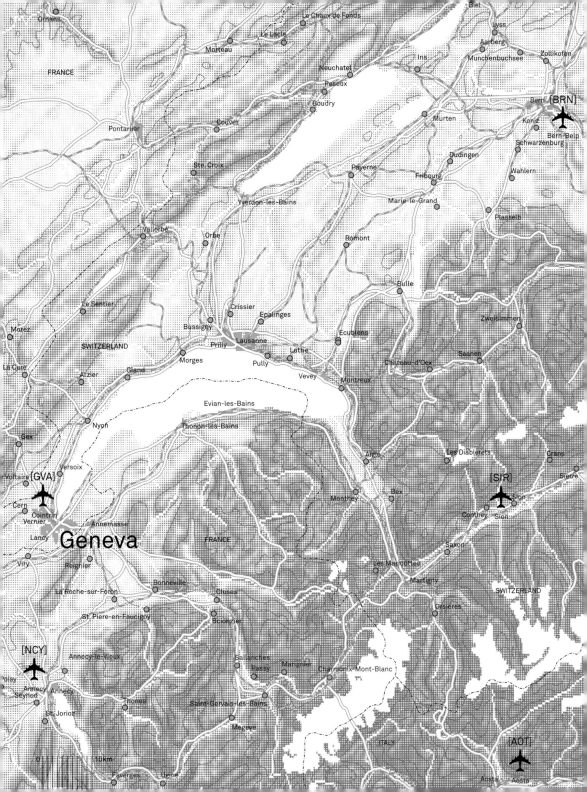

Hamburg Germany

	8.3 E	11.3 E		
			– 54.2 N	

	CNT	OIL	DRY
	17	18	10
Elevation (m)			16

Metropolitan density

Inhabitants	1,970,000
Built-up area (km²)	829
Population density (inhabitants/km²)	**2,376**

Kenworthy Laube, 1990

Population

Inhabitants 2002	**2,593,000**

demographia.com

Metropolitan development

Year	1965	2002
Total metropolitan inhabitants	2,300,000	2,593,000
Inhabitants in metropolitan core	1,855,000	1,726,000
Core share	**80.7%**	**66.6%**
Inhabitants in metropolitan periphery	445,000	867,000
Periphery share	19.3%	33.4%

demographia.com

Employment

	Metr. Area	CBD
Area (km²)	829	4.7
Area share	100%	0.6%
Employment	980,725	153,590
Employment share	100%	15.7%
Employment density (employment/km²)	**1,183**	**32,679**

demographia.com, 1990

Traffic and transport

Public transport market share	40.0%
Private vehicle market share	60.0%
Average commuting time (minutes)	**31**

publicpurpose.com, 1990

Road use

Average road speed (km/hour)	29.9
Vehicle density (vehicle km/km²)	**63,260**

publicpurpose.com, 1990

Economy

Gross regional product per capita (€)	33,452
Unemployment rate	8.3%

Regio Randstad, 2002

Railway use

Passenger density (passenger km/km)	16,654
Rail vehicle density (vehicle km/km²)	**455,121**

publicpurpose.com, 1990

Health

Hospital beds per 1,000 inhabitants	**6**
Average life expectancy at birth	76

Eurostat, 1996

Climate

Average January temperature (°C)	-1.1
Average July temperature (°C)	**21.1**

weatherbase.com

Crime

Crimes per 100,000 inhabitants	**15,940**

Eurostat, 1996

Pollution

NOX (tonnes/km²)	51.0
CO (tonnes/km²)	213.1
VOC (tonnes/km²)	33.2
Total pollution (tonnes/km²)	**297.3**

demographia.com, 1990

Hong Kong China

112.5 E	115.6 E								
		MET	CNT	OIL	DRY	PAX	CRG		@ TEL
		28	1	13	9	17	2		17
	Elevation (m)			24					

Population

Inhabitants 2000	**9,180,000**
Inhabitants 1970	3,937,000
demographia.com	

Metropolitan development

Year	1965
Total metropolitan inhabitants	3,275,000
Inhabitants in metropolitan core	1,452,000
Core share	**44.3%**
Inhabitants in metropolitan periphery	1,823,000
Periphery share	55.7%
demographia.com	

Employment

	Metr. Area	CBD
Area (km²)	6,937	15.3
Area share	100%	0.2%
Employment	2,573,165	193,520
Employment share	100%	7.5%
Employment density (employment/km²)	**371**	**12,648**
demographia.com, 1990		

Economy

Average income per capita (€)	**16,666**
Unemployment rate	5.0%
asiaweek.com, 2000	

Health

Hospital beds per 1,000 inhabitants	**6**
Average life expectancy at birth	79
asiaweek.com, 2000	

Crime

Crimes per 100,000 inhabitants	**1,100**
asiaweek.com, 2000	

Residential density

Year	1985
Inhabitants	5,415,000
Residential area (km²)	52
Residential density (inhabitants/km²)	**104,135**
demographia.com	

Change in density (1970–1990)

Change in inhabitants	1,586,000
Change in area (km²)	75
Change in density (inhabitants/km²)	**21,147**
demographia.com	

Traffic and transport

Public transport market share	61.1%
Private vehicle market share	38.9%
Average commuting time (minutes)	**30**
publicpurpose.com, 1990; asiaweek.com, 2000	

Road use

Average road speed (km/hour)	25.7
Vehicle density (vehicle km/km²)	**113,856**
publicpurpose.com, 1990	

Railway use

Passenger density (passenger km/km)	110,340
Rail vehicle density (vehicle km/km²)	**6,795,116**
publicpurpose.com, 1990	

Climate

Average January temperature (°C)	14.4
Average July temperature (°C)	**31.7**
weatherbase.com	

Pollution

NOX (tonnes/km²)	240.5
CO (tonnes/km²)	757.9
VOC (tonnes/km²)	72.2
Total pollution (tonnes/km²)	**1,070.7**
publicpurpose.com, 1990	

Houston United States

- 30.3 N

- 28.9 N

	CNT	OIL	DRY	PAX	MOV
	24	2	12	13	13

Elevation (m)   29

Population

Inhabitants 2003	**5,176,000**
Inhabitants 1970	1,678,000
Inhabitants 1960	1,140,000

US Census

Metropolitan development

Year	1965	2003
Total metropolitan inhabitants	1,490,000	5,176,000
Inhabitants in metropolitan core	1,100,000	2,010,000
Core share	**73.8%**	**38.8%**
Inhabitants in metropolitan periphery	390,000	3,166,000
Periphery share	26.2%	61.2%

demographia.com

Employment

	Metr. Area	CBD
Area (km²)	3,354	3.9
Area share	100%	0.1%
Employment	1,779,289	264,940
Employment share	100%	14.9%
Employment density (employment/km²)	**530**	**67,933**

demographia.com, 2000

Economy

Average income per capita (€)	**15,194**
Gross regional product per capita (€)	31,839
Unemployment rate	4.2%

demographia.com; bestplaces.net, 1998

Metropolitan density

Inhabitants	3,823,000
Built-up area (km²)	3,354
Population density (inhabitants/km²)	**1,140**

US Census, 2000

Residential density

Year	1985
Inhabitants	2,104,000
Residential area (km²)	803
Residential density (inhabitants/km²)	**2,620**

demographia.com

Change in density (1970–1990)

Change in inhabitants	1,224,000
Change in area (km²)	1,931
Change in density (inhabitants/km²)	**634**

demographia.com

Traffic and transport

Public transport market share	1.0%
Private vehicle market share	99.0%
Average commuting time (minutes)	**24**

publicpurpose.com, 1990; bestplaces.net, 1998

Road use

Average road speed (km/hour)	61.1
Vehicle density (vehicle km/km²)	**39,039**

publicpurpose.com, 1990

Railway use

Rail vehicle density (vehicle km/km²)	**31,072**

publicpurpose.com, 1990

Climate

Average January temperature (°C)	5.0
Average July temperature (°C)	**34.4**

weatherbase.com

Pollution

NOX (tonnes/km²)	25.1
CO (tonnes/km²)	26.3
VOC (tonnes/km²)	26.3
Total pollution (tonnes/km²)	**77.6**

demographia.com, 1990

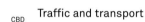

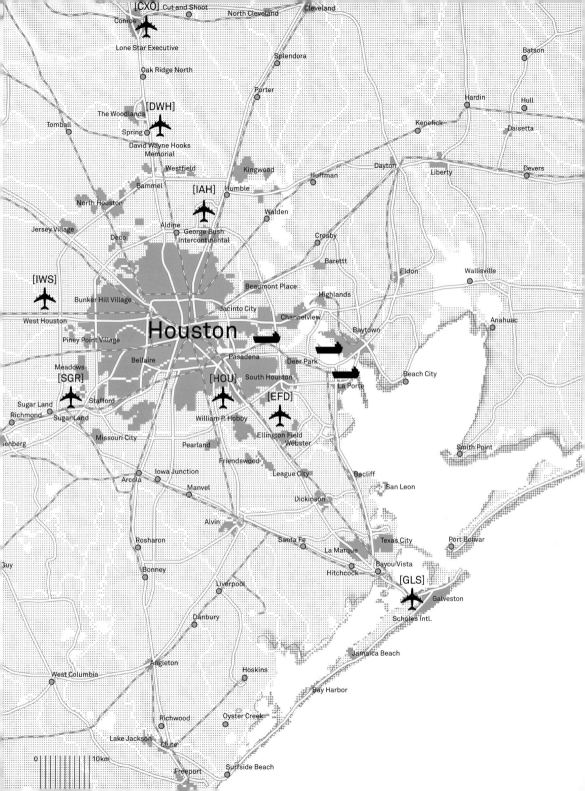

Hyderabad India

77.1 E	80.1 E	
		18.2 N

MET
39

Elevation (m)	545

16.7 N

Population

Inhabitants 2000	6,390,000
demographia.com	

Residential density

Year	1985
Inhabitants	3,022,000
Residential area (km²)	228
Residential density (inhabitants/km²)	13,254
demographia.com	

Metropolitan development

Year	1965	2000
Total metropolitan inhabitants	1,350,000	6,390,000
Inhabitants in metropolitan core	950,000	4,306,000
Core share	70.4%	67,4%
Inhabitants in metropolitan periphery	400,000	2,084,000
Periphery share	29.6%	32,6%
demographia.com		

Climate

Average January temperature (°C)	17.2
Average July temperature (°C)	30.0
weatherbase.com	

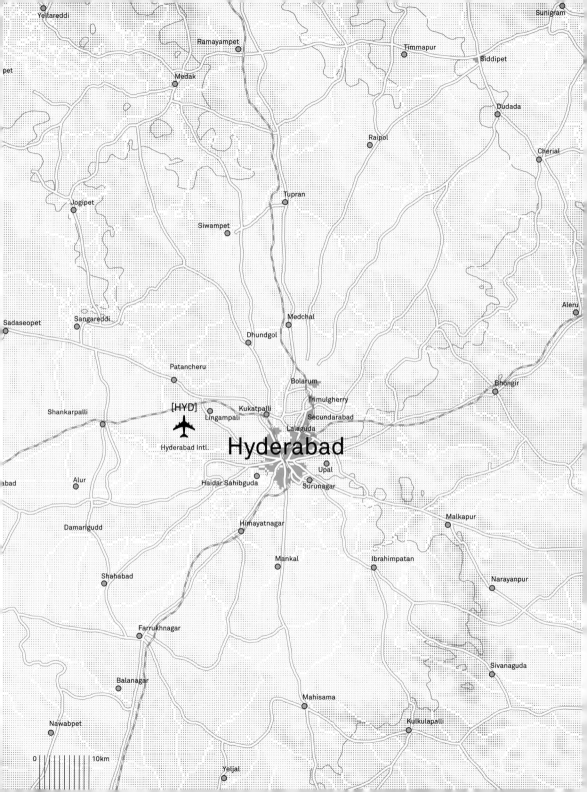

Yellareddi
Sunigram
Ramayampet
Timmapur
Siddipet
Medak
Dudada
Raipol
Cherial
Tupran
Jogipet
Siwampet
Aleru
Sadaseopet
Sangareddi
Medchal
Dhundgol
Patancheru
Bhongir
Bolarum
Shankarpalli
[HYD]
Trimulgherry
Kukatpalli
Lingampali
Secundarabad
Lalaguda
Hyderabad Intl.
Hyderabad
abad
Alur
Upal
Haidar Sahibguda
Surunagar
Malkapur
Damarigudd
Himayatnagar
Mankal
Ibrahimpatan
Narayanpur
Shahabad
Sivanaguda
Farrukhnagar
Balanagar
Mahisama
Kulkulapalli
Nawabpet
0   10km
Yeljal

Indianapolis United States

87.6 W   84.6 W
- 40.5 N

- 39.1 N   Elevation (m)   241

CRG
17

Metropolitan density

Inhabitants	1,219,000
Built-up area (km²)	1,432
Population density (inhabitants/km²)	**851**

US Census, 2000

Population

Inhabitants 2000	**1,219,000**
Inhabitants 1985	700,807

US Census

Metropolitan development

Year	1965	2000
Total metropolitan inhabitants	502,000	1,219,000
Inhabitants in metropolitan core	427,000	782,000
Core share	**85.1%**	**64.2%**
Inhabitants in metropolitan periphery	75,000	437,000
Periphery share	14.9%	35.8%

demographia.com

Employment

	Metr. Area	CBD
Area (km²)	1,432	–
Area share	100%	–
Employment	651,123	85,799
Employment share	100%	13.2%
Employment density (employment/km²)	**455**	–

demographia.com, 2000

Traffic and transport

Average commuting time (minutes)	**21**

bestplaces.net, 1998

Road use

Vehicle density (vehicle km/km²)	**29,568**

publicpurpose.com, 1990

Economy

Average income per capita (€)	**17,132**
Unemployment rate	2.4%

bestplaces.net, 1998

Railway use

Rail vehicle density (vehicle km/km²)	**13,734**

publicpurpose.com, 1990

Climate

Average January temperature (°C)	-7.2
Average July temperature (°C)	**29.4**

weatherbase.com

Crime

Crimes per 100,000 inhabitants	**5,322**

bestplaces.net, 1998

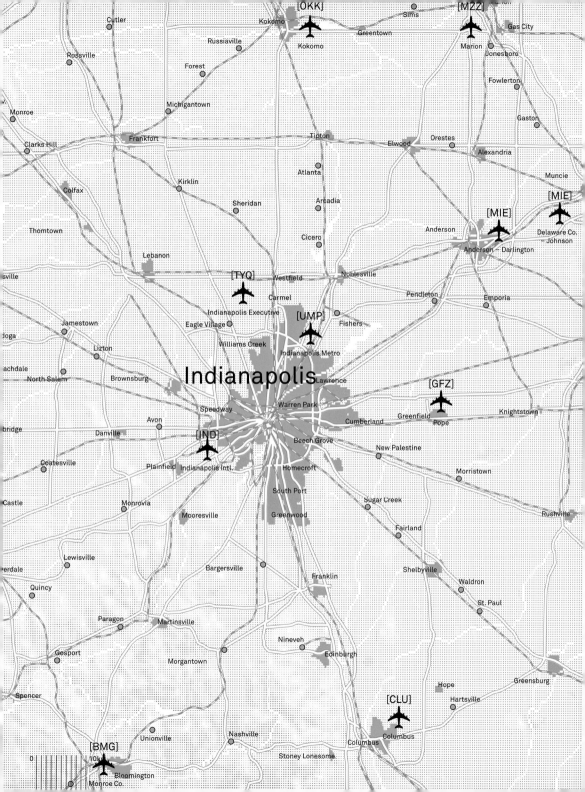

Istanbul Turkey

27.4 Es   30.4 E
                     41.7 N

                     40.2 N

MET
24
Elevation (m)   37

Population

Inhabitants 2000   **10,430,000**
demographia.com

Metropolitan development

Year	1965	2000
Total metropolitan inhabitants	1,950,000	10,430,000
Inhabitants in metropolitan core	1,625,000	8,803,000
Core share	**83.3%**	**84.4%**
Inhabitants in metropolitan periphery	325,000	1,627,000
Periphery share	16.7%	15.6%

demographia.com

Metropolitan density

Inhabitants	10,430,000
Built-up area (km²)	1,269
Population density (inhabitants/km²)	**8,219**

demographia.com

Residential density

Year	1985
Inhabitants	5,389,000
Residential area (km²)	427
Residential density (inhabitants/km²)	**12,620**

demographia.com

Climate

Average January temperature (°C)	2.8
Average July temperature (°C)	**27.8**

weatherbase.com

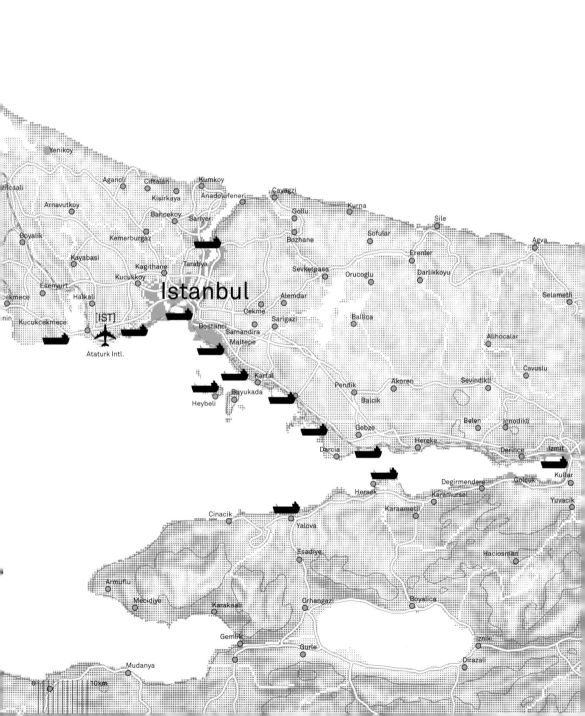

Jerusalem-Tel Aviv Israel

33.6 E   36.6 E
      32.6 N

31.2 N   Elevation (m)   759-49

Population

Inhabitants 2002   **1,040,000**
citypopulation.de

Climate

Average January temperature (°C)	4.4
Average July temperature (°C)	**30.6**

weatherbase.com

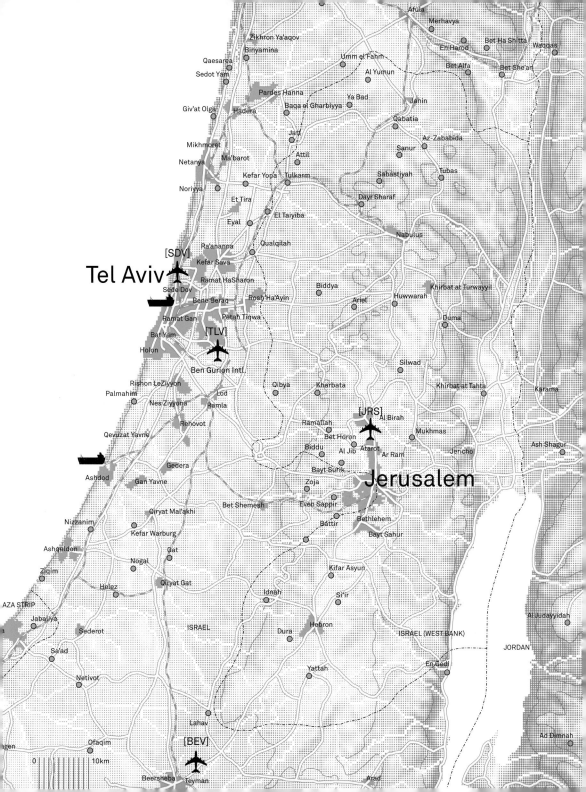

Johannesburg South Africa

26.6 E   29.6 E
|- 25.4 S

MET
47

|- 26.8 S   Elevation (m)   1700

Population

Inhabitants 2000   **5,530,000**
demographia.com

Metropolitan density

Inhabitants	5,100,000
Built-up area (km²)	1,300
Population density (inhabitants/km²)	**3,923**

demographia.com, 1996

Metropolitan development

Year	1965	1999
Total metropolitan inhabitants	2,200,000	5,250,000
Inhabitants in metropolitan core	575,000	1,481,000
Core share	**26.1%**	**28.2%**
Inhabitants in metropolitan periphery	1,625,000	3,769,000
Periphery share	73.9%	71.8%

demographia.com

Climate

Average January temperature (°C)	15.6
Average July temperature (°C)	**18.9**

weatherbase.com

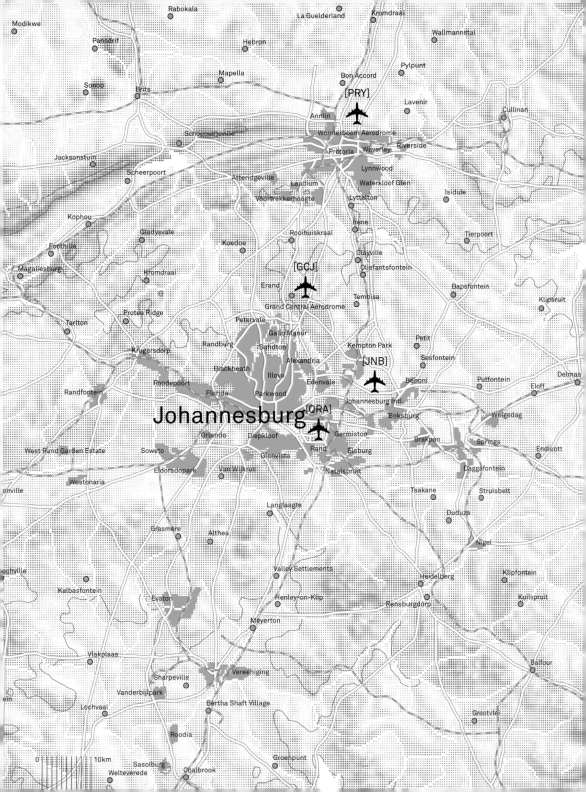

Kaohsiung China (Taiwan)

119.3 E 122.3 E

23.3 N

21.8 N

CNT OIL DRY

3   9   4

Elevation (m)   9

Population

Inhabitants 2001   **1,494,457**
Inhabitants 1985   1,202,000
citypopulation.de

Traffic and transport

Average commuting time (minutes)   **62**
asiaweek.com, 2000

Economy

Average income per capita (€)   **13,396**
Unemployment rate   3.4%
asiaweek.com, 2000

Health

Hospital beds per 1,000 inhabitants   **7**
Average life expectancy at birth   75
asiaweek.com, 2000

Crime

Crimes per 100,000 inhabitants   **2,600**
asiaweek.com, 2000

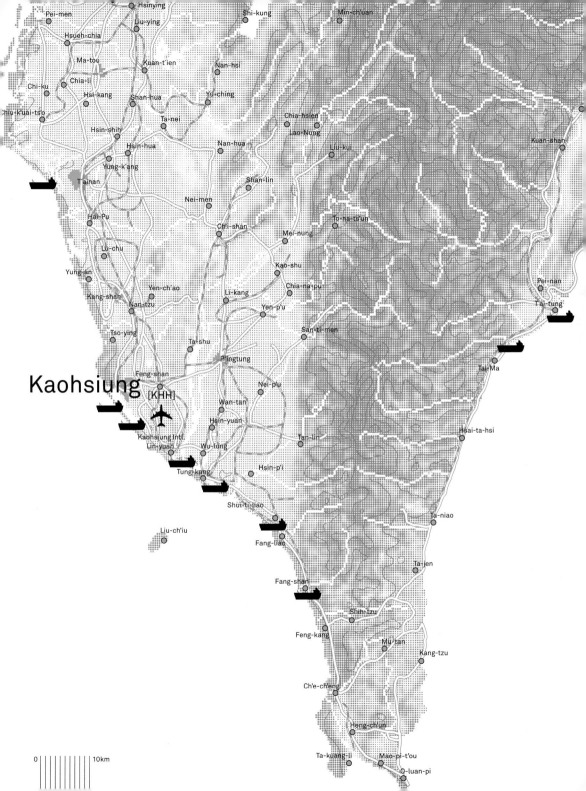

Pei-men
Hsinying
Shi-kung
Min-ch'uan
Liu-ying
Hsueh-chia
Ma-tou
Kuan-t'ien
Nan-hsi
Chia-li
Chi-ku
Hsi-kang
Shan-hua
Yu-ching
Chiu-k'uai-ts'o
Ta-nei
Chia-hsien
Hsin-shih
Lao-Nung
Kuan-shan
Hsin-hua
Nan-hua
Liu-kui
Yung-k'ang
Shan-lin
Tainan
Nei-men
To-ha-ts'un
Hai-Pu
Ch'i-shan
Mei-nung
Lu-chu
Kao-shu
Pei-nan
Yung-an
Yen-ch'ao
Chia-na-pu
T'ai-tung
Kang-shan
Nan-tzu
Li-kang
Yen-p'u
Tso-ying
Ta-shu
San-ti-men
Tai-Ma

Kaohsiung
[KHH]
P'ingtung
Feng-shan
Nei-p'u
Hsai-ta-hsi
Kaohsiung Intl.
Wan-tan
Lin-yuan
Wu-tung
Tan-lin
Hsin-yuan
Ta-niao
Tung-kang
Hsin-p'i
Shui-ti-liao
Liu-ch'iu
Ta-jen
Fang-liao
Fang-shan
Shih-tzu
Mu-tan
Feng-kang
Kang-tzu
Ch'e-ch'eng
Heng-ch'un
Ta-kuang-li
Mao-pi-t'ou
O-luan-pi

0   10km

Karachi Pakistan

66.1 E	69.1 E	25.7 N
		24.3 N

MET 20

Elevation (m) 22

Population

Inhabitants 2000 **11,020,000**
demographia.com

Metropolitan development

Year	1965	1996
Total metropolitan inhabitants	2,100,000	10,032,000
Inhabitants in metropolitan core	1,550,000	9,296,000
Core share	**73.8%**	**92.7%**
Inhabitants in metropolitan periphery	550,000	736,000
Periphery share	26.2%	7.3%

demographia.com

Metropolitan density

Inhabitants	10,032,000
Built-up area (km²)	932
Population density (inhabitants/km²)	**10,764**

demographia.com, 1996

Residential density

Year	1985
Inhabitants	6,351,000
Residential area (km²)	492
Residential density (inhabitants/km²)	**12,909**

demographia.com

Traffic and transport

Average commuting time (minutes)	**45**

asiaweek.com, 2000

Economy

Average income per capita (€)	**1,904**
Unemployment rate	8.0%

asiaweek.com, 2000

Health

Hospital beds per 1,000 inhabitants	**1**
Average life expectancy at birth	62

asiaweek.com, 2000

Climate

Average January temperature (°C)	12.8
Average July temperature (°C)	**31.7**

weatherbase.com

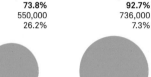

Kinshasa Democratic Republic of Congo

13.8 E 16.8 E
- 3.5 S

MET
45
- 5.0 S
Elevation (m)   312

Population

Inhabitants 2000   **5,750,000**
demographia.com

Residential density

Year	1985
Inhabitants	2,794,000
Residential area (km²)	148
Residential density (inhabitants/km²)	**18,878**
demographia.com	

Climate

Average January temperature (˚C)	22.8
Average July temperature (˚C)	**26.1**
weatherbase.com	

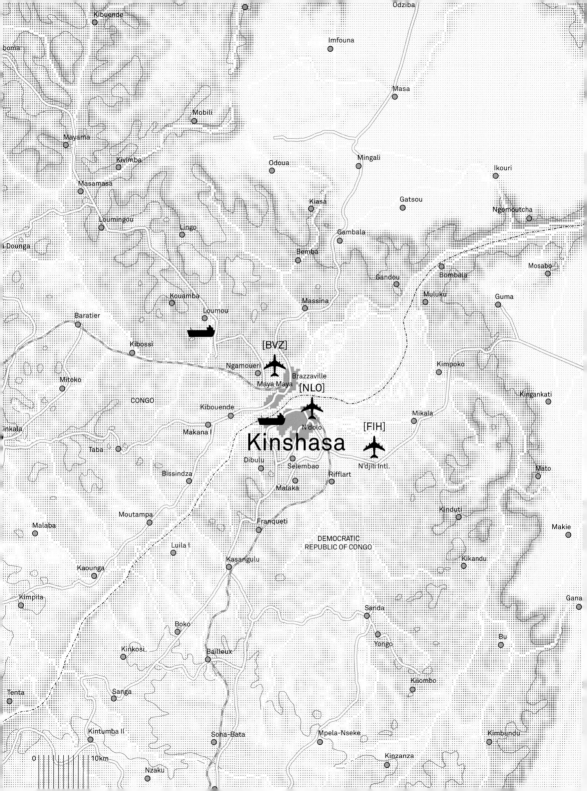

Kobe-Osaka-Kyoto Japan

	MET	CNT	OIL	DRY		CRG		@ TEL
	7	5+18	21+23	21+20		18		24

Elevation (m)   59-15-41

Population

Inhabitants 2000	**16,930,000**

demographia.com

Metropolitan density

Inhabitants	16,930,000
Built-up area (km²)	2,720
Population density (inhabitants/km²)	**6,224**

demographia.com, 2000

Residential density

Year	1991
Inhabitants	13,872,000
Residential area (km²)	1,281
Residential density (inhabitants/km²)	**10,829**

demographia.com

Metropolitan development

Year	1965	2000
Total metropolitan inhabitants	13,070,000	16,930,000
Inhabitants in metropolitan core	3,156,000	2,599,000
Core share	**24.1%**	**15.4%**
Inhabitants in metropolitan periphery	9,914,000	14,331,000
Periphery share	75.9%	84.6%

demographia.com

Employment

	Metr. Area	CBD
Area (km²)	2,720	120.6
Area share	100%	4.4%
Employment	7,500,000	1,740,000
Employment share	100%	23%
Employment density (employment/km²)	**2,757**	**14,428**

demographia.com, 2000

Traffic and transport

Average commuting time (minutes)	**40**

publicpurpose.com, 1990

Economy

Average income per capita (€)	**30,666**
Gross regional product per capita (€)	20,039
Unemployment rate	5.6%

demographia.com; asiaweek.com, 2000

Health

Hospital beds per 1,000 inhabitants	**14**
Average life expectancy at birth	75

asiaweek.com, 2000

Climate (Kobe)

Average January temperature (°C)	-1.1
Average July temperature (°C)	**30.6**

weatherbase.com

Crime

Crimes per 100,000 inhabitants	**3,340**

asiaweek.com, 2000

Kuala Lumpur Malaysia

CNT OIL DRY
8   19   16

Elevation (m)   22

Population

Inhabitants 1990	**3,025,000**
Inhabitants 1985	2,019,000
Inhabitants 1970	1,452,000

Kenworthy Laube

Metropolitan density

Inhabitants	3,025,000
Built-up area (km²)	531
Population density (inhabitants/km²)	**5,697**

Kenworthy Laube, 1990

Change in density (1970–1990)

Change in inhabitants	1,572,000
Change in area (km²)	382
Change in density (inhabitants/km²)	**4,115**

demographia.com

Traffic and transport

Public transport market share	83.1%
Private vehicle market share	16.9%

publicpurpose.com, 1990

Road use

Average road speed (km/hour)	29.4
Vehicle density (vehicle km/km²)	**82,140**

publicpurpose.com, 1990

Railway use

Rail vehicle density (vehicle km/km²)	**469,872**

publicpurpose.com, 1990

Health

Hospital beds per 1,000 inhabitants	**4**
Average life expectancy at birth	73

asiaweek.com, 2000

Climate

Average January temperature (°C)	22.8
Average July temperature (°C)	**31.7**

weatherbase.com

Pollution

NOX (tonnes/km²)	65.6
CO (tonnes/km²)	528.6
VOC (tonnes/km²)	134.0
Total pollution (tonnes/km²)	**728.2**

demographia.com, 1990

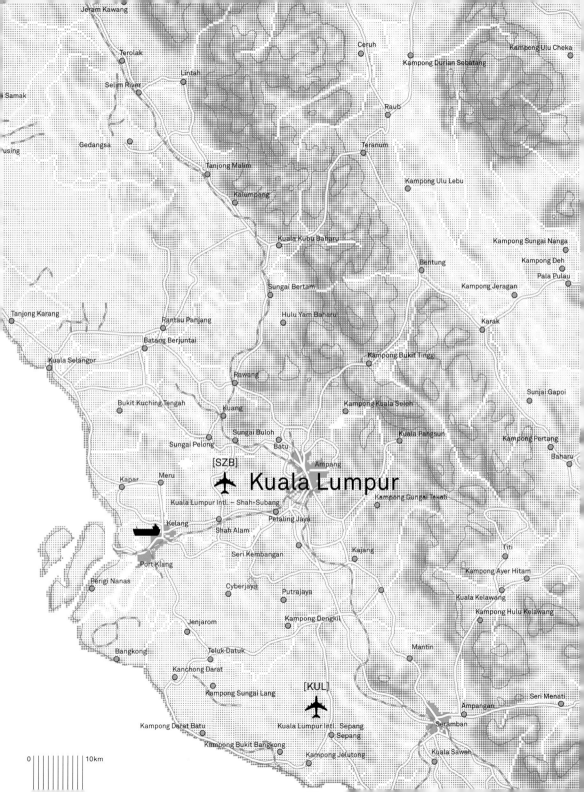

Jeram Kawang

Terolak

Lintah

Selim River

Ceruh

Kampong Ulu Cheka

Kampong Durian Sebatang

Samak

Raub

using

Gedangsa

Teranum

Tanjong Malim

Kampong Ulu Lebu

Kalumpang

Kampong Sungai Nanga

Kuala Kubu Baharu

Kampong Deh

Bentung

Pala Pulau

Sungai Bertam

Kampong Jeragan

Tanjong Karang

Hulu Yam Baharu

Karak

Rantau Panjang

Batang Berjuntai

Kampong Bukit Tinggi

Kuala Selangor

Rawang

Sunjai Gapoi

Bukit Kuching Tengah

Kampong Kuala Seleh

Kuang

Kuala Pangsun

Kampong Pertang

Sungai Buloh

Baharu

Sungai Pelong

Batu

[SZB]

✈ **Kuala Lumpur**

Ampang

Kapar

Meru

Kuala Lumpur Intl. – Shah-Subang

Kampong Sungai Tekali

Kelang

Petaling Jaya

Shah Alam

Seri Kembangan

Kajang

Titi

Port Klang

Kampong Ayer Hitam

Perigi Nanas

Cyberjaya

Kuala Kelawang

Putrajaya

Kampong Hulu Kelawang

Jenjarom

Kampong Dengkil

Mantin

Bangkong

Teluk Datuk

Kanchong Darat

Kampong Sungai Lang

[KUL]

✈

Seri Menati

Ampangan

Kampong Darat Batu

Kuala Lumpur Intl. Sepang

Seramban

Kampong Bukit Bangkong

Sepang

Kuala Sawah

Kampong Jelutong

0 |||||||||| 10km

Lagos Nigeria

1.8 E   4.8 E
         — 7.5 N

MET
25
— 6.0 N   Elevation (m)   38

Population

Inhabitants 2000   **10,030,000**
demographia.com

Metropolitan development

Year	1965
Total metropolitan inhabitants	1,500,000
Inhabitants in metropolitan core	665,000
Core share	**44.3%**
Inhabitants in metropolitan periphery	835,000
Periphery share	55.7%
demographia.com	

Residential density

Year	1985
Inhabitants	6,054,000
Residential area (km²)	145
Residential density (inhabitants/km²)	**41,752**
demographia.com	

Climate

Average January temperature (°C)	26.1
Average July temperature (°C)	**26.1**
weatherbase.com	

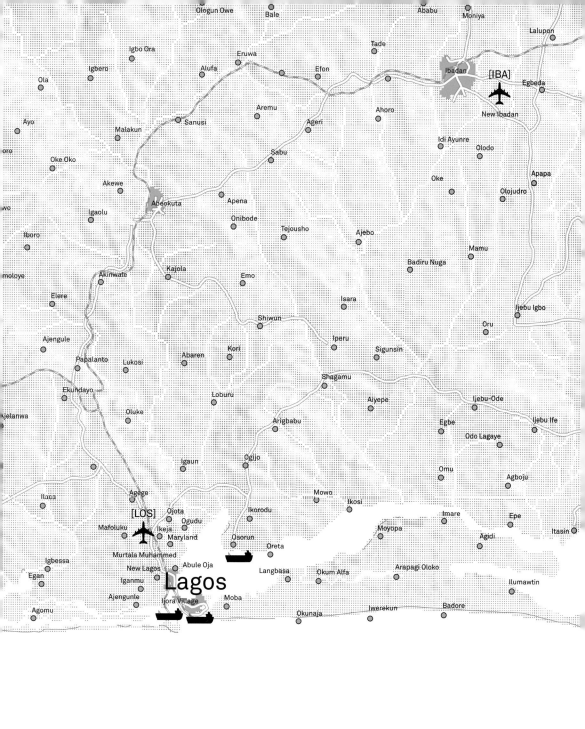

Lahore Pakistan

72.9 E 75.9 E
- 32.3 N

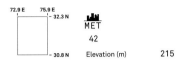

MET
42

- 30.8 N Elevation (m) 215

Population

Inhabitants 2000   **5,920,000**
demographia.com

Residential density

Year	1985
Inhabitants	3,603,000
Residential area (km²)	148
Residential density (inhabitants/km²)	**24,345**

demographia.com

Metropolitan development

Year	1965	2000
Total metropolitan inhabitants	1,450,000	5,920,000
Inhabitants in metropolitan core	1,350,000	5,063,000
Core share	**93.1%**	**93.4%**
Inhabitants in metropolitan periphery	100,000	389,000
Periphery share	6.9%	6.6%

demographia.com

Climate

Average January temperature (°C)	8.9
Average July temperature (°C)	**33.9**

weatherbase.com

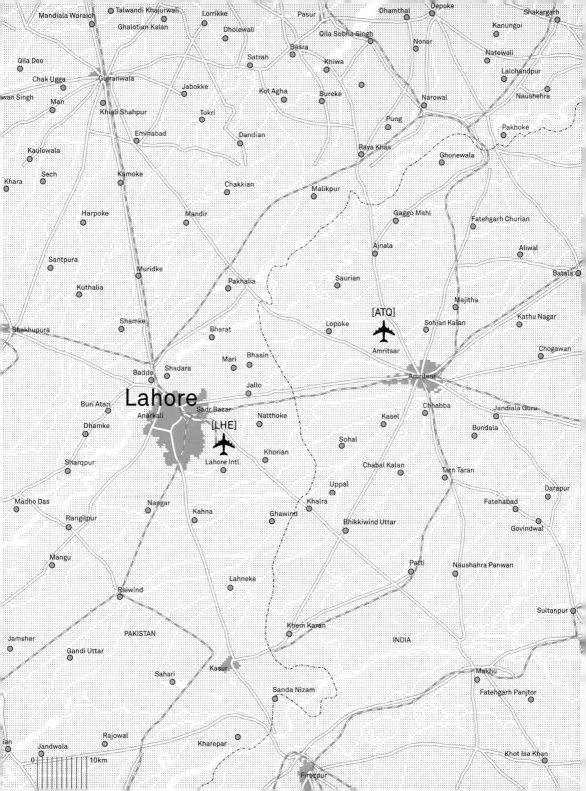

Las Vegas United States

116.5 W   113.5 W
— 36.8 N

— 34.5 N   Elevation (m)   659

PAX   **MOV**
12   9

Population

Inhabitants 2000   **1,314,000**
US Census

Metropolitan density

Inhabitants	1,314,000
Built-up area (km²)	741
Population density (inhabitants/km²)	**1,773**

US Census, 2000

Metropolitan development

Year	1965	2000
Total metropolitan inhabitants	639,000	1,314,000
Inhabitants in metropolitan core	476,000	478,000
Core share	**74.5%**	**36.4%**
Inhabitants in metropolitan periphery	163,000	836,000
Periphery share	25.5%	63.6%

demographia.com

Traffic and transport

Average commuting time (minutes)	**20**

bestplaces.net, 1998

Road use

Vehicle density (vehicle km/km²)	**56,421**

publicpurpose.com, 1990

Economy

Average income per capita (€)	**17,186**
Gross regional product per capita (€)	30,047
Unemployment rate	4.0%

demographia.com; bestplaces.net, 1998

Railway use

Rail vehicle density (vehicle km/km²)	**7,364**

publicpurpose.com, 1990

Climate

Average January temperature (°C)	1.1
Average July temperature (°C)	**40.0**

weatherbase.com

Crime

Crimes per 100,000 inhabitants	**6,198**

bestplaces.net, 1998

Le Havre France

CNT   OIL   DRY
15   7   22

Elevation (m)   103

Population

Inhabitants 2003   **815,089**
Eurostat, 1996

Economy

Unemployment rate   6.7%
Eurostat, 1996

Health

Hospital beds per 1,000 inhabitants   **4**
Eurostat, 1996

Climate

Average January temperature (˚C)   1.1
Average July temperature (˚C)   **18.3**
weatherbase.com

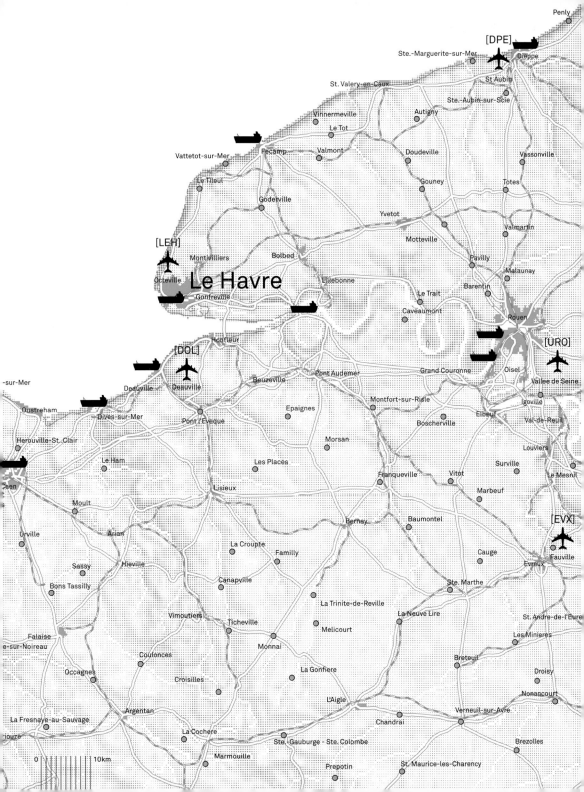

Lima Peru

MET
32

Elevation (m)   13

Population

Inhabitants 2000	**7,420,000**
demographia.com	

Residential density

Year	1985
Inhabitants	5,447,000
Residential area (km²)	311
Residential density (inhabitants/km²)	**17,514**
demographia.com	

Metropolitan development

Year	1965	2000
Total metropolitan inhabitants	2,300,000	7,420,000
Inhabitants in metropolitan core	340,000	316,000
Core share	**14.8%**	**4.3%**
Inhabitants in metropolitan periphery	1,960,000	7,104,000
Periphery share	85.2%	95.7%
demographia.com		

Climate

Average January temperature (°C)	20.0
Average July temperature (°C)	**19.4**
weatherbase.com	

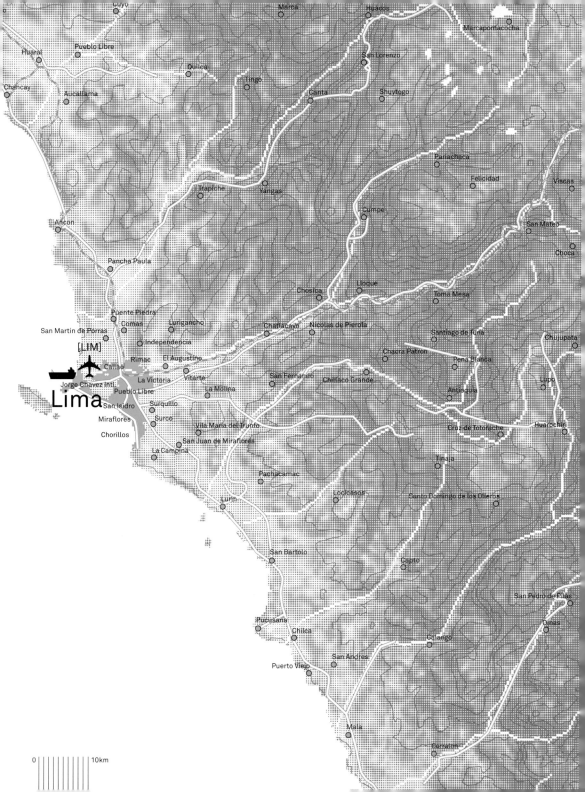

Cuyo

MARCA

Huacos

Marcapomacocha

Pueblo Libre

Huaral

San Lorenzo

Chancay

Quilca

Tingo

Canta

Shuytogo

Aucallama

Pariachaca

Felicidad

Viscas

Trapiche

Yangas

Cumpe

San Mateo

Ancon

Choca

Pancha Paula

Chosica

Lloque

Toma Mesa

Puente Piedra

Santiago de Tuna

Chujupata

Comas

Lurigancho

Chattacayo

Nicolas de Pierola

San Martin de Porras

Independencia

Chacra Patron

Pena Blanca

[LIM]

El Augustino

✈

Lupo

Callao

Rimac

Vitarte

San Fernando

Chillaco Grande

Antioquia

Jorge Chavez Intl.

La Victoria

La Molina

Pueblo Libre

Huarochiri

Lima

Surquillo

Cruz de Totorache

San Isidro

Surco

Vila Maria del Trunfo

Miraflores

La Campina

San Juan de Miraflores

Tinaja

Chorillos

Pachacamac

Locloasos

Santo Domingo de los Olleros

Lurin

San Bartolo

Capto

San Pedro de Pilas

Pucusana

Omas

Chilca

Calango

San Andres

Puerto Viejo

Mala

Corralon

0   10km

Lisbon Portugal

10.3 W 7.3 W
— 39.6 N

— 38.2 N   Elevation (m)   123

Population

Inhabitants 2002   **3,000,000**
Regio Randstad

Metropolitan density

Inhabitants   2,250,000
Built-up area (km²)   557
Population density (inhabitants/km²)   **4,039**
demographia.com, 2001

Traffic and transport

Public transport market share   58.0%
Private vehicle market share   42.0%
Average commuting time (minutes)   **31**
publicpurpose.com, 1990; Eurostat, 1996

Economy

Gross regional product per capita (€)   17,467
Unemployment rate   3.5%
Eurostat, 1996

Health

Hospital beds per 1,000 inhabitants   **6**
Eurostat, 1996

Climate

Average January temperature (°C)   7.2
Average July temperature (°C)   **27.8**
weatherbase.com

Crime

Crimes per 100,000 inhabitants   **9,780**
Eurostat, 1996

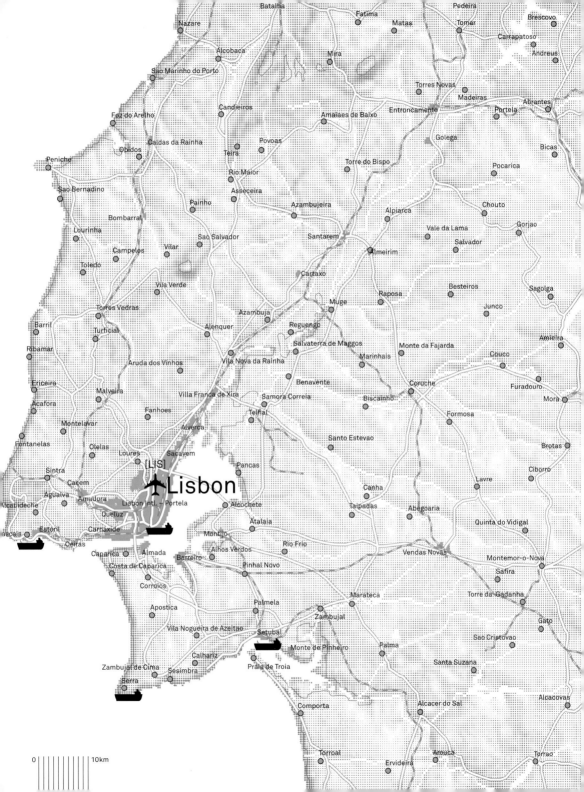

London United Kingdom

1.5 W	1.5 E					
	52.1 N	MET	PAX	CRG	MOV	@ TEL
		11	4 + 20	13	15	2
	50.6 N	Elevation (m)	62			

Population

Inhabitants 2001   **13,945,000**
demographia.com

Metropolitan development

Year	1965	2001
Total metropolitan inhabitants	12,930,000	13,945,000
Inhabitants in metropolitan core	3,175,000	2,766,000
Core share	**24.6%**	**19.8%**
Inhabitants in metropolitan periphery	9,755,000	11,779,000
Periphery share	75.4%	80.2%
demographia.com		

Residential density

Year	1985
Inhabitants	9,442,000
Residential area (km²)	2,263
Residential density (inhabitants/km²)	**4,172**
demographia.com	

Employment

	Metr. Area	CBD
Area (km²)	1,186	29.8
Area share	100%	2.5%
Employment	6,000,000	1,260,500
Employment share	100%	21.0%
Employment density (employment/km²)	**5,059**	**42,299**
demographia.com, 1990		

Traffic and transport

Public transport market share	26.3%
Private vehicle market share	73.7%
Average commuting time (minutes)	**37**
publicpurpose.com, 1990; Eurostat, 1996	

Road use

Average road speed (km/hour)	30.2
Vehicle density (vehicle km/km²)	**53,812**
publicpurpose.com, 1990	

Economy

Gross regional product per capita (€)	37,180
Unemployment rate	6.7%
Regio Randstad, 2002	

Railway use

Passenger density (passenger km/km)	26,058
Rail vehicle density (vehicle km/km²)	**942,892**
publicpurpose.com, 1990	

Climate

Average January temperature (°C)	1.1
Average July temperature (°C)	**21.7**
weatherbase.com	

Pollution

NOX (tonnes/km²)	69.5
CO (tonnes/km²)	410.8
VOC (tonnes/km²)	71.8
Total pollution (tonnes/km²)	**552.1**
demographia.com, 1990	

Los Angeles United States

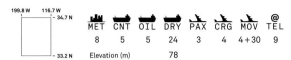

	MET	CNT	OIL	DRY	PAX	CRG	MOV	@ TEL
	8	5	5	24	3	4	4+30	9
Elevation (m)			78					

199.8 W 116.7 W — 34.7 N — 33.2 N

Population

Inhabitants 2003	**17,263,000**
Inhabitants 1970	8,351,000
Inhabitants 1960	6,489,000

demographia.com

Metropolitan development

Year	1965	2003
Total metropolitan inhabitants	7,475,000	17,263,000
Inhabitants in metropolitan core	2,660,000	3,820,000
Core share	**35.6%**	**22.1%**
Inhabitants in metropolitan periphery	4,815,000	13,443,000
Periphery share	64.4%	77.9%

demographia.com

Employment

	Metr. Area	CBD
Area (km²)	5,457	15.3
Area share	100%	0.3%
Employment	6,813,757	512,238
Employment share	100%	7.5%
Employment density (employment/km²)	**1,249**	**33,480**

demographia.com, 1990

Economy

Average income per capita (€)	**17,492**
Gross regional product per capita (€)	260789
Unemployment rate	5.5%

demographia.com; bestplaces.net, 1998

Crime

Crimes per 100,000 inhabitants	**4,588**

bestplaces.net, 1998

Residential density

Year	1985
Inhabitants	9,636,000
Residential area (km²)	2,874
Residential density (inhabitants/km²)	**3,353**

demographia.com

Change in density (1970–1990)

Change in inhabitants	3,051,000
Change in area (km²)	1,543
Change in density (inhabitants/km²)	**1,977**

demographia.com

Traffic and transport

Public transport market share	1.8%
Private vehicle market share	98.2%
Average commuting time (minutes)	**25**

publicpurpose.com, 1990; bestplaces.net, 1998

Road use

Average road speed (km/hour)	45.1
Vehicle density (vehicle km/km²)	**78,907**

publicpurpose.com, 1990

Railway use

Passenger density (passenger km/km)	6,322
Rail vehicle density (vehicle km/km²)	**72,120**

publicpurpose.com, 1990

Climate

Average January temperature (°C)	8.9
Average July temperature (°C)	**27.8**

weatherbase.com

Pollution

NOX (tonnes/km²)	44.4
CO (tonnes/km²)	405.2
VOC (tonnes/km²)	48.3
Total pollution (tonnes/km²)	**498.1**

demographia.com, 1990

Louisville United States

87.2 W 84.1 W
- 38.9 N

- 37.5 N   Elevation (m)   145

CRG
10

Population

Inhabitants 2000	**864,000**
Inhabitants 1985	298,000

US Census

Metropolitan density

Inhabitants	864,000
Built-up area (km²)	1,013
Population density (inhabitants/km²)	**853**

US Census, 2000

Traffic and transport

Average commuting time (minutes)	**19**

bestplaces.net, 1998

Economy

Average income per capita (€)	**13,114**
Unemployment rate	3.2%

bestplaces.net, 1998

Railway use

Rail vehicle density (vehicle km/km²)	**29,900**

publicpurpose.com, 1990

Climate

Average January temperature (°C)	-3.9
Average July temperature (°C)	**31.1**

weatherbase.com

Crime

Crimes per 100,000 inhabitants	**5,965**

bestplaces.net, 1998

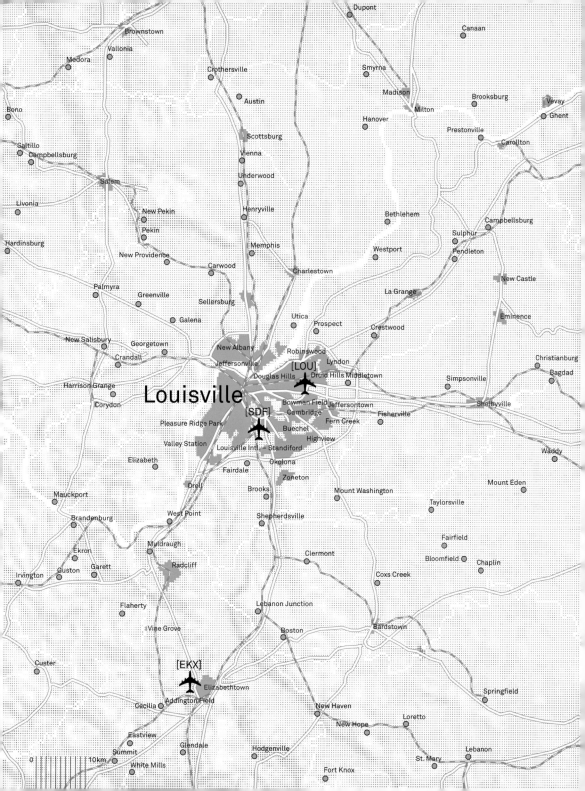

Madrid Spain

PAX
16

@
TEL
18

Elevation (m)   582

Metropolitan density

Inhabitants	4,900,000
Built-up area (km²)	932
Population density (inhabitants/km²)	**5,258**

demographia.com, 2000

Population

Inhabitants 2002   5,300,000
Regio Randstad

Metropolitan development

Year	1965	2001
Total metropolitan inhabitants	2,575,000	5,087,000
Inhabitants in metropolitan core	2,450,000	2,939,000
Core share	**95.1%**	**57.8%**
Inhabitants in metropolitan periphery	125,000	2,148,000
Periphery share	4.9%	42.2%

Traffic and transport

Public transport market share	56.2%
Private vehicle market share	42.8%
Average commuting time (minutes)	**33**

publicpurpose.com, 1990; Eurostat, 1996

Economy

Gross regional product per capita (€)	22,660
Unemployment rate	7.2%

Regio Randstad, 2002

Climate

Average January temperature (°C)	0.0
Average July temperature (°C)	**32.2**

weatherbase.com

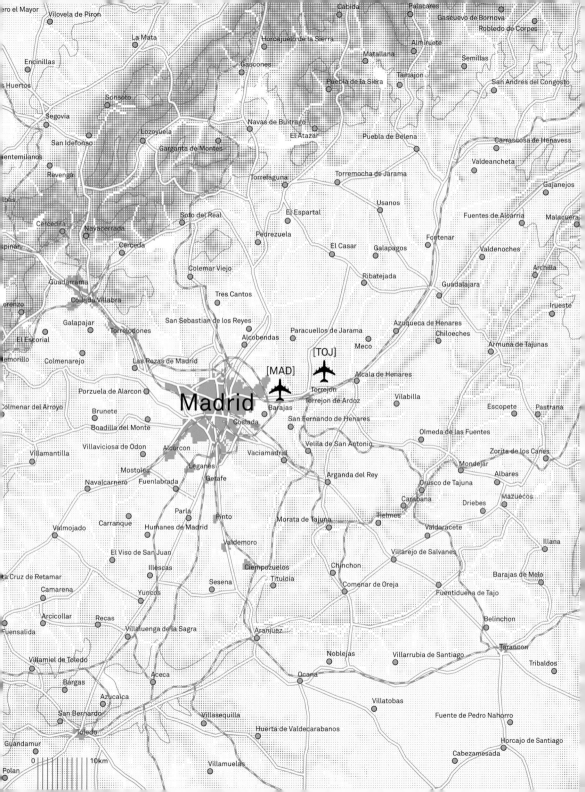

Manila Philipines

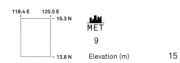

119.4 E   120.5 E

- 15.3 N

MET

9

- 13.8 N   Elevation (m)   15

Population

Inhabitants 2000	**14,140,000**
Inhabitants 1970	3,967,000
Inhabitants 1960	2,462,000

demographia.com

Metropolitan development

Year	1965
Total metropolitan inhabitants	2,900,000
Inhabitants in metropolitan core	1,190,000
Core share	**41.0%**
Inhabitants in metropolitan periphery	1,710,000
Periphery share	59.0%

demographia.com

Employment

	Metr. Area	CBD
Area (km²)	1,943	36.0
Area share	100%	1.9%
Employment	2,718,000	815,400
Employment share	100%	30.0%
Employment density (employment/km²)	**1,399**	**22,650**

demographia.com, 2000

Economy

Average income per capita (€)	**6,825**
Unemployment rate	11.1%

asiaweek.com, 2000

Health

Hospital beds per 1,000 inhabitants	**27**
Average life expectancy at birth	66

asiaweek.com, 2000

Crime

Crimes per 100,000 inhabitants	**1,550**

asiaweek.com, 2000

Metropolitan density

Inhabitants	14,140,000
Built-up area (km²)	1,943
Population density (inhabitants/km²)	**7,277**

demographia.com, 2000

Residential density

Year	1985
Inhabitants	8,485,000
Residential area (km²)	487
Residential density (inhabitants/km²)	**17,427**

demographia.com

Change in density (1970–1990)

Change in inhabitants	3,982,000
Change in area (km²)	185
Change in density (inhabitants/km²)	**21,524**

demographia.com

Traffic and transport

Public transport market share	57.9%
Private vehicle market share	43.1%
Average commuting time (minutes)	**45**

publicpurpose.com, 1990; asiaweek.com, 2000

Road use

Average road speed (km/hour)	25.4
Vehicle density (vehicle km/km²)	**48,907**

publicpurpose.com, 1990

Railway use

Passenger density (passenger km/km)	133,444
Rail vehicle density (vehicle km/km²)	**8,224,354**

publicpurpose.com, 1990

Climate

Average January temperature (°C)	21.7
Average July temperature (°C)	**31.1**

weatherbase.com

Pollution

NOX (tonnes/km²)	182.2
CO (tonnes/km²)	1,337.5
VOC (tonnes/km²)	222.0
Total pollution (tonnes/km²)	**1,741.7**

demographia.com, 1990

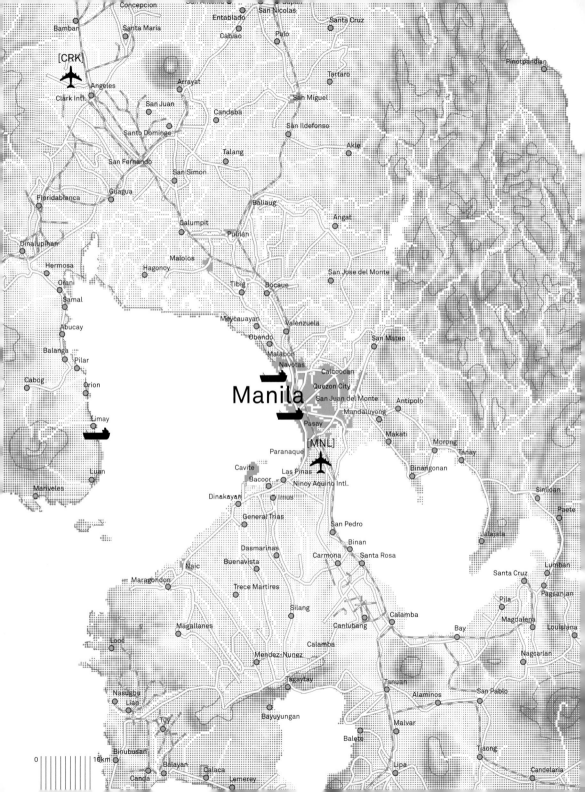

Melbourne Australia

143.5 E   146.5 E
- 37.2 S
- 38.7 S   Elevation (m)   132

Population

Inhabitants 2001	**3,367,000**
Inhabitants 1970	2,503,000
Inhabitants 1960	1,985,000

Kenworthy Laube; demographia.com

Metropolitan development

Year	1965	2001
Total metropolitan inhabitants	2,055,000	3,367,000
Inhabitants in metropolitan core	75,000	91,000
Core share	**3.6%**	**2.7%**
Inhabitants in metropolitan periphery	1,980,000	3,276,000
Periphery share	96.4%	97.3%

demographia.com

Employment

	Metr. Area	CBD
Area (km²)	2,025	2.3
Area share	100%	0.1%
Employment	1,186,864	126,286
Employment share	100%	10.6%
Employment density (employment/km²)	**586**	**54,907**

demographia.com

Metropolitan density

Inhabitants	3,023,000
Built-up area (km²)	2,025
Population density (inhabitants/km²)	**1,493**

Kenworthy Laube, 1990

Residential density

Year	1985
Inhabitants	2,852,000
Residential area (km²)	847
Residential density (inhabitants/km²)	**3,367**

demographia.com

Change in density (1970–1990)

Change in inhabitants	519,000
Change in area (km²)	1,049
Change in density (inhabitants/km²)	**495**

demographia.com

Traffic and transport

Public transport market share	6.6%
Private vehicle market share	93.4%

publicpurpose.com, 1990

Road use

Average road speed (km/hour)	45.1
Vehicle density (vehicle km/km²)	**32,377**

publicpurpose.com, 1990

Railway use

Rail vehicle density (vehicle km/km²)	**119,749**

publicpurpose.com, 1990

Climate

Average January temperature (°C)	13.3
Average July temperature (°C)	**12.8**

weatherbase.com

Pollution

NOX (tonnes/km²)	27.0
CO (tonnes/km²)	267.2
VOC (tonnes/km²)	34.0
Total pollution (tonnes/km²)	**328.2**

demographia.com, 1990

Memphis United States

91.3 W 88.2 W
– 35.7 N

– 34.3 N
Elevation (m) 81

CRG MOV
1   27

Population

Inhabitants 2000   **972,000**
Inhabitants 1985   646,356
US Census

Metropolitan density

Inhabitants   972,000
Built-up area (km²)   1,063
Population density (inhabitants/km²)   **914**
US Census , 2000

Traffic and transport

Average commuting time (minutes)   **21**
bestplaces.net, 1998

Road use

Vehicle density (vehicle km/km²)   **26,300**
publicpurpose.com, 1990

Economy

Average income per capita (€)   **13,710**
Unemployment rate   3.6%
bestplaces.net, 1998

Railway use

Rail vehicle density (vehicle km/km²)   **21,013**
publicpurpose.com, 1990

Climate

Average January temperature (°C)   0.0
Average July temperature (°C)   **33.3**
weatherbase.com

Crime

Crimes per 100,000 inhabitants   **8,369**
bestplaces.net, 1998

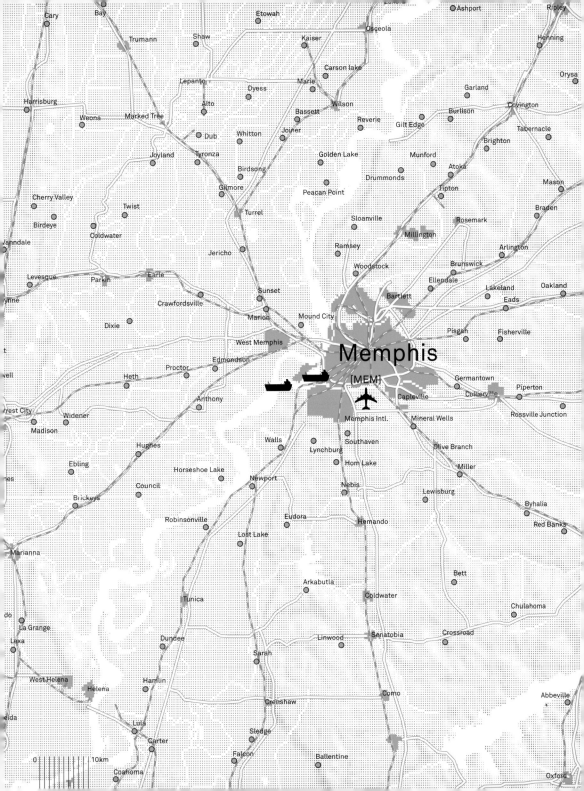

Mexico City Mexico

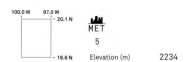

100.0 W   97.0 W

— 20.1 N

— 18.6 N

MET

5

Elevation (m)   2234

@
TEL

20

Population

Inhabitants 2000	**19,620,000**
Inhabitants 1985	8,831,079

demographia.com

Metropolitan development

Year	1965	1999
Total metropolitan inhabitants	6,100,000	19,100,000
Inhabitants in metropolitan core	3,050,000	8,605,000
Core share	**50.0%**	**45.1%**
Inhabitants in metropolitan periphery	3,050,000	10,495,000
Periphery share	50.0%	54.9%

demographia.com

Metropolitan density

Inhabitants	17,250,000
Built-up area (km²)	1,476
Population density (inhabitants/km²)	**11,687**

demographia.com, 1990

Residential density

Year	1985
Inhabitants	16,901,000
Residential area (km²)	1,351
Residential density (inhabitants/km²)	**12,510**

demographia.com

Climate

Average January temperature (°C)	7.2
Average July temperature (°C)	**23.3**

weatherbase.com

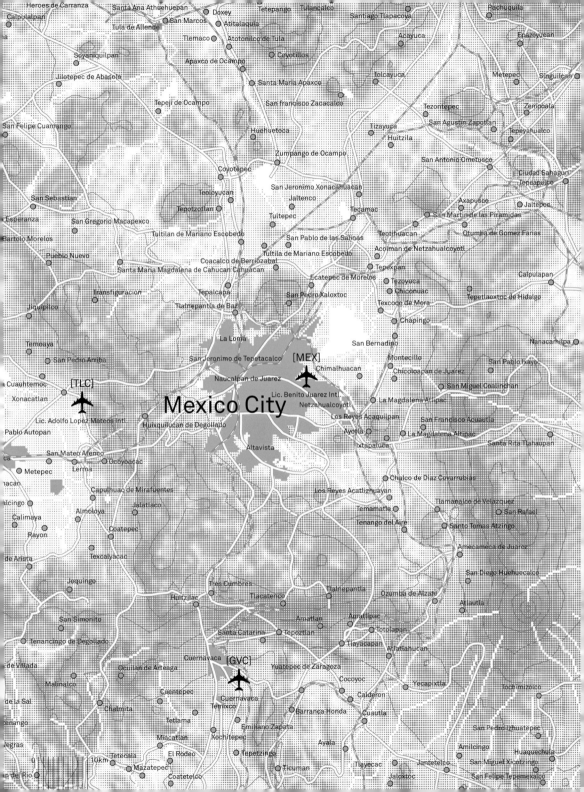

Miami United States

81.6 W   78.6 W
— 26.9 N

— 25.5 N   Elevation (m)   4

PAX   CRG   MOV   @TEL
19   6   12   8

Metropolitan density

Inhabitants	4,919,000
Built-up area (km²)	2,890
Population density (inhabitants/km²)	**1,702**

US Census, 2000

Population

Inhabitants 2003	**5,289,000**
Inhabitants 1985	1,608,000
Inhabitants 1960	853,000

US Census

Metropolitan development

Year	1965	2003
Total metropolitan inhabitants	1,500,000	5,289,000
Inhabitants in metropolitan core	325,000	377,000
Core share	**21.7%**	**7.1%**
Inhabitants in metropolitan periphery	1,175,000	4,912,000
Periphery share	78.3%	92.9%

demographia.com

Change in density (1970–1990)

Change in inhabitants	695,000
Change in area (km²)	440
Change in density (inhabitants/km²)	**1,580**

demographia.com

Employment

	Metr. Area	CBD
Area (km²)	2,890	-
Area share	100%	-
Employment	1,474,533	75,057
Employment share	100%	5.1%
Employment density (employment/km²)	**510**	-

demographia.com, 2000

Traffic and transport

Average commuting time (minutes)	**23**

bestplaces.net, 1998

Road use

Vehicle density (vehicle km/km²)	**62,721**

publicpurpose.com, 1990

Economy

Average income per capita (€)	**11,051**
Gross regional product per capita (€)	22,182
Unemployment rate	5.5%

bestplaces.net, 1998

Railway use

Passenger density (passenger km/km)	8,899
Rail vehicle density (vehicle km/km²)	**89,894**

publicpurpose.com, 1996

Climate

Average January temperature (°C)	15.6
Average July temperature (°C)	**31.7**

weatherbase.com

Crime

Crimes per 100,000 inhabitants	**10,724**

bestplaces.net, 1998

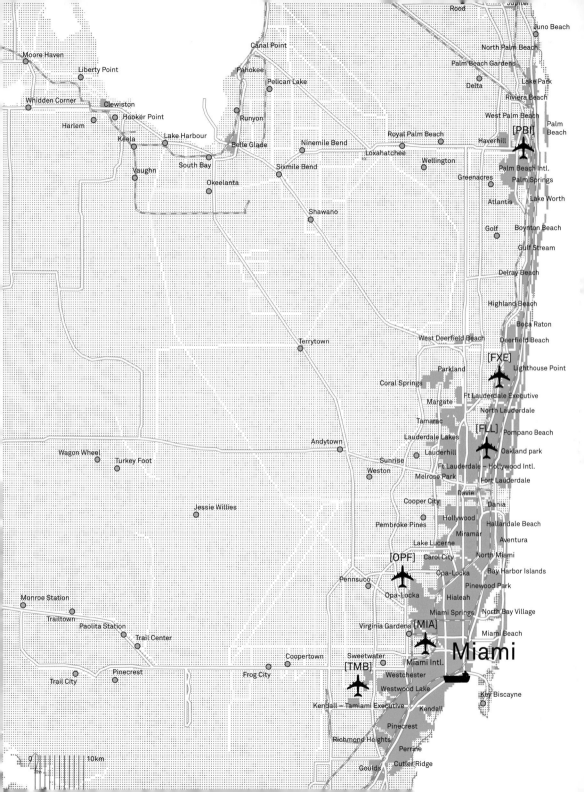

Milan Italy

7.6 E 10.6 E
46.2 N
44.7 N

Elevation (m)		211

Population

Inhabitants 2001	**4,050,000**
demographia.com	

Metropolitan density

@
TEL
25

Inhabitants	4,050,000
Built-up area (km²)	1,865
Population density (inhabitants/km²)	**2,172**
demographia.com, 2001	

Metropolitan development

Year	1965	1996
Total metropolitan inhabitants	2,775,000	3,790,000
Inhabitants in metropolitan core	1,665,000	1,306,000
Core share	**60.0%**	**34.5%**
Inhabitants in metropolitan periphery	1,110,000	2,484,000
Periphery share	40.0%	65.5%
demographia.com		

Economy

Gross regional product per capita (€)	29,179
Unemployment rate	3.8%
Regio Randstad, 2002	

Health

Hospital beds per 1,000 inhabitants	**5**
Eurostat, 1996	

Climate

Average January temperature (°C)	-3.9
Average July temperature (°C)	**28.3**
weatherbase.com	

Crime

Crimes per 100,000 inhabitants	**11,830**
Eurostat, 1996	

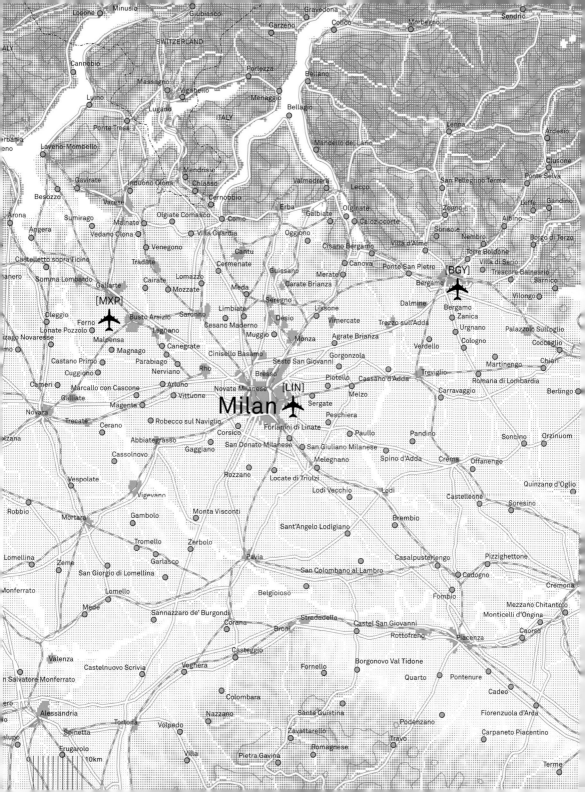

Minneapolis-St. Paul United States

94.5 W	91.5 W			
	45.6 N		PAX	MOV
			15	8
	44.2 N	Elevation (m)	254	

Metropolitan density

Inhabitants	2,389,000
Built-up area (km²)	2,315
Population density (inhabitants/km²)	**1,032**

US Census, 2000

Population

Inhabitants 2000	**2,389,000**
Inhabitants 1985	1,788,000
Inhabitants 1970	1,701,000

US Census

Metropolitan development

Year	1965	2000
Total metropolitan inhabitants	987,000	2,389,000
Inhabitants in metropolitan core	833,000	670,000
Core share	**84.4%**	**28.0%**
Inhabitants in metropolitan periphery	154,000	1,719,000
Periphery share	15.6%	72.0%

demographia.com

Change in density (1970–1990)

Change in inhabitants	379,000
Change in area (km²)	1,051
Change in density (inhabitants/km²)	**361**

demographia.com

Employment

	Metr. Area	CBD
Area (km²)	2,315	-
Area share	100%	-
Employment	1,307,624	168,673
Employment share	100%	12.9%
Employment density (employment/km²)	**565**	-

demographia.com, 2000

Traffic and transport

Average commuting time (minutes)	**19**

bestplaces.net, 1998

Road use

Vehicle density (vehicle km/km²)	**25,520**

publicpurpose.com, 1990

Economy

Average income per capita (€)	**16,558**
Gross regional product per capita (€)	33,312
Unemployment rate	2.2%

demographia.com; bestplaces.net, 1998

Railway use

Rail vehicle density (vehicle km/km²)	**26,857**

publicpurpose.com, 1990

Climate

Average January temperature (°C)	-15.6
Average July temperature (°C)	**29.4**

weatherbase.com

Crime

Crimes per 100,000 inhabitants	**8,636**

bestplaces.net, 1998

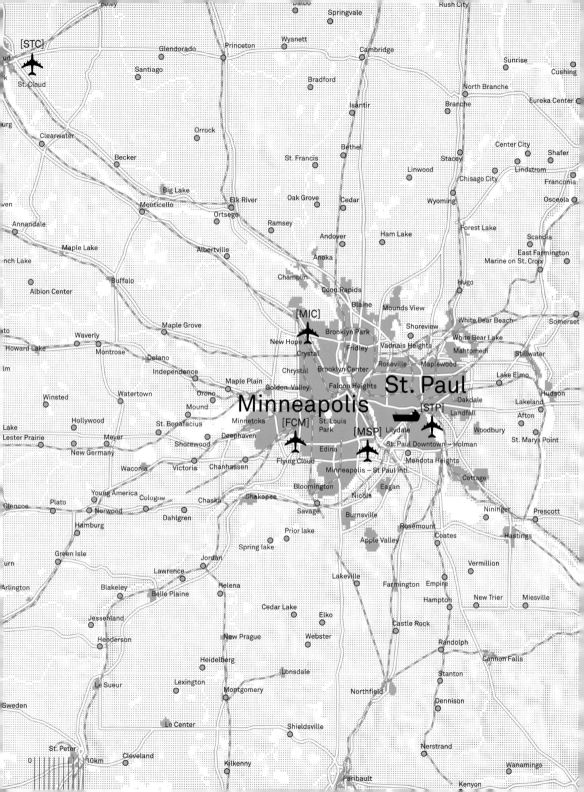

Monterey United States

123.3 W   120.3 W
— 37.3 N

— 35.9 N   Elevation (m)   15

@
TEL
28

Population

Inhabitants 2004   **32,797**
bestplaces.net

Traffic and transport

Average commuting time (minutes)   **18**
bestplaces.net, 1998

Economy

Average income per capita (€)   **21,308**
Unemployment rate   9.2%
bestplaces.net, 1998

Climate

Average January temperature (°C)   6.1
Average July temperature (°C)   **20.0**
weatherbase.com

Crime

Crimes per 100,000 inhabitants   **6,151**
bestplaces.net, 1998

Pollution

NOX (tonnes/km²)   62.5
CO (tonnes/km²)   167.1
VOC (tonnes/km²)   27.8
Total pollution (tonnes/km²)   **257.4**
demographia.com, 1990

148

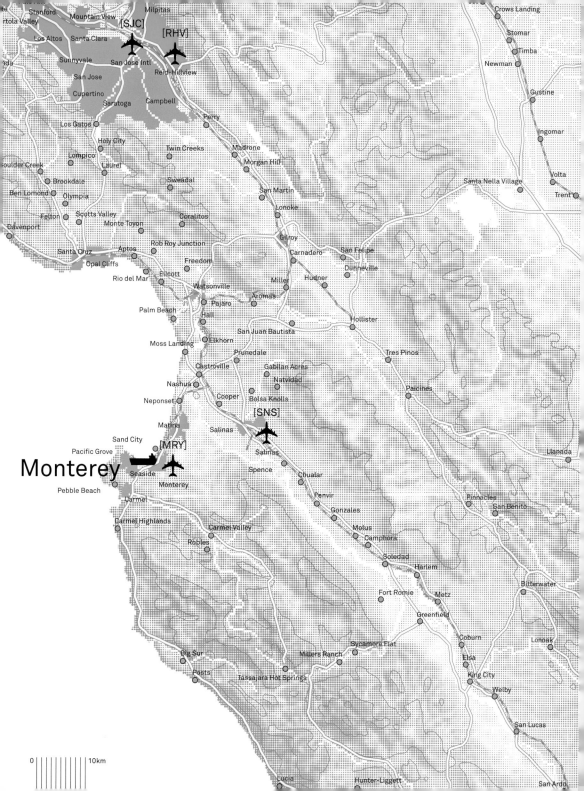

Montreal Canada

74,9 W 71.9 W
46.2 N
44.7 N   Elevation (m)   36

Population

Inhabitants 2001   **3,216,000**
StatsCanada

Metropolitan density

Inhabitants	3,216,000
Built-up area (km²)	1,738
Population density (inhabitants/km²)	**1,850**

StatsCanada, 2001

Residential density

Year	1985
Inhabitants	2,827,000
Residential area (km²)	425
Residential density (inhabitants/km²)	**6,652**

demographia.com

Change in density (1970–1990)

Change in inhabitants	376,000
Change in area (km²)	557
Change in density (inhabitants/km²)	**675**

demographia.com

Employment

	Metr. Area	CBD
Area (km²)	1,738	12.2
Area share	100%	0.7%
Employment	1,365,929	273,203
Employment share	100%	20.0%
Employment density (employment/km²)	**786**	**22,394**

demographia.com, 2001

Traffic and transport

Public transport market share	11.6%
Private vehicle market share	88.4%

publicpurpose.com, 1990

Road use

Average road speed (km/hour)	43.3
Vehicle density (vehicle km/km²)	**41.155**

publicpurpose.com, 1990

Railway use

Passenger density (passenger km/km)	34,956
Rail vehicle density (vehicle km/km²)	**327,717**

publicpurpose.com, 1990

Climate

Average January temperature (°C)	-13.9
Average July temperature (°C)	**26.1**

weatherbase.com

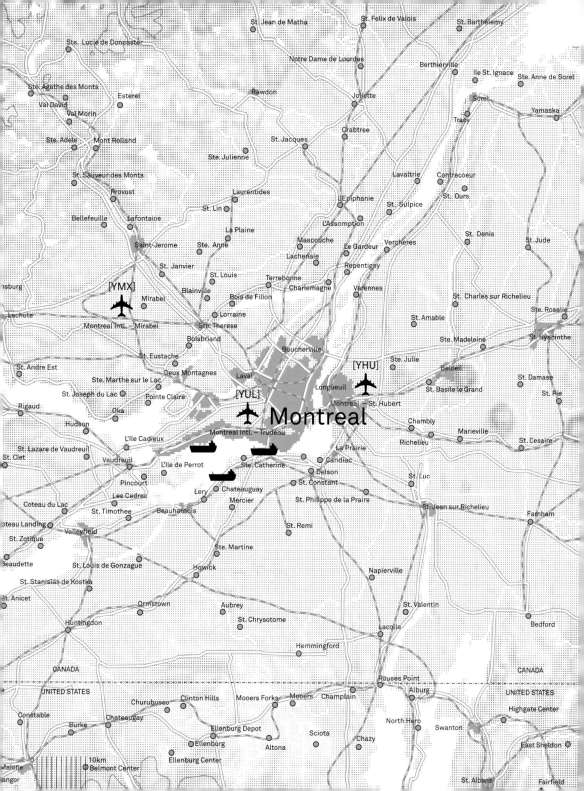

Moscow Russia

36.0 E   39.1 E

- 56.5 N

MET

18

- 55.1 N   Elevation (m)   190

Population

Inhabitants 2000	13,100,000
demographia.com	

Residential density

Year	1985
Inhabitants	9,873,000
Residential area (km²)	981
Residential density (inhabitants/km²)	**10,064**
demographia.com	

Metropolitan development

Year	1965	1999
Total metropolitan inhabitants	8,450,000	13,000,000
Inhabitants in metropolitan core	6,475,000	10,126,000
Core share	**76.6%**	**77.9%**
Inhabitants in metropolitan periphery	1,975,000	2,874,000
Periphery share	23.4%	22.1%
demographia.com		

Climate

Average January temperature (°C)	-11.7
Average July temperature (°C)	**21.7**
weatherbase.com	

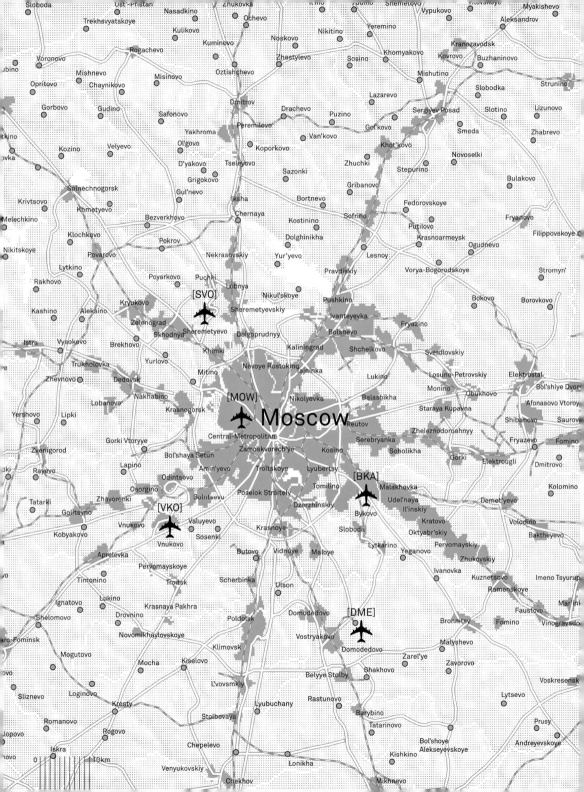

Mumbai India

71.9 E 74.9 E
19.7 N

MET

4

18.3 N   Elevation (m)   14

Population

Inhabitants 2001	**20,043,000**
Inhabitants 1985	8,243,405

demographia.com

Metropolitan development

Year	1965	2001
Total metropolitan inhabitants	4,700,000	20,043,000
Inhabitants in metropolitan core	4,500,000	11,914,000
Core share	**95.7%**	**59.4%**
Inhabitants in metropolitan periphery	200,000	8,129,000
Periphery share	4.3%	40.6%

demographia.com

Metropolitan density

Inhabitants	14,300,000
Built-up area (km²)	738
Population density (inhabitants/km²)	**19,377**

demographia.com, 1990

Residential density

Year	1991
Inhabitants	12,101,000
Residential area (km²)	246
Residential density (inhabitants/km²)	**49,191**

demographia.com

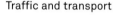

Traffic and transport

Average commuting time (minutes)	**30**

asiaweek.com, 2000

Economy

Average income per capita (€)	**2,012**
Unemployment rate	3.0%

asiaweek.com, 2000

Health

Hospital beds per 1,000 inhabitants	**1**
Average life expectancy at birth	62

asiaweek.com, 2000

Climate

Average January temperature (˚C)	18.3
Average July temperature (˚C)	**29.4**

weatherbase.com

Crime

Crimes per 100,000 inhabitants	**10**

asiaweek.com, 2000

Nagoya Japan

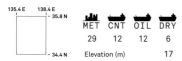

	MET	CNT	OIL	DRY
	29	12	12	6

135.4 E 138.4 E
35.8 N
34.4 N

Elevation (m)   17

Population

Inhabitants 2000	8,837,000

demographia.com

Metropolitan development

Year	1965	2000
Total metropolitan inhabitants	6,078,000	8,837,000
Inhabitants in metropolitan core	1,935,000	2,171,000
Core share	31.8%	24.6%
Inhabitants in metropolitan periphery	4,143,000	6,666,000
Periphery share	68.2%	75.4%

demographia.com

Employment

	Metr. Area	CBD
Area (km²)	2,823	86.0
Area share	100%	3.0%
Employment	4,000,000	1,250,000
Employment share	100%	31.3%
Employment density (employment/km²)	1,417	14,535

demographia.com, 2000

Metropolitan density

Inhabitants	8,837,000
Built-up area (km²)	2,823
Population density (inhabitants/km²)	3,130

demographia.com, 2000

Residential density

Year	1985
Inhabitants	4,452,000
Residential area (km²)	795
Residential density (inhabitants/km²)	5,600

demographia.com

Traffic and transport

Average commuting time (minutes)	26

demographia.com, 1990

Climate

Average January temperature (°C)	-0.6
Average July temperature (°C)	30.0

weatherbase.com

New Delhi India

75.9 N 78.9 E
- 29.4 N

- 28.0 N

MET
13
Elevation (m)   216

Population

Inhabitants 2000	**13,730,000**
Inhabitants 1985	5,729,283

demographia.com

Metropolitan development

Year	1965	2001
Total metropolitan inhabitants	2,900,000	13,783,000
Inhabitants in metropolitan core	2,575,000	13,783,000
Core share	**88,8%**	**100%**
Inhabitants in metropolitan periphery	325,000	–
Periphery share	11.2%	–

demographia.com

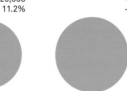

Metropolitan density

Inhabitants	10,300,000
Built-up area (km²)	583
Population density (inhabitants/km²)	**17,677**

demographia.com, 1998

Residential density

Year	1985
Inhabitants	6,993,000
Residential area (km²)	357
Residential density (inhabitants/km²)	**19,588**

demographia.com

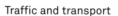

Traffic and transport

Average commuting time (minutes)	**45**

asiaweek.com, 2000

Economy

Average income per capita (€)	**2,355**
Unemployment rate	5.7%

asiaweek.com, 2000

Health

Hospital beds per 1,000 inhabitants	**4**
Average life expectancy at birth	63

asiaweek.com, 2000

Climate

Average January temperature (°C)	8.9
Average July temperature (°C)	**33.9**

weatherbase.com

Crime

Crimes per 100,000 inhabitants	**520**

asiaweek.com, 2000

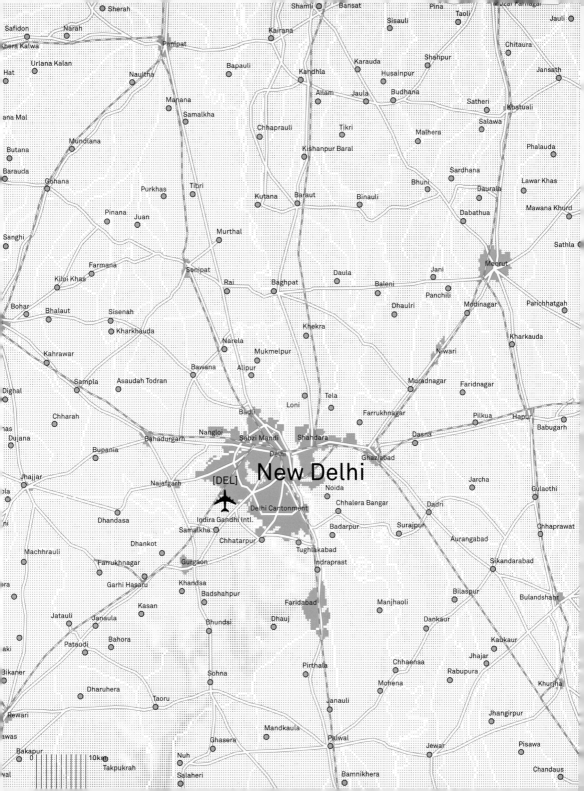

New Orleans United States

91.4 W 88.4 W
— 30.9 N

— 29.4 N

CNT OIL DRY
25   4   2

Elevation (m)   1

Population

Inhabitants 2000	**1,009,000**
demographia.com	

Metropolitan density

Inhabitants	1,009,000
Built-up area (km²)	513
Population density (inhabitants/km²)	**1,967**
demographia.com, 2000	

Metropolitan development

Year	1965	2000
Total metropolitan inhabitants	660,000	1,009,000
Inhabitants in metropolitan core	570,000	485,000
Core share	**86.4%**	**48.1%**
Inhabitants in metropolitan periphery	90,000	524,000
Periphery share	13.6%	51.9%
demographia.com		

Employment

	Metr. Area	CBD
Area (km²)	513	-
Area share	100%	-
Employment	515,264	93,292
Employment share	100%	18.1%
Employment density (employment/km²)	**1,004**	-
demographia.com, 2000		

Traffic and transport

Average commuting time (minutes)	**24**
bestplaces.net, 1998	

Road use

Vehicle density (vehicle km/km²)	**36,842**
publicpurpose.com, 1990	

Economy

Average income per capita (€)	**12,262**
Unemployment rate	4.5%
bestplaces.net, 1998	

Railway use

Rail vehicle density (vehicle km/km²)	**57,530**
publicpurpose.com, 1990	

Climate

Average January temperature (°C)	6.1
Average July temperature (°C)	**32.8**
weatherbase.com	

Crime

Crimes per 100,000 inhabitants	**7,677**
bestplaces.net, 1998	

New York United States

	MET	CNT	OIL	DRY	PAX	CRG	MOV	@ TEL
	3	13	6	21	22+23	11+20	20	1

75.5 W — 72.4 W
41.3 N
39.9 N

Elevation (m) 40

Population

Inhabitants 2003 21,767,000
demographia.com

Metropolitan density

Inhabitants	20,270,000
Built-up area (km²)	11,518
Population density (inhabitants/km²)	**1,760**

demographia.com, 2000

Metropolitan development

Year	1965	2003
Total metropolitan inhabitants	16,325,000	21,767,000
Inhabitants in metropolitan core	8,085,000	8,086,000
Core share	**49.5%**	**37.1%**
Inhabitants in metropolitan periphery	8,240,000	13,681,000
Periphery share	50.5%	62.9%

demographia.com

Employment

	Metr. Area	CBD
Area (km²)	11,518	28.2
Area share	100%	0.2%
Employment	9,357,218	3,192,229
Employment share	100%	34.1%
Employment density (employment/km²)	**812**	**113,200**

demographia.com, 2000

Traffic and transport

Public transport market share	9.8%
Private vehicle market share	90.2%
Average commuting time (minutes)	**35**

publicpurpose.com, 1990; bestplaces.net, 1998

Road use

Average road speed (km/hour)	38.3
Vehicle density (vehicle km/km²)	**47,703**

publicpurpose.com, 1990

Economy

Average income per capita (€)	**19,173**
Gross regional product per capita (€)	35,044
Unemployment rate	5.3%

demographia.com; bestplaces.net, 1998

Railway use

Passenger density (passenger km/km)	44,805
Rail vehicle density (vehicle km/km²)	**238,081**

publicpurpose.com, 1990

Climate

Average January temperature (°C)	-3.3
Average July temperature (°C)	**29.4**

weatherbase.com

Crime

Crimes per 100,000 inhabitants 4,032
bestplaces.net, 1998

Pollution

NOX (tonnes/km²)	40.9
CO (tonnes/km²)	359.5
VOC (tonnes/km²)	39.4
Total pollution (tonnes/km²)	**439.8**

demographia.com, 1990

Orlando United States

82.9 W 79.8 W
29.3 N

27.9 N

Elevation (m) 36

PAX 24   **MOV** 24

Population

Inhabitants 2000	**1,157,000**
US Census	

Metropolitan density

Inhabitants	1,157,000
Built-up area (km²)	1,173
Population density (inhabitants/km²)	**986**
US Census, 2000	

Metropolitan development

	1965	2000
Year	1965	2000
Total metropolitan inhabitants	73,000	1,157,000
Inhabitants in metropolitan core	52,000	186,000
Core share	**71.2%**	**16.1%**
Inhabitants in metropolitan periphery	21,000	971,000
Periphery share	28.8%	83.9%
demographia.com		

Employment

	Metr. Area	CBD
Area (km²)	1,173	–
Area share	100%	–
Employment	590,850	39,700
Employment share	100%	6.7%
Employment density (employment/km²)	**504**	–
demographia.com, 2000		

Traffic and transport

Average commuting time (minutes)	**23**
bestplaces.net, 1998	

Road use

Vehicle density (vehicle km/km²)	**29,043**
publicpurpose.com, 1990	

Economy

Average income per capita (€)	**16,135**
Unemployment rate	2.6%
bestplaces.net, 1998	

Railway use

Rail vehicle density (vehicle km/km²)	**12,048**
publicpurpose.com, 1990	

Climate

Average January temperature (°C)	10.0
Average July temperature (°C)	**33.3**
weatherbase.com	

Crime

Crimes per 100,000 inhabitants	**13,618**
bestplaces.net, 1998	

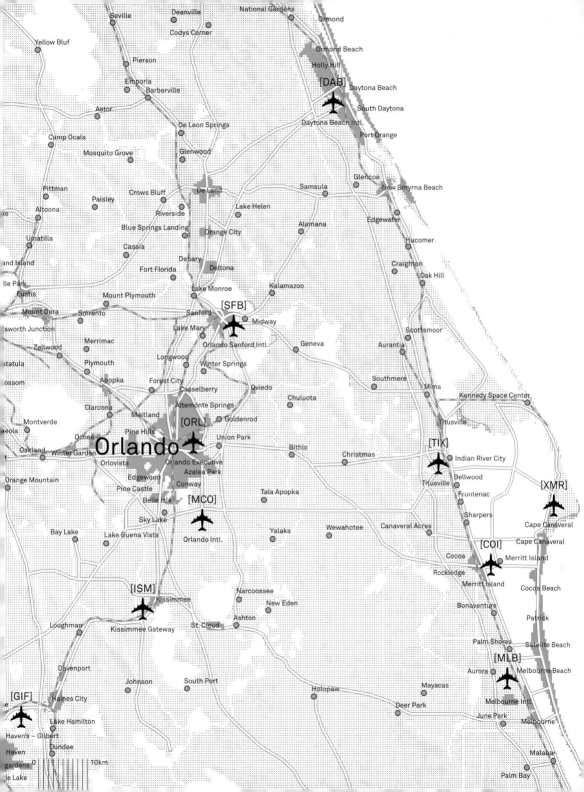

Oslo Norway

9.0 E   12.0 E
— 60.2 N

— 58.7 N   Elevation (m)   17

Population

Inhabitants 2000   **780,000**
demographia.com

Metropolitan density

Inhabitants   780,000
Built-up area (km²)   298
Population density (inhabitants/km²)   **2,617**
demographia.com, 2000

Climate

Average January temperature (°C)   -6.7
Average July temperature (°C)   **21.7**
weatherbase.com

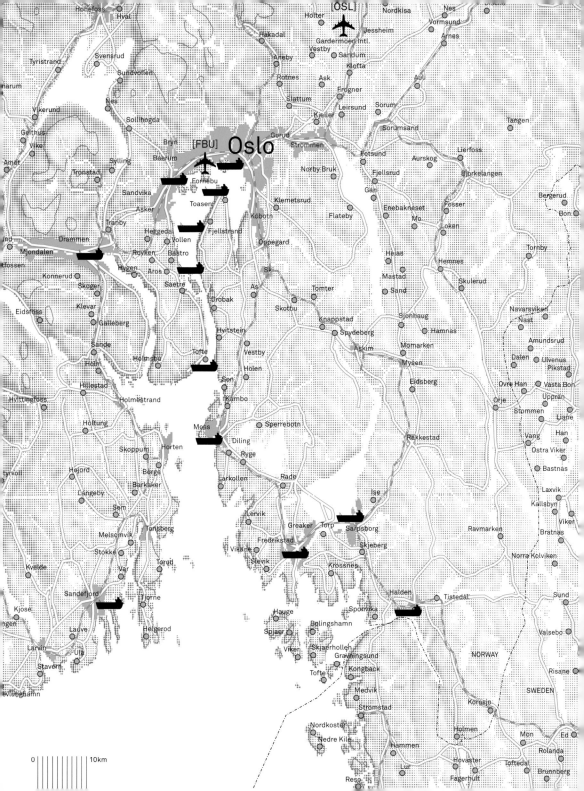

Paris France

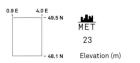

0.9 E 4.0 E						
49.5 N						
48.1 N	MET	PAX	CRG	MOV	TEL	
	23	8	8	6	4	
	Elevation (m)	96				

Population

Inhabitants 2000	**10,600,000**
Inhabitants 1985	9,057,000
Inhabitants 1970	8,537,000
Inhabitants 1960	7,369,000
demographia.com	

Metropolitan development

Year	1965	1999
Total metropolitan inhabitants	8,000,000	9,645,000
Inhabitants in metropolitan core	2,800,000	2,125,000
Core share	**35.0%**	**22.0%**
Inhabitants in metropolitan periphery	5,200,000	7,520,000
Periphery share	65.0%	78.0%
demographia.com		

Employment

	Metr. Area	CBD
Area (km²)	2,721	30.6
Area share	100%	1.1%
Employment	5,109,107	1,165,000
Employment share	100%	22.8%
Employment density (employment/km²)	**1,878**	**38,072**
demographia.com, 1999		

Economy

Gross regional product per capita (€)	25,874
Unemployment rate	8.1%
Regio Randstad, 2002	

Health

Hospital beds per 1,000 inhabitants	**5**
Eurostat, 1996	

Metropolitan density

Inhabitants	9,645,000
Built-up area (km²)	2,721
Population density (inhabitants/km²)	**3,545**
demographia.com, 1999	

Change in density (1970–1990)

Change in inhabitants	1,416,000
Change in area (km²)	1,085
Change in density (inhabitants/km²)	**1,308**

Traffic and transport

Public transport market share	27.0%
Private vehicle market share	73.0%
Average commuting time (minutes)	**35**
publicpurpose.com, 1990	

Road use

Average road speed (km/hour)	25.7
Vehicle density (vehicle km/km²)	**51,821**
publicpurpose.com, 1990	

Railway use

Passenger density (passenger km/km)	48,587
Rail vehicle density (vehicle km/km²)	**527,163**
publicpurpose.com, 1990	

Climate

Average January temperature (°C)	1.1
Average July temperature (°C)	**23.9**
weatherbase.com	

Pollution

NOX (tonnes/km²)	49.0
CO (tonnes/km²)	315.1
VOC (tonnes/km²)	92.7
Total pollution (tonnes/km²)	**456.8**
demographia.com, 1990	

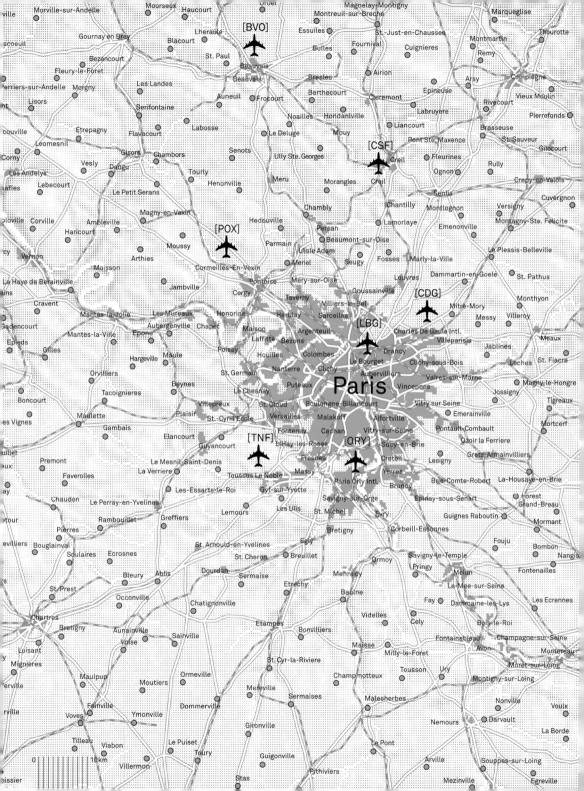

Perth Australia

114.6 E   117.6 E
- 32.9 S

- 41.4 S   Elevation (m)   20

Population

Inhabitants 2001	**1,340,000**
demographia.com	

@
TEL
27

Metropolitan density

Inhabitants	1,143,000
Built-up area (km²)	1,075
Population density (inhabitants/km²)	**1,063**
Kenworthy Laube, 1990	

Metropolitan development

Year	1965	2001
Total metropolitan inhabitants	485,000	1,340,000
Inhabitants in metropolitan core	95,000	13,000
Core share	**19.6%**	**1.0%**
Inhabitants in metropolitan periphery	390,000	1,327,000
Periphery share	80.4%	99.0%
demographia.com		

Change in density (1970–1990)

Change in inhabitants	439,000
Change in area (km²)	498
Change in density (inhabitants/km²)	**882**
demographia.com	

Employment

	Metr. Area	CBD
Area (km²)	1,075	7.5
Area share	100%	0.7%
Employment	469,419	99,819
Employment share	100%	21.3%
Employment density (employment/km²)	**437**	**13,309**
demographia.com, 1990		

Traffic and transport

Public transport market share	3.6%
Private vehicle market share	96.5%
Average commuting time (minutes)	**23**
publicpurpose.com, 1990	

Road use

Average road speed (km/hour)	45.1
Vehicle density (vehicle km/km²)	**25,804**
publicpurpose.com, 1990	

Railway use

Rail vehicle density (vehicle km/km²)	**80,240**
publicpurpose.com, 1990	

Climate

Average January temperature (°C)	16.7
Average July temperature (°C)	**17.8**
weatherbase.com	

Pollution

NOX (tonnes/km²)	21.6
CO (tonnes/km²)	198.4
VOC (tonnes/km²)	25.1
Total pollution (tonnes/km²)	**245.1**
demographia.com, 1990	

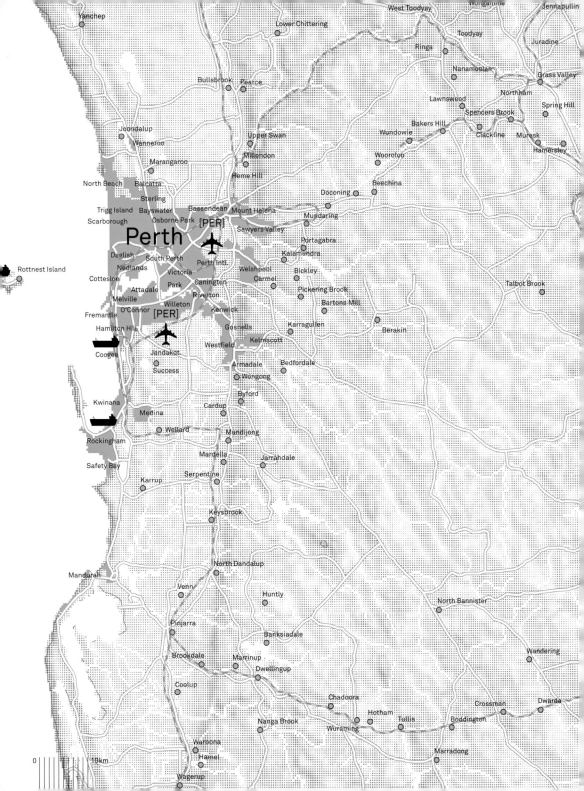

Philadelphia United States

76.6 W 73.6 W
40.6 N
39.2 N

MET
41
Elevation (m) 3

CRG 30 **MOV** 14

Population

Inhabitants 2000	**6,010,000**
Inhabitants 1985	4,112,000
Inhabitants 1970	4,021,000
Inhabitants 1960	3,635,000

demographia.com

Metropolitan development

Year	1965	2000
Total metropolitan inhabitants	4,200,000	6,010,000
Inhabitants in metropolitan core	2,030,000	1,479,000
Core share	**48.3%**	**24.6%**
Inhabitants in metropolitan periphery	2,170,000	4,531,000
Periphery share	51.7%	75.4%

demographia.com

Employment

	Metr. Area	CBD
Area (km²)	4,659	-
Area share	100%	-
Employment	2,433,682	247,945
Employment share	100%	10.2%
Employment density (employment/km²)	**522**	-

demographia.com, 2000

Economy

Average income per capita (€)	**14,465**
Unemployment rate	3.9%

bestplaces.net, 1998

Crime

Crimes per 100,000 inhabitants	**7,294**

bestplaces.net, 1998

Metropolitan density

Inhabitants	6,010,000
Built-up area (km²)	4,659
Population density (inhabitants/km²)	**1,290**

demographia.com, 2000

Residential density

Year	1985
Inhabitants	4,025,000
Residential area (km²)	1,219
Residential density (inhabitants/km²)	**3,302**

demographia.com

Change in density (1970–1990)

Change in inhabitants	201,000
Change in area (km²)	1,468
Change in density (inhabitants/km²)	**137**

demographia.com

Traffic and transport

Average commuting time (minutes)	**27**

bestplaces.net, 1998

Road use

Vehicle density (vehicle km/km²)	**34,916**

publicpurpose.com, 1990

Railway use

Rail vehicle density (vehicle km/km²)	**70,679**

publicpurpose.com, 1990

Climate

Average January temperature (°C)	**-4.4**
Average July temperature (°C)	**30.6**

weatherbase.com

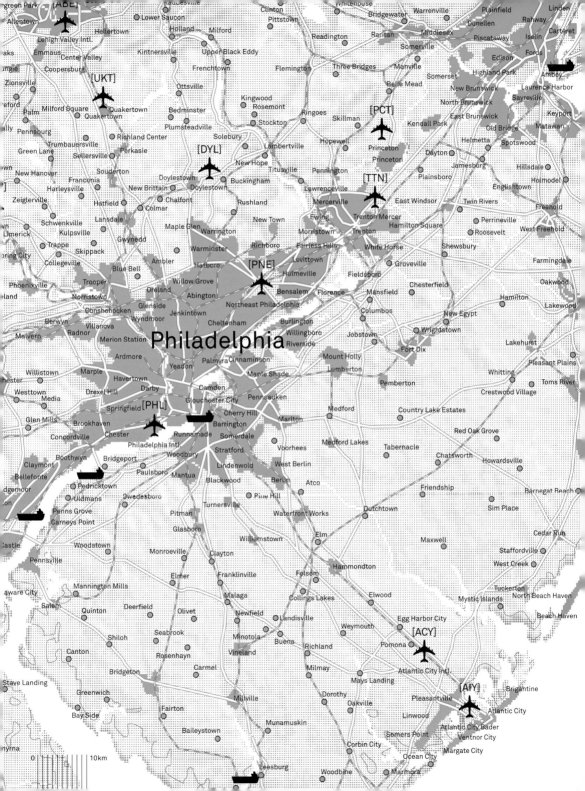

Phoenix United States

113.3 W   110.3 W
- 34.1 N

- 32.6 N   Elevation (m)   338

PAX   MOV
11   5

Population

Inhabitants 2000	**2,907,000**
Inhabitants 1985	1,409,000
Inhabitants 1970	863,000

US Census

Metropolitan development

Year	1965	2000
Total metropolitan inhabitants	216,000	2,907,000
Inhabitants in metropolitan core	106,000	1,321,000
Core share	**49.1%**	**45.4%**
Inhabitants in metropolitan periphery	110,000	1,586,000
Periphery share	50.9%	54.6%

demographia.com

Metropolitan density

Inhabitants	2,907,000
Built-up area (km²)	2,069
Population density (inhabitants/km²)	**1,405**

US Census, 2000

Change in density (1970–1990)

Change in inhabitants	1,143,000
Change in area (km²)	914
Change in density (inhabitants/km²)	**1,251**

demographia.com

Employment

	Metr. Area	CBD
Area (km²)	2,069	3.9
Area share	100%	0.2%
Employment	998,114	35.267
Employment share	100%	3.5%
Employment density (employment/km²)	**482**	**9,043**

demographia.com, 2000

Traffic and transport

Public transport market share	0.7%
Private vehicle market share	99.3%
Average commuting time (minutes)	**22**

publicpurpose.com, 1990; bestplaces.net, 1998

Road use

Average road speed (km/hour)	51.5
Vehicle density (vehicle km/km²)	**34,639**

publicpurpose.com, 1990

Economy

Average income per capita (€)	**16,310**
Unemployment rate	2.6%

bestplaces.net, 1998

Railway use

Rail vehicle density (vehicle km/km²)	**15,529**

publicpurpose.com, 1990

Climate

Average January temperature (°C)	5.0
Average July temperature (°C)	**40.6**

weatherbase.com

Crime

Crimes per 100,000 inhabitants	**7,720**

bestplaces.net, 1998

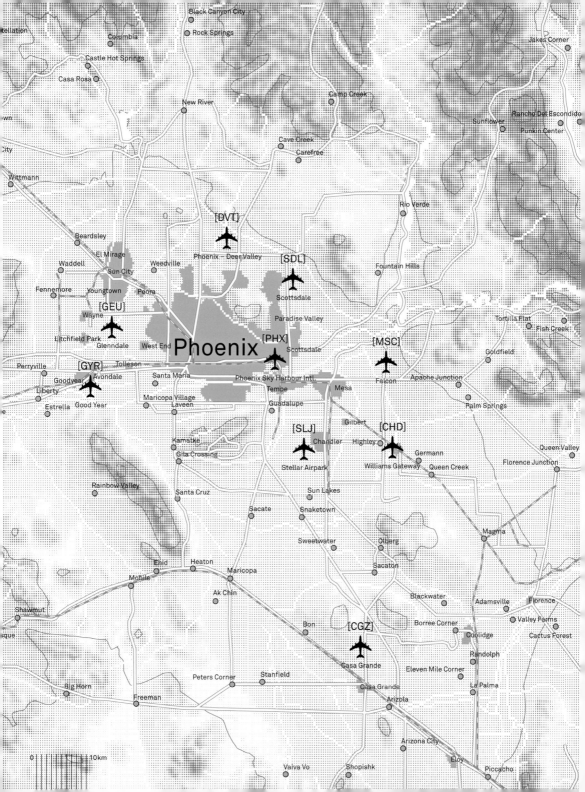

Pittsburgh United States

81.2 W   78.2 W
41.1 N

39.7 N   Elevation (m)   351

Population

Inhabitants 2000	**1,753,000**
Inhabitants 1985	1,810,000
Inhabitants 1970	1,846,000
Inhabitants 1960	1,804,000

US Census

Metropolitan development

Year	1965	2000
Total metropolitan inhabitants	1,533,000	1,753,000
Inhabitants in metropolitan core	677,000	335,000
Core share	**44.2%**	**19.1%**
Inhabitants in metropolitan periphery	856,000	1,418,000
Periphery share	55.8%	80.9%

demographia.com

Employment

	Metr. Area	CBD
Area (km²)	2,207	-
Area share	100%	-
Employment	965,310	114,814
Employment share	100%	11.9%
Employment density (employment/km²)	**437**	-

demographia.com, 2000

Economy

Average income per capita (€)	**14,210**
Unemployment rate	4.0%

bestplaces.net, 1998

Crime

Crimes per 100,000 inhabitants	**6,124**

bestplaces.net, 1998

MOV
19

Metropolitan density

Inhabitants	1,753,000
Built-up area (km²)	2,207
Population density (inhabitants/km²)	**794**

US Census, 2000

Change in density (1970–1990)

Change in inhabitants	-168,000
Change in area (km²)	655
Change in density (inhabitants/km²)	**-256**

demographia.com

Traffic and transport

Average commuting time (minutes)	**20**

bestplaces.net, 1998

Road use

Vehicle density (vehicle km/km²)	**25,462**

publicpurpose.com, 1990

Railway use

Rail vehicle density (vehicle km/km²)	**43,355**

publicpurpose.com, 1990

Climate

Average January temperature (°C)	-6.7
Average July temperature (°C)	**28.3**

weatherbase.com

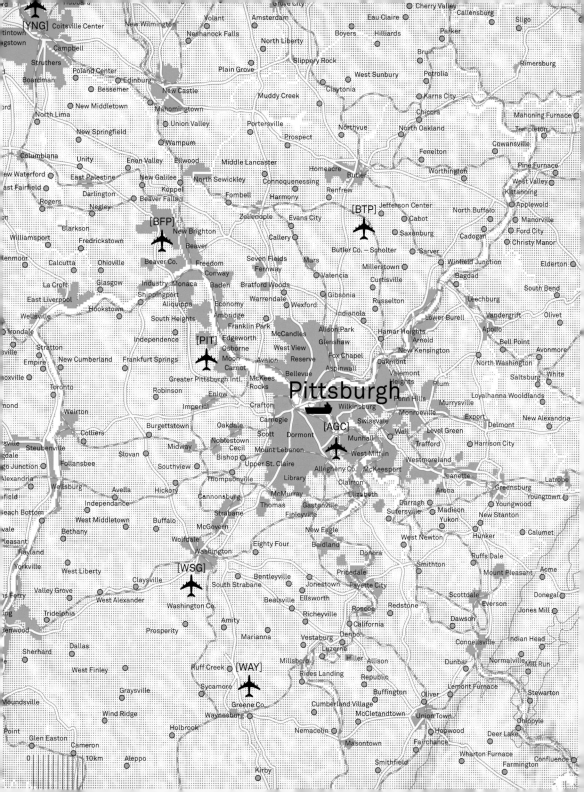

Randstad Holland The Netherlands

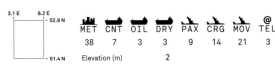

	MET	CNT	OIL	DRY	PAX	CRG	MOV	@ TEL
	38	7	3	3	9	14	21	3

3.1 E — 6.2 E
52.9 N — 51.4 N

Elevation (m)   2

Population

Inhabitants 2002　　　**6,600,000**
Regio Randstad

Metropolitan density

Inhabitants	6,600,000
Built-up area (km²)	1,419
Population density (inhabitants/km²)	**4,651**

Regio Randstad, 2002

Metropolitan development (Amsterdam)

Year	1965	1992
Total metropolitan inhabitants	1,730,000	1,875,000
Inhabitants in metropolitan core	866,000	713,000
Core share	**50.1%**	**38.0%**
Inhabitants in metropolitan periphery	864,000	1,162,000
Periphery share	49.9%	62.0%

demographia.com

Employment (Amsterdam)

	Metr. Area	CBD
Area (km²)	324	8.3
Area Share	100%	2.6%
Employment	320,168	80,722
Employment share	100%	25.2%
Employment density (employment/km²)	**988**	**9,726**

demographia.com, 2000

Traffic and transport (Amsterdam)

Public transport market share	49.0%
Private vehicle market share	51.0%
Average commuting time (minutes)	**28**

publicpurpose.com, 1990

Road use (Amsterdam)

Average road speed (km/hour)	34.9
Vehicle density (vehicle km/km²)	**67,713**

publicpurpose.com, 1990

Economy

Gross regional product per capita (€)	31,212
Unemployment rate	4.0%

Regio Randstad, 2002

Railway use (Amsterdam)

Passenger density (passenger km/km)	7,906
Rail vehicle density (vehicle km/km²)	**473,939**

publicpurpose.com, 1990

Health (Amsterdam)

Hospital beds per 1,000 inhabitants	**5**

Eurostat, 1996

Climate (Amsterdam)

Average January temperature (°C)	1.1
Average July temperature (°C)	**20.6**

weatherbase.com

Crime (Amsterdam)

Crimes per 100,000 inhabitants	**11,850**

Eurostat, 1996

Pollution (Amsterdam)

NOX (tonnes/km²)	62.5
CO (tonnes/km²)	167.2
VOC (tonnes/km²)	27.8
Total pollution (tonnes/km²)	**257.5**

demographia.com, 1990

Rhine-Ruhr Germany

5.4 N   8.4 N
- 52.0 N

MET
19

- 50.6 N   Elevation (m)   161

Population

Inhabitants 2002	**11,100,000**
Regio Randstad	

Residential density

Year	1985
Inhabitants	7,604,000
Residential area (km²)	1,823
Residential density (inhabitants/km²)	**4,171**

Metropolitan development

Year	1965
Total metropolitan inhabitants	5,200,000
Inhabitants in metropolitan core	729,000
Core share	**14.0%**
Inhabitants in metropolitan periphery	4,471,000
Periphery share	86.0%
demographia.com	

Traffic and transport (Essen)

Public transport market share	29.0%
Private vehicle market share	71.0%
Average commuting time (minutes)	**24**
publicpurpose.com, 1990; Eurostat, 1996	

Economy

Gross regional product per capita (€)	27,419
Unemployment rate	6.9%
Regio Randstad, 2002	

Health

Hospital beds per 1,000 inhabitants	**8**
Eurostat, 1996	

Climate (Essen)

Average January temperature (°C)	0.0
Average July temperature (°C)	**21.1**
weatherbase.com	

Crime

Crimes per 100,000 inhabitants	**9,880**
Eurostat, 1996	

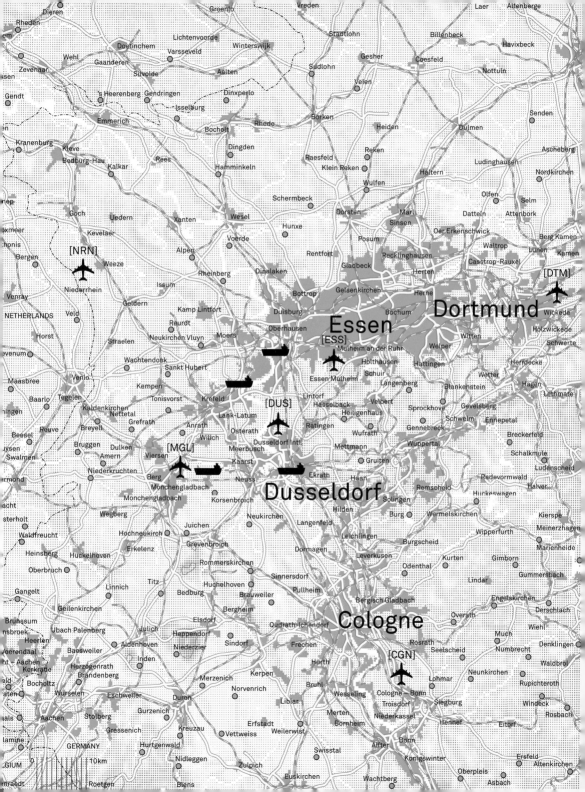

Rio de Janeiro Brazil

44.7 W   41.7 W
- 22.0 S

MET
21

Elevation (m)   6

- 23.4 S

@
TEL
30

Metropolitan density

Inhabitants	10,810,000
Built-up area (km²)	1,166
Population density (inhabitants/km²)	**9,271**

demographia.com, 2000

Population

Inhabitants 2000	**10,810,000**

demographia.com

Metropolitan development

Year	1965	2000
Total metropolitan inhabitants	5,250,000	10,810,000
Inhabitants in metropolitan core	3,600,000	5,852,000
Core share	**68.6%**	**54.1%**
Inhabitants in metropolitan periphery	1,650,000	4,958,000
Periphery share	31.4%	45.9%

Climate

Average January temperature (°C)	23.3
Average July temperature (°C)	**27.2**

weatherbase.com

Rome Italy

PAX
29

Population

Inhabitants 2002	**3,900,000**
Regio Randstad	

Residential density

Year	1985
Inhabitants	2,944,000
Residential area (km²)	179
Residential density (inhabitants/km²)	**16,447**
demographia.com	

Metropolitan development

Year	1965	1996
Total metropolitan inhabitants	2,500,000	3,235,000
Inhabitants in metropolitan core	2,340,000	2,650,000
Core share	**93.6%**	**81.9%**
Inhabitants in metropolitan periphery	160,000	585,000
Periphery share	6.4%	18.1%
demographia.com		

Economy

Gross regional product per capita (€)	26,000
Unemployment rate	3.3%
Eurostat, 1996	

Health

Hospital beds per 1,000 inhabitants	**7**
Eurostat, 1996	

Climate

Average January temperature (°C)	3.9
Average July temperature (°C)	**28.3**
weatherbase.com	

Crime

Crimes per 100,000 inhabitants	**7,660**
Eurostat, 1996	

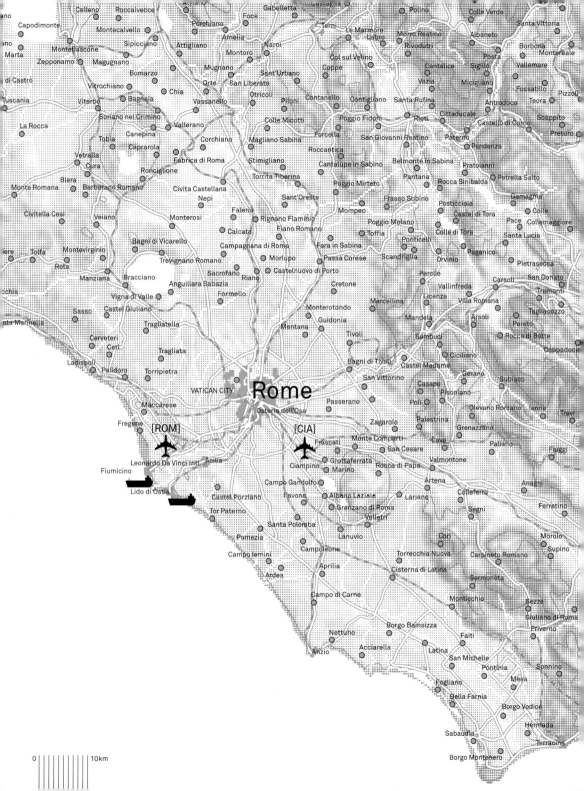

Sacramento United States

122.8 W 119.7 W
39.9 N
37.9 N

Elevation (m)	5

Population

Inhabitants 2000	**1,393,000**
Inhabitants 1985	796,000
Inhabitants 1970	641,000

US Census

Metropolitan development

Year	1965	2000
Total metropolitan inhabitants	212,000	1,393,000
Inhabitants in metropolitan core	138,000	407,000
Core share	**65.1%**	**29.2%**
Inhabitants in metropolitan periphery	74,000	986,000
Periphery share	34.9%	70.8%

demographia.com

Employment

	Metr. Area	CBD
Area (km²)	956	4.7
Area share	100%	0.2%
Employment	484,810	46,078
Employment share	100%	7.5%
Employment density (employment/km²)	**507**	**9,804**

demographia.com, 2000

Economy

Average income per capita (€)	**16,374**
Gross regional product per capita (€)	27,011
Unemployment rate	5.0%

demographia.com; bestplaces.net, 1998

Crime

Crimes per 100,000 inhabitants	**6,611**

bestplaces.net, 1998

@ TEL
22

Metropolitan density

Inhabitants	1,393,000
Built-up area (km²)	956
Population density (inhabitants/km²)	**1,457**

demographia.com, 2000

Change in density (1970–1990)

Change in inhabitants	455,000
Change in area (km²)	207
Change in density (inhabitants/km²)	**2,198**

demographia.com

Traffic and transport

Public transport market share	0.5%
Private vehicle market share	99.5%
Average commuting time (minutes)	**19**

publicpurpose.com, 1990

Road use

Average road speed (km/hour)	63.9
Vehicle density (vehicle km/km²)	**43,880**

publicpurpose.com, 1990

Railway use

Passenger density (passenger km/km)	3,439
Rail vehicle density (vehicle km/km²)	**27,684**

publicpurpose.com, 1996

Climate

Average January temperature (°C)	3.3
Average July temperature (°C)	**33.9**

weatherbase.com

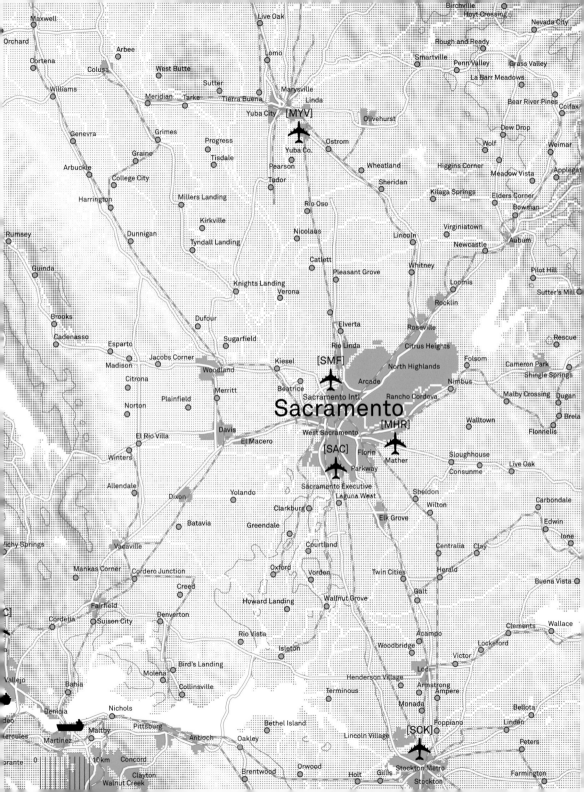

San Francisco-Oakland United States

	MET	CNT	OIL	DRY	PAX	CRG	MOV	@ TEL
	35	14	8	14	14	24+27	26+28	5

123.7 W — 120.7 W
38.4 N
37.0 N

Elevation (m) 39

Population

Inhabitants 2003	7,154,000

demographia.com

Metropolitan development

Year	1965	2003
Total metropolitan inhabitants	3,730,000	7,154,000
Inhabitants in metropolitan core	1,128,000	1,160,000
Core share	**30.2%**	**16.2%**
Inhabitants in metropolitan periphery	2,602,000	5,994,000
Periphery share	69.8%	83.8%

demographia.com

Employment

	Metr. Area	CBD
Area (km²)	2,038	3.9
Area share	100%	0.2%
Employment	3,153,201	415,984
Employment share	100%	13.2%
Employment density (employment/km²)	**1,547**	**106,663**

demographia.com, 1990

Economy

Average income per capita (€)	**23,376**
Gross regional product per capita (€)	37,132
Unemployment rate	2.1%

bestplaces.net, 1998

Crime

Crimes per 100,000 inhabitants	**5,725**

bestplaces.net, 1998

Metropolitan density

Inhabitants	4,767,000
Built-up area (km²)	2,038
Population density (inhabitants/km²)	**2,339**

demographia.com, 1990

Residential density

Year	1985
Inhabitants	3,790,000
Residential area (km²)	1,108
Residential density (inhabitants/km²)	**3,421**

demographia.com

Change in density (1970–1990)

Change in inhabitants	642,000
Change in area (km²)	782
Change in density (inhabitants/km²)	**821**

demographia.com

Traffic and transport

Public transport market share	4.7%
Private vehicle market share	95.3%
Average commuting time (minutes)	**25**

publicpurpose.com, 1990; bestplaces.net, 1998

Road use

Average road speed (km/hour)	44.2
Vehicle density (vehicle km/km²)	**53,904**

publicpurpose.com, 1990

Railway use

Passenger density (passenger km/km)	3,564
Rail vehicle density (vehicle km/km²)	**131,649**

publicpurpose.com, 1990

Climate

Average January temperature (°C)	7.8
Average July temperature (°C)	**18.9**

weatherbase.com

Pollution

NOX (tonnes/km²)	34.0
CO (tonnes/km²)	313.9
VOC (tonnes/km²)	34.7
Total pollution (tonnes/km²)	**382.6**

demographia.com, 1990

Santiago de Chile Chile

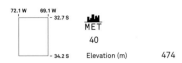

72.1 W   69.1 W
                      – 32.7 S

MET
40
                 Elevation (m)   474
                      – 34.2 S

Population

Inhabitants 2004   **6,061,000**
demographia.com

Metropolitan development

Year	1965	2004
Total metropolitan inhabitants	2,400,000	6,061,000
Inhabitants in metropolitan core	233,000	200,000
Core share	**9.7%**	**3.3%**
Inhabitants in metropolitan periphery	2,167,000	5,861,000
Periphery share	90.3%	96.7%

demographia.com

Metropolitan density

Inhabitants	4,937,000
Built-up area (km²)	974
Population density (inhabitants/km²)	**5,069**

demographia.com, 1992

Residential density

Year	1985
Inhabitants	4,700,000
Residential area (km²)	331
Residential density (inhabitants/km²)	**14,199**

demographia.com

Climate

Average January temperature (°C)	12.2
Average July temperature (°C)	**13.9**

weatherbase.com

São Paulo Brazil

47.8 W   44.8 W
— 22.9 S

— 24.4 S

MET	CNT	OIL	DRY
6	21	16	11

Elevation (m)   803

@
TEL
14

Metropolitan density

Inhabitants	17,720,000
Built-up area (km²)	1,981
Population density (inhabitants/km²)	**8,945**

demographia.com, 2000

Population

Inhabitants 2000	**17,720,000**

demographia.com

Metropolitan development

Year	1965	2000
Total metropolitan inhabitants	5,450,000	17,720,000
Inhabitants in metropolitan core	4,425,000	10,406,000
Core share	**81.2%**	**58.7%**
Inhabitants in metropolitan periphery	1,025,000	7,314,000
Periphery share	18.8%	41.3%

demographia.com

Climate

Average January temperature (°C)	19.4
Average July temperature (°C)	**23.3**

weatherbase.com

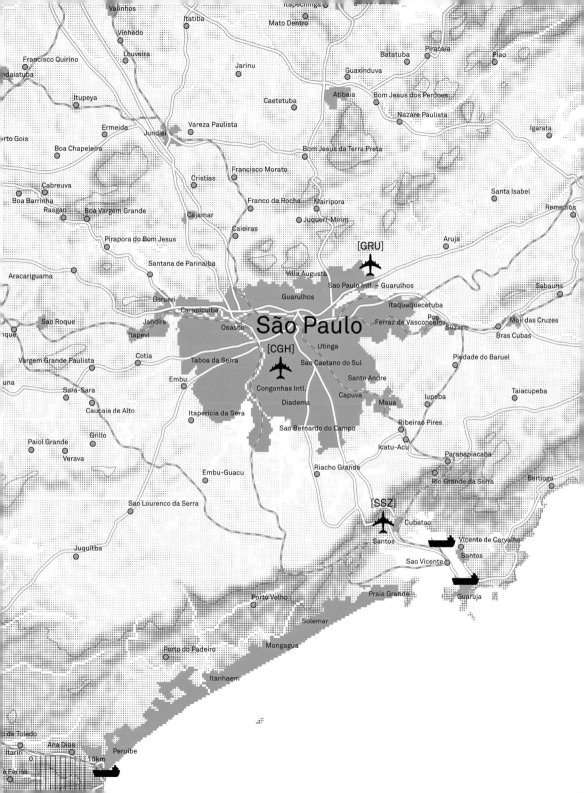

Seattle United States

123.9 W 120.8 W
48.3 N
46.9 N

Elevation (m) 6

PAX 27
MOV 23
@ TEL 12

Metropolitan density

Inhabitants	2,712,000
Built-up area (km²)	2,471
Population density (inhabitants/km²)	**1,098**

US Census, 2000

Population

Inhabitants 2000	**2,712,000**
Inhabitants 1985	1,392,000
Inhabitants 1970	1,238,000

US Census

Metropolitan development

	1965	2000
Year	1965	2000
Total metropolitan inhabitants	790,000	2,712,000
Inhabitants in metropolitan core	612,000	563,000
Core share	**77.5%**	**20.8%**
Inhabitants in metropolitan periphery	178,000	2,149,000
Periphery share	22.5%	79.2%

demographia.com

Change in density (1970–1990)

Change in inhabitants	506,000
Change in area (km²)	906
Change in density (inhabitants/km²)	**558**

demographia.com

Employment

	Metr. Area	CBD
Area (km²)	2,471	8.8
Area share	100%	0.4%
Employment	1,409,497	367,085
Employment share	100%	26.0%
Employment density (employment/km²)	**570**	**41,714**

demographia.com, 2000

Traffic and transport

Average commuting time (minutes)	**21**

bestplaces.net, 1998

Road use

Vehicle density (vehicle km/km²)	**43,487**

publicpurpose.com, 1990

Economy

Average income per capita (€)	**21,277**
Gross regional product per capita (€)	31,142
Unemployment rate	3.4%

demographia.com; bestplaces.net, 1998

Railway use

Rail vehicle density (vehicle km/km²)	**74,763**

publicpurpose.com, 1990

Climate

Average January temperature (°C)	2.2
Average July temperature (°C)	**23.3**

weatherbase.com

Crime

Crimes per 100,000 inhabitants	**9,164**

bestplaces.net, 1998

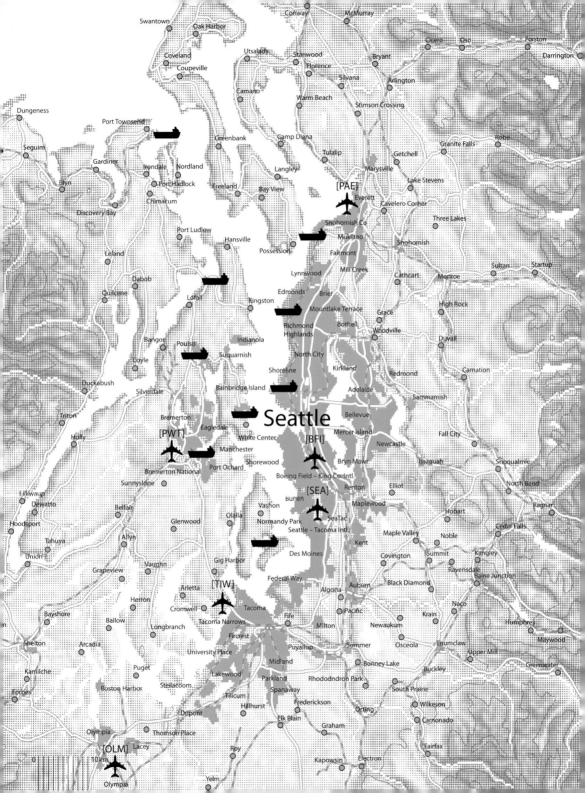

Seoul-Incheon South Korea

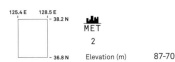

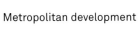

	125.4 E	128.5 E
		38.2 N

MET
2

Elevation (m) 87-70

CRG @
15+26 TEL 16

36.8 N

Population

Inhabitants 2002	**22,877,000**

demographia.com

Metropolitan development

Year	1965	2002
Total metropolitan inhabitants	3,700,000	22,877,000
Inhabitants in metropolitan core	3,588,000	10,280,000
Core share	**97.0%**	**44.9%**
Inhabitants in metropolitan periphery	112,000	12,597,000
Periphery share	3.0%	55.1%

demographia.com

Employment

	Metr. Area	CBD
Area (km²)	1,191	21.2
Area share	100%	1.8%
Employment	7,122,689	1,226,830
Employment share	100%	17.2%
Employment density (employment/km²)	**5,980**	**57,869**

demographia.com, 2000

Economy

Average income per capita (€)	**11,909**
Unemployment rate	6.9%

asiaweek.com, 2000

Health

Hospital beds per 1,000 inhabitants	**5**
Average life expectancy at birth	71

asiaweek.com, 2000

Crime

Crimes per 100,000 inhabitants	**3,640**

bestplaces.net, 1998

Metropolitan density

Inhabitants	19,920,000
Built-up area (km²)	1,191
Population density (inhabitants/km²)	**16,725**

demographia.com, 2000

Residential density

Year	1985
Inhabitants	13,665,000
Residential area (km²)	885
Residential density (inhabitants/km²)	**15,441**

demographia.com

Change in density (1970–1990)

Change in inhabitants	2,540,000
Change in area (km²)	88
Change in density (inhabitants/km²)	**28,749**

demographia.com

Traffic and transport

Public transport market share	47.8%
Private vehicle market share	52.2%
Average commuting time (minutes)	**41**

publicpurpose.com, 1990

Road use

Average road speed (km/hour)	24.0
Vehicle density (vehicle km/km²)	**141,864**

publicpurpose.com, 1990

Railway use

Passenger density (passenger km/km)	134,190
Rail vehicle density (vehicle km/km²)	**4,490,766**

publicpurpose.com, 1990

Climate

Average January temperature (°C)	-6.1
Average July temperature (°C)	**27.8**

weatherbase.com

Pollution

NOX (tonnes/km²)	300.0
CO (tonnes/km²)	971.0
VOC (tonnes/km²)	121.2
Total pollution (tonnes/km²)	**1,392.3**

demographia.com, 1990

Shanghai China

119.9 E 122.9 E
- 32.0 N

- 30.5 N

MET	CNT	OIL	DRY
14	20	22	23

Elevation (m) 7

Population

Inhabitants 2000	**13,580,000**
Inhabitants 1985	6,726,000

demographia.com

Metropolitan density

Inhabitants	9,000,000
Built-up area (km²)	549
Population density (inhabitants/km²)	**16,393**

demographia.com, 1998

Traffic and transport

Average commuting time (minutes)	**40**

asiaweek.com, 2000

Economy

Average income per capita (€)	**4,434**
Unemployment rate	4.6%

asiaweek.com, 2000

Health

Hospital beds per 1,000 inhabitants	**6**
Average life expectancy at birth	71

asiaweek.com, 2000

Climate

Average January temperature (°C)	1.1
Average July temperature (°C)	**31.1**

weatherbase.com

Crime

Crimes per 100,000 inhabitants	**210**

asiaweek.com, 2000

Singapore 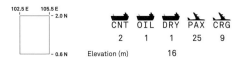 Singapore

	CNT	OIL	DRY	PAX	CRG	@ TEL
	2	1	1	25	9	26

102.5 E   105.5 E
2.0 N
0.6 N

Elevation (m)   16

Population

Inhabitants 2003	**4,163,000**
Inhabitants 1970	2,075,000
Inhabitants 1960	1,646,000

citypopulation.de

Metropolitan development

Year	1965
Total metropolitan inhabitants	1,825,000
Inhabitants in metropolitan core	1,100,000
Core share	**60.3%**
Inhabitants in metropolitan periphery	725,000
Periphery share	39.7%

demographia.com

Employment

	Metr. Area	CBD
Area (km²)	319	7.2
Area share	100%	2.3%
Employment	1,537,011	280,000
Employment share	100%	18.2%
Employment density (employment/km²)	**4,818**	**38,889**

demographia.com, 1995

Economy

Average income per capita (€)	**29,149**
Unemployment rate	3.3%

asiaweek.com, 2000

Health

Hospital beds per 1,000 inhabitants	**3**
Average life expectancy at birth	77

asiaweek.com, 2000

Crime

Crimes per 100,000 inhabitants	**1,000**

bestplaces.net, 2000

Metropolitan density

Inhabitants	2,987,000
Built-up area (km²)	319
Population density (inhabitants/km²)	**9,364**

demographia.com, 1995

Residential density

Year	1985
Inhabitants	2,556,000
Residential area (km²)	202
Residential density (inhabitants/km²)	**12,653**

demographia.com

Change in density (1970–1990)

Change in inhabitants	631,000
Change in area (km²)	153
Change in density (inhabitants/km²)	**4,131**

demographia.com

Traffic and transport

Public transport market share	31.2%
Private vehicle market share	68.8%
Average commuting time (minutes)	**30**

publicpurpose.com, 1990; asiaweek.com, 1998

Road use

Average road speed (km/hour)	32.5
Vehicle density (vehicle km/km²)	**85,564**

publicpurpose.com, 1990

Railway use

Passenger density (passenger km/km)	58,520
Rail vehicle density (vehicle km/km²)	**1,593,712**

publicpurpose.com, 1990

Climate

Average January temperature (°C)	23.9
Average July temperature (°C)	**30.6**

weatherbase.com

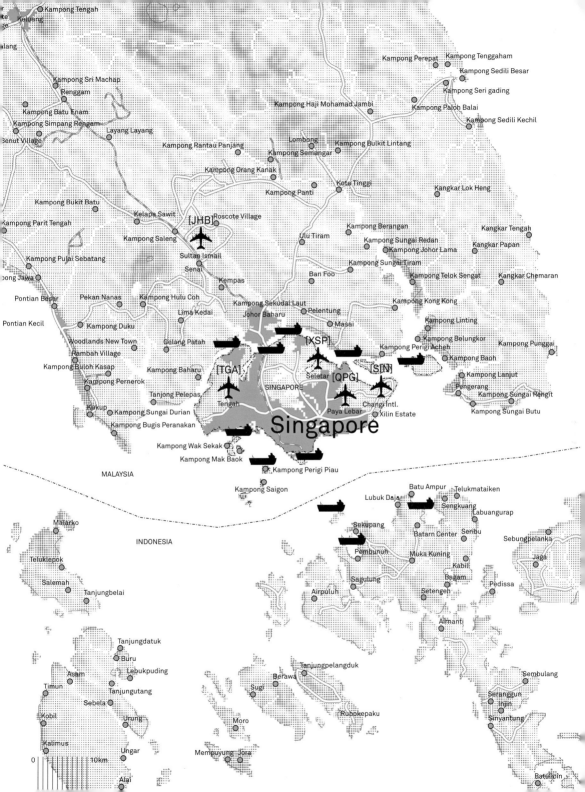

St. Louis United States

91.7 W — 88.6 W
- 39.3 N
- 37.9 N

PAX 28   MOV 11

Elevation (m) 163

Metropolitan density

Inhabitants	2,078,000
Built-up area (km²)	2,147
Population density (inhabitants/km²)	**968**

US Census, 2000

Population

Inhabitants 2000	**2,078,000**
Inhabitants 1985	1,849,000
Inhabitants 1970	1,883,000

US Census

Metropolitan development

Year	1965	2000
Total metropolitan inhabitants	1,401,000	2,078,000
Inhabitants in metropolitan core	857,000	348,000
Core share	**61.3%**	**16.7%**
Inhabitants in metropolitan periphery	544,000	1,730,000
Periphery share	38.8%	83.2%

demographia.com

Change in density (1970–1990)

Change in inhabitants	64,000
Change in area (km²)	153
Change in density (inhabitants/km²)	**418**

demographia.com

Employment

	Metr. Area	CBD
Area (km²)	2,147	-
Area share	100%	-
Employment	1,157,017	123,697
Employment share	100%	10.7%
Employment density (employment/km²)	**539**	-

demographia.com

Traffic and transport

Average commuting time (minutes)	**22**

bestplaces.net, 1998

Road use

Vehicle density (vehicle km/km²)	**38,520**

publicpurpose.com, 1990

Economy

Average income per capita (€)	**12,538**
Unemployment rate	3.3%

bestplaces.net, 1998

Railway use

Passenger density (passenger km/km)	7,747
Rail vehicle density (vehicle km/km²)	**32,722**

publicpurpose.com, 1996

Climate

Average January temperature (°C)	-6.1
Average July temperature (°C)	**31.7**

weatherbase.com

Crime

Crimes per 100,000 inhabitants	**13,998**

bestplaces.net, 1998

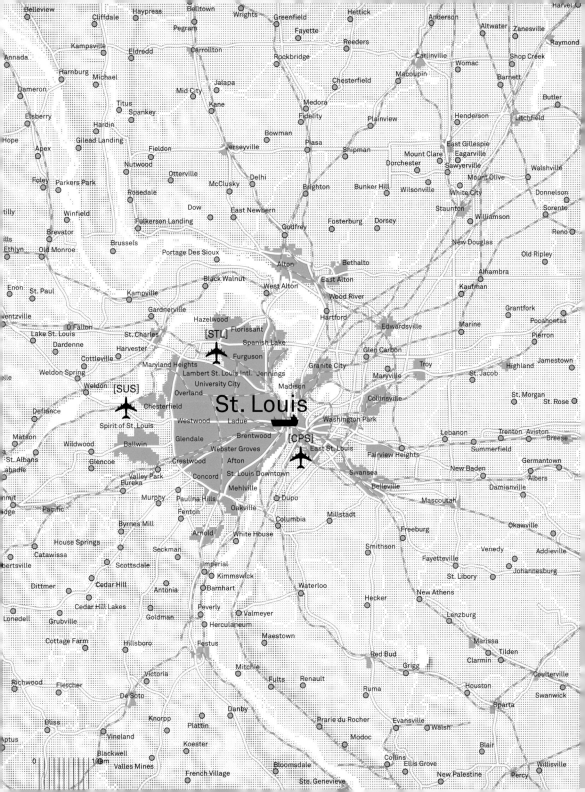

St. Petersburg Russia

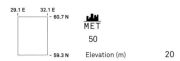

29.1 E	32.1 E		
		60.7 N	
	MET		
	50		
		59.3 N	
	Elevation (m)	20	

Population

Inhabitants 2000	**5,410,000**
demographia.com	

Residential density

Year	1985
Inhabitants	4,569,000
Residential area (km²)	360
Residential density (inhabitants/km²)	**12,692**
demographia.com	

Metropolitan development

Year	1965	1999
Total metropolitan inhabitants	4,000,000	5,275,000
Inhabitants in metropolitan core	3,100,000	4,160,000
Core share	**77.5%**	**78.9%**
Inhabitants in metropolitan periphery	900,000	1,115,000
Periphery share	22.5%	21.1%
demographia.com		

Climate

Average January temperature (°C)	-9.4
Average July temperature (°C)	**21.1**
weatherbase.com	

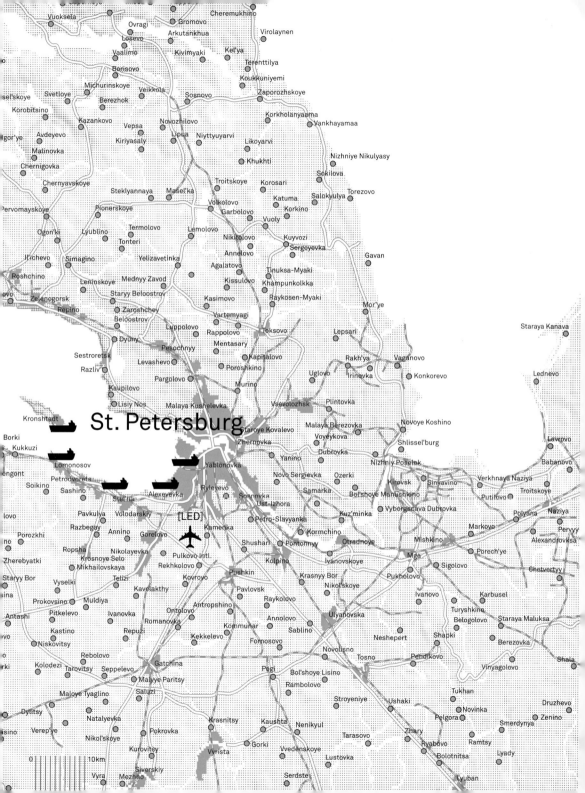

Stockholm Sweden

16.2 E 19.3 E
- 60.1 N
- 58.6 N

Elevation (m) 61

Population

Inhabitants 2002 **1,684,000**
demographia.com

@
TEL
23

Metropolitan density

Inhabitants	1,479,000
Built-up area (km²)	409
Population density (inhabitants/km²)	**3,614**

demographia.com, 2000

Metropolitan development

Year	1965	2002
Total metropolitan inhabitants	1,180,000	1,684,000
Inhabitants in metropolitan core	800,000	758,000
Core share	**67.8%**	**45.0%**
Inhabitants in metropolitan periphery	380,000	926,000
Periphery share	32.2%	55.0%

demographia.com

Employment

	Metr. Area	CBD
Area (km²)	409	4.1
Area share	100%	1.0%
Employment	499,094	111,233
Employment share	100%	22.3%
Employment density (employment/km²)	**1,220**	**27,130**

demographia.com, 2000

Traffic and transport

Public transport market share	54.0%
Private vehicle market share	46.0%
Average commuting time (minutes)	**27**

publicpurpose.com, 1990; Eurostat, 1996

Road use

Average road speed (km/hour)	26.7
Vehicle density (vehicle km/km²)	**73,509**

publicpurpose.com, 1990

Economy

Gross regional product per capita (€)	43,667
Unemployment rate	4.4%

Regio Randstad, 2002

Railway use

Passenger density (passenger km/km)	23,349
Rail vehicle density (vehicle km/km²)	**1,139,158**

publicpurpose.com, 1990

Health

Average life expectancy at birth	78

Eurostat, 1996

Climate

Average January temperature (°C)	-5.6
Average July temperature (°C)	**21.1**

weatherbase.com

Crime

Crimes per 100,000 inhabitants	**19,810**

Eurostat, 1996

Pollution

NOX (tonnes/km²)	94.6
CO (tonnes/km²)	1,103.1
VOC (tonnes/km²)	141.7
Total pollution (tonnes/km²)	**1,339.4**

demographia.com

Sydney Australia

	149.6 E	152.6 E	
		– 33.1 S	
		– 34.6 S	

Elevation (m)   6

Population

Inhabitants 2001	**3,997,000**
demographia.com	

Metropolitan development

Year	1965	2001
Total metropolitan inhabitants	2,340,000	3,997,000
Inhabitants in metropolitan core	168,000	140,000
Core share	**7.2%**	**3.5%**
Inhabitants in metropolitan periphery	2,172,000	3,857,000
Periphery share	92.8%	96.5%
domographia.com		

Employment

	Metr. Area	CBD
Area (km²)	2,103	4.1
Area share	100%	0.2%
Employment	1,524,403	175,620
Employment share	100%	11.5%
Employment density (employment/km²)	**725**	**42,834**
demographia.com, 1990		

@ TEL 13

Metropolitan density

Inhabitants	3,539,000
Built-up area (km²)	2,103
Population density (inhabitants/km²)	**1,683**
Kenworthy Laube, 1990	

Residential density

Year	1985
Inhabitants	3,396,000
Residential area (km²)	875
Residential density (inhabitants/km²)	**3,881**
demographia.com	

Change in density (1970–1990)

Change in inhabitants	731,000
Change in area (km²)	1,028
Change in density (inhabitants/km²)	**711**
demographia.com	

Traffic and transport

Public transport market share	13.6%
Private vehicle market share	86.4%
Average commuting time (minutes)	**31**
publicpurpose.com, 1990	

Road use

Average road speed (km/hour)	37.0
Vehicle density (vehicle km/km²)	**32,491**
publicpurpose.com, 1990	

Railway use

Rail vehicle density (vehicle km/km²)	**254,345**
publicpurpose.com, 1990	

Climate

Average January temperature (°C)	18.3
Average July temperature (°C)	**16.7**
weatherbase.com	

Pollution

NOX (tonnes/km²)	39.8
CO (tonnes/km²)	347.9
VOC (tonnes/km²)	37.8
Total pollution (tonnes/km²)	**425.5**
demographia.com, 1990	

Taichung China (Taiwan)

119.2 E   122.2 E
                    ⌐ 24.9 N

                                ⌐ 23.4 N

CNT   OIL   DRY
22   14   5

Elevation (m)   112

Population

Inhabitants 2001   **983,694**
Inhabitants 1985   593,000
citypopulation.de

Climate

Average January temperature (°C)   11.1
Average July temperature (°C)   **31.7**
weatherbase.com

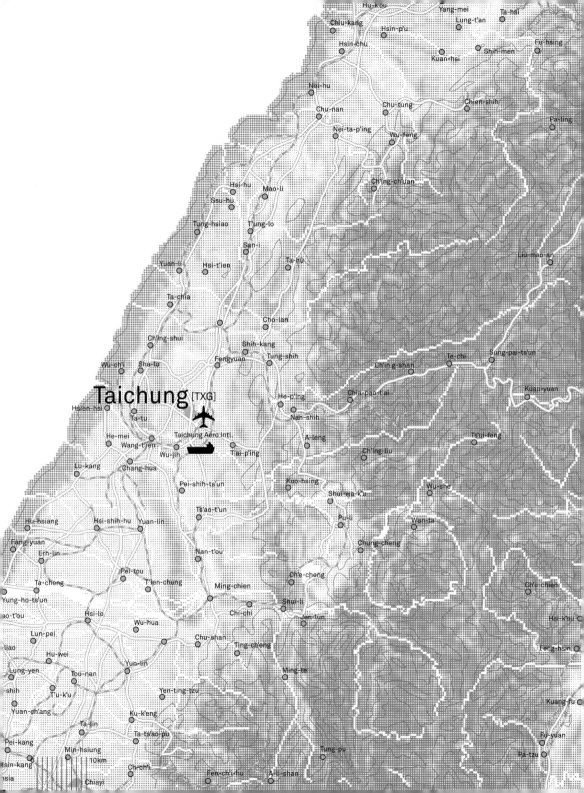

Taipei China (Taiwan)

	MET	CNT	OIL	DRY		CRG		@ TEL
	33	11	20	20		16		15
	Elevation (m)			6				

119.7 E 122.7 E
25.4 N
23.9 N

Population

Inhabitants 2000	**7,260,000**
demographia.com	

Metropolitan density

Inhabitants	5,960,000
Built-up area (km²)	259
Population density (inhabitants/km²)	**23,012**
demographia.com, 1995	

Residential density

Year	1985
Inhabitants	5,550,000
Residential area (km²)	357
Residential density (inhabitants/km²)	**15,546**
demographia.com	

Metropolitan development

Year	1965	2000
Total metropolitan inhabitants	1,425,000	7,260,000
Inhabitants in metropolitan core	1,025,000	3,247,000
Core share	**71.9%**	**44.7%**
Inhabitants in metropolitan periphery	400,000	4,013,000
Periphery share	28.1%	55.3%
demographia.com		

Traffic and transport

Average commuting time (minutes)	**24**
asiaweek.com, 2000	

Economy

Average income per capita (€)	**13,782**
Unemployment rate	2.8%
asiaweek.com, 2000	

Health

Hospital beds per 1,000 inhabitants	**8**
Average life expectancy at birth	79
asiaweek.com, 2000	

Climate

Average January temperature (°C)	12.8
Average July temperature (°C)	**33.3**
weatherbase.com	

Crime

Crimes per 100,000 inhabitants	**1,060**
asiaweek.com, 2000	

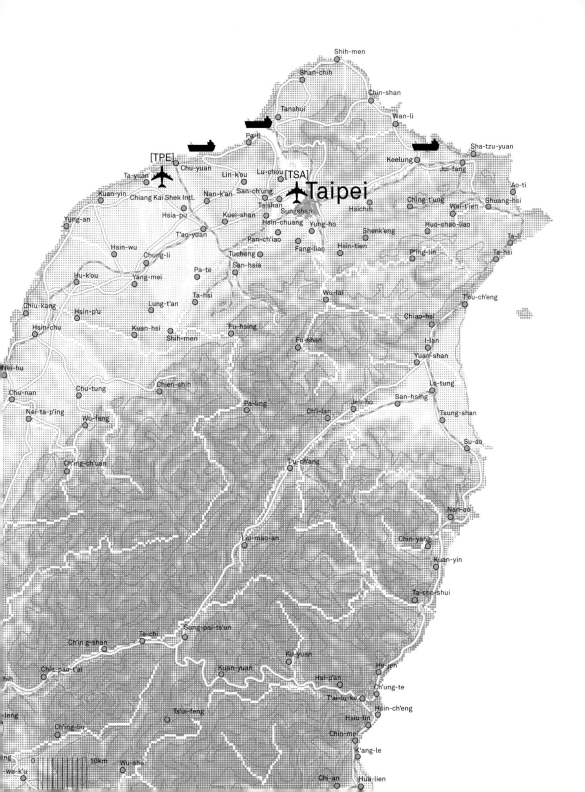

Tangier Morocco

7.1 W 4.1 W
- 36.8 N

- 35.4 N   Elevation (m)   21

Population

Inhabitants 1994   **497,147**
Inhabitants 1985   266,346
citypopulation.de

Climate

Average January temperature (°C)   8.3
Average July temperature (°C)   **28.3**
weatherbase.com

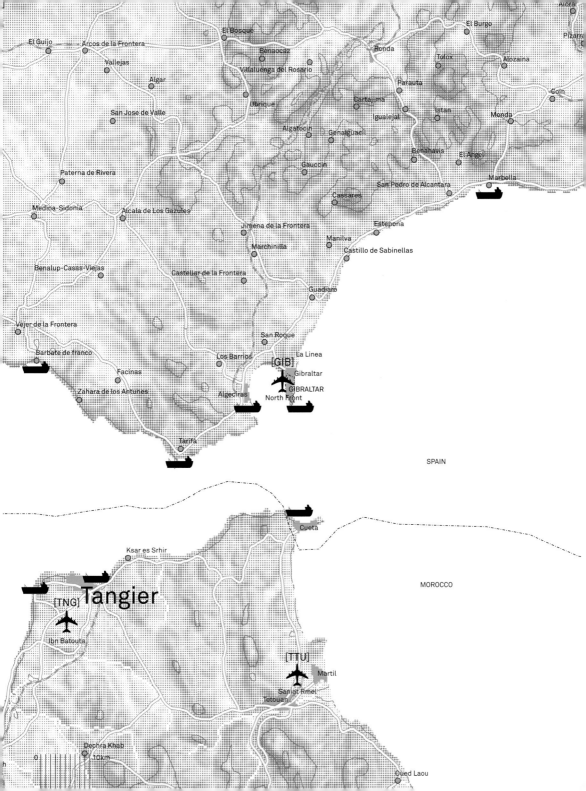

Tehran Iran

MET
22

Elevation (m)	1191

Population

Inhabitants 2000	**10,740,000**
demographia.com	

Residential density

Year	1985
Inhabitants	7,354,000
Residential area (km²)	290
Residential density (inhabitants/km²)	**25,359**
demographia.com	

Metropolitan development

Year	1965	2000
Total metropolitan inhabitants	2,000,000	10,740,000
Inhabitants in metropolitan core	1,900,000	7,681,000
Core share	**95.0%**	**71.5%**
Inhabitants in metropolitan periphery	100,000	3,059,000
Periphery share	5.0%	28.5%
demographia.com		

Climate

Average January temperature (°C)	-1.7
Average July temperature (°C)	**36.1**
weatherbase.com	

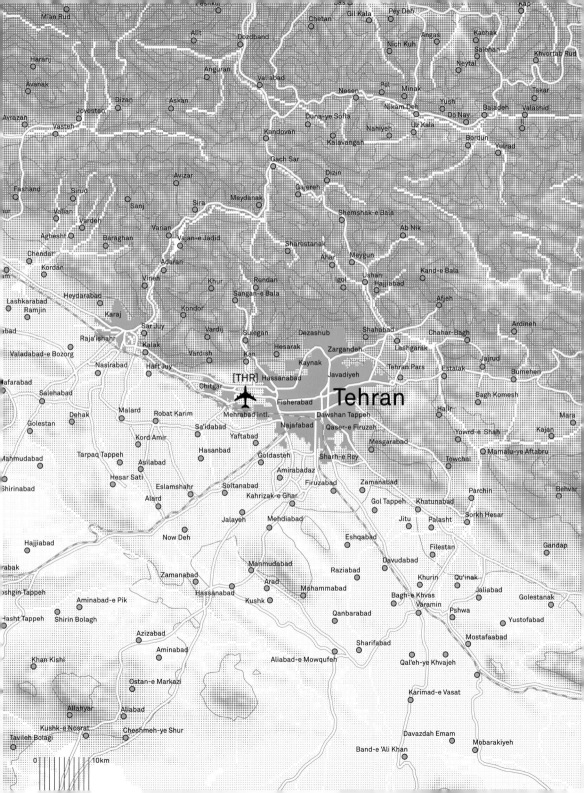

Tianjin China

115.8 E 118.8 E

39.9 N

38.5 N

MET
26

Elevation (m)	5

Population

Inhabitants 2000	**9,920,000**
demographia.com	

Metropolitan development

Year	1965	2000
Total metropolitan inhabitants	4,426,000	9,920,000
Inhabitants in metropolitan core	3,220,000	5,096,000
Core share	**72.8%**	**51.4%**
Inhabitants in metropolitan periphery	1,206,000	4,824,000
Periphery share	27.2%	48.6%

Residential density

Year	1985
Inhabitants	4,622,000
Residential area (km²)	127
Residential density (inhabitants/km²)	**36,394**
demographia.com	

Climate

Average January temperature (°C)	-6.7
Average July temperature (°C)	**30.0**
weatherbase.com	

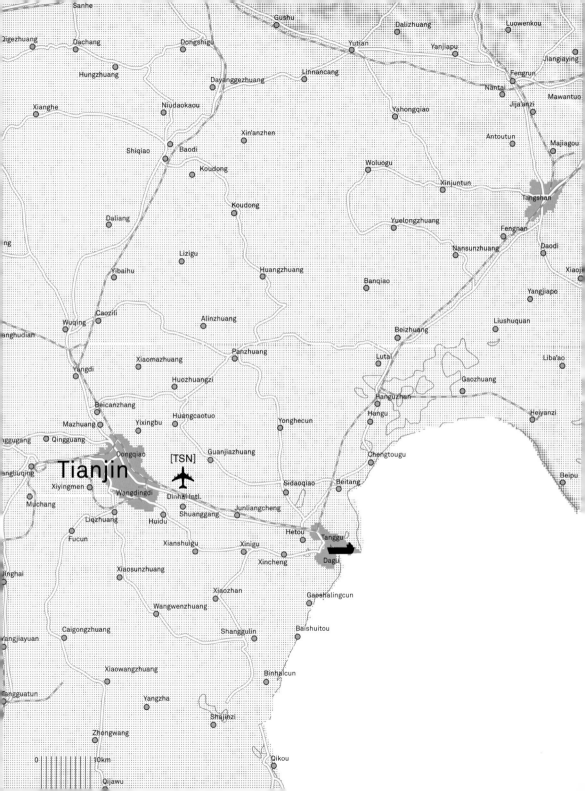

Tokyo-Yokohama Japan

	MET	CNT	OIL	DRY	PAX	CRG		@ TEL
	1	9+10	10+25	17+25	5+30	5+23		6
Elevation (m)				8				

138.6 E 141.6 E — 36.3 N — 34.8 N

Population

Inhabitants 2000	**33,190,000**

demographia.com

Metropolitan development

Year	1965	2000
Total metropolitan inhabitants	21,017,000	33,190,000
Inhabitants in metropolitan core	8,893,000	8,130,000
Core share	**42.3%**	**24.5%**
Inhabitants in metropolitan periphery	12,124,000	25,060,000
Periphery share	57.7%	75.5%

demographia.com

Employment

	Metr. Area	CBD
Area (km²)	5,258	222.4
Area share	100%	4.2%
Employment	23,200,000	7,975,000
Employment share	100%	34.5%
Employment density (employment/km²)	**4,393**	**35,859**

demographia.com, 2000

Economy

Average income per capita (€)	**30,129**
Gross regional product per capita (€)	35,052
Unemployment rate	4.6%

demographia.com, 1998; asiaweek.com, 2000

Health

Hospital beds per 1,000 inhabitants	**12**
Average life expectancy at birth	77

asiaweek.com, 2000

Crime

Crimes per 100,000 inhabitants	**2,240**

asiaweek.com, 2000

Metropolitan density

Inhabitants	33,190,000
Built-up area (km²)	5,258
Population density (inhabitants/km²)	**6,312**

demographia.com, 2000

Residential density

Year	1985
Inhabitants	25,434,000
Residential area (km²)	2,819
Residential density (inhabitants/km²)	**9,022**

demographia.com

Change in density (1970–1990)

Change in inhabitants	10,326,000
Change in area (km²)	2,664
Change in density (inhabitants/km²)	**3,876**

demographia.com

Traffic and transport

Public transport market share	49.0%
Private vehicle market share	51.0%
Average commuting time (minutes)	**56**

publicpurpose.com, 1990; asiaweek.com, 2000

Road use

Average road speed (km/hour)	24.5
Vehicle density (vehicle km/km²)	**73,795**

publicpurpose.com, 1990

Railway use

Passenger density (passenger km/km)	143,292
Rail vehicle density (vehicle km/km²)	**1,021,163**

publicpurpose.com, 1990

Climate

Average January temperature (°C)	1.7
Average July temperature (°C)	**27.8**

weatherbase.com

Pollution

NOX (tonnes/km²)	45.9
CO (tonnes/km²)	149.4
VOC (tonnes/km²)	20.8
Total pollution (tonnes/km²)	**216.2**

demographia.com, 1990

Toronto Canada

	80.7 W	77.7 W			

MET **48**
PAX **26**
MOV **22**

44.1 N
42.7 N

Elevation (m) 173

Population

Inhabitants 2000 5,470,000
demographia.com

Metropolitan density

Inhabitants	5,470,000
Built-up area (km²)	1,652
Population density (inhabitants/km²)	**3,311**

demographia.com, 2001

Residential density

Year	1985
Inhabitants	2,972,000
Residential area (km²)	399
Residential density (inhabitants/km²)	**7,449**

demographia.com

Employment

	Metr. Area	CBD
Area (km²)	1,652	1.8
Area share	100%	0.1%
Employment	2,290,000	302,200
Employment share	100%	13.2%
Employment density (employment/km²)	**1,386**	**167,889**

demographia.com, 2000

Traffic and transport

Public transport market share	11.5%
Private vehicle market share	88.5%
Average commuting time (minutes)	**25**

publicpurpose.com, 1990

Road use

Average road speed (km/hour)	34.9
Vehicle density (vehicle km/km²)	**68,723**

publicpurpose.com, 1990

Railway use

Passenger density (passenger km/km)	52,882
Rail vehicle density (vehicle km/km²)	**252,709**

publicpurpose.com, 1990

Climate

Average January temperature (°C)	-9.4
Average July temperature (°C)	**27.8**

weatherbase.com

Pollution

NOX (tonnes/km²)	112.0
CO (tonnes/km²)	667.2
VOC (tonnes/km²)	90.0
Total pollution (tonnes/km²)	**869.1**

demographia.com, 1990

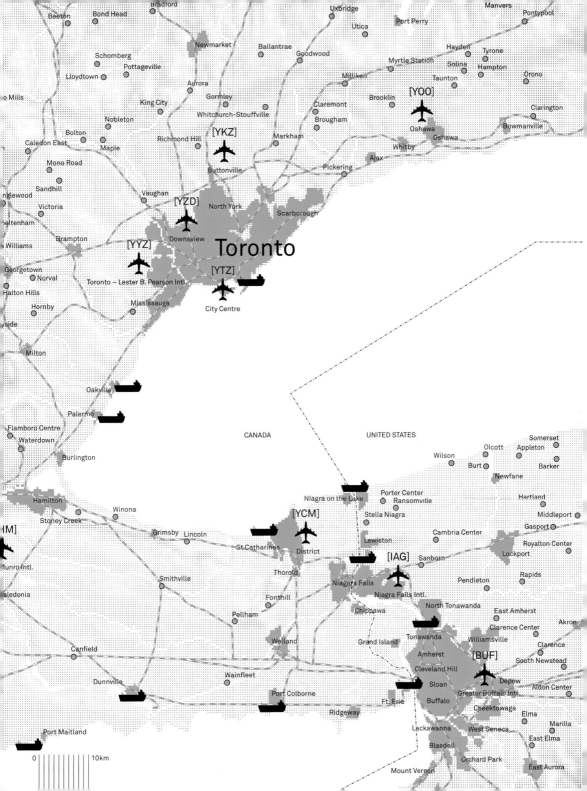

Vancouver Canada

124.1 W 121.0 W
- 49.6 N

- 48.2 N Elevation (m) 2

Population

Inhabitants 2001	**2,118,000**
StatsCanada	

Metropolitan density

Inhabitants	2,118,000
Built-up area (km²)	1,391
Population density (inhabitants/km²)	**1,523**
StatsCanada, 2001	

Change in density (1970–1990)

Change in inhabitants	515,000
Change in area (km²)	425
Change in density (inhabitants/km²)	**1,212**
demographia.com	

Employment

	Metr. Area	CBD
Area (km²)	1,391	3.4
Area share	100%	0.2%
Employment	792,485	104,000
Employment share	100%	13.1%
Employment density (employment/km²)	**570**	**30,588**
demographia.com, 2001		

Traffic and transport

Public transport market share	6.2%
Private vehicle market share	93.8%
publicpurpose.com, 1990	

Road use

Average road speed (km/hour)	38.0
Vehicle density (vehicle km/km²)	**49,904**
publicpurpose.com, 1990	

Railway use

Passenger density (passenger km/km)	24,404
Rail vehicle density (vehicle km/km²)	**168,506**
publicpurpose.com, 1990	

Climate

Average January temperature (°C)	0.6
Average July temperature (°C)	**21.1**
weatherbase.com	

Washington-Baltimore United States

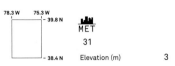

78.3 W   75.3 W
39.8 N

38.4 N

MET
31

Elevation (m)   3

MOV **@ TEL**
25   7

Metropolitan density

Inhabitants	7,430,000
Built-up area (km²)	4,763
Population density (inhabitants/km²)	**1,560**

demographia.com, 2000

Population

Inhabitants 2002	**7,910,000**
Inhabitants 1985	4,518,000
Inhabitants 1970	4,064,000

demographia.com

Metropolitan development

Year	1965	2002
Total metropolitan inhabitants	3,965,000	7,910,000
Inhabitants in metropolitan core	1,715,000	1,192,000
Core share	**43.3%**	**15.1%**
Inhabitants in metropolitan periphery	2,250,000	6,718,000
Periphery share	56.7%	84.9%

demographia.com

Change in density (1970–1990)

Change in inhabitants	1,192,000
Change in area (km²)	2,529
Change in density (inhabitants/km²)	**471**

demographia.com

Employment

	Metr. Area	CBD
Area (km²)	4,763	-
Area share	100%	-
Employment	3,487,712	538,935
Employment share	100%	15.5%
Employment density (employment/km²)	**732**	-

demographia.com, 2000

Traffic and transport

Public transport market share	4.3%
Private vehicle market share	95.7%
Average commuting time (minutes)	**26**

publicpurpose.com, 1990; bestplaces.net, 1998

Road use

Average road speed (km/hour)	42.3
Vehicle density (vehicle km/km²)	**39,922**

publicpurpose.com, 1990

Economy

Average income per capita (€)	**21,867**
Gross regional product per capita (€)	33,053
Unemployment rate	2.3%

demographia.com; bestplaces.net, 1998

Railway use

Passenger density (passenger km/km)	19,421
Rail vehicle density (vehicle km/km²)	**72,701**

publicpurpose.com, 1996

Climate

Average January temperature (°C)	-4.4
Average July temperature (°C)	**31.1**

weatherbase.com

Crime

Crimes per 100,000 inhabitants	**8,062**

bestplaces.net, 1998

Pollution

NOX (tonnes/km²)	30.1
CO (tonnes/km²)	252.1
VOC (tonnes/km²)	28.2
Total pollution (tonnes/km²)	**310.4**

demographia.com, 1990

World comparison of metropolitan data

Anchorage

Detroit
Chicago
Minneapolis-St.Paul
Indianapolis
St.Louis
Memphis

Toronto
Montreal
Cincinnati
Pittsburgh
Boston
New York
Philadelphia
Washington-Baltimore

Vancouver
Seattle
Denver
Sacramento
San Francisco-Oakland

Las Vegas
Los Angeles
Phoenix
Dallas-Ft.Worth
Houston
Monterey
New Orleans

Louisville
Charlotte
Atlanta
Orlando
Miami

Oslo
Hamburg
Rhine-Ruhr
Frankfurt
Randstad Holland
Antwerp-Brussels
London
Le Havre
Paris
Geneva
Milan
Lisbon
Madrid
Barcelona

Tangie

Mexico City

Lagos

Bogotá
Lima

Santiago de Chile

Rio de Janeiro
São Paulo
Buenos Aires

Stockholm
St.Petersburg
Copenhagen
Moscow

Berlin
Rome
Istanbul
Athens

Jerusalem-Tel Aviv
Baghdad
Tehran
Cairo

Dubai
Lahore
Hyderabad
Karachi
New Delhi
Mumbai

Beijing
Tianjin
Shanghai
Hong Kong

Dhaka
Calcutta

Seoul-Incheon
Busan

Tokyo-Yokohama
Nagoya
Kobe-Osaka-Kyoto

Taipei
Taichung
Kaohsiung

Manila

Bangkok
Bangalore
Chennai

Kuala Lumpur
Singapore
Djakarta

Kinshasa
Johannesburg
Durban

Perth
Melbourne
Sydney
Auckland

The world's 50 largest cities [🏛 MET]

The world's 50 largest cities in terms of inhabitants (c. 2000)

demographia.com, citypopulation.de, Eurostat, Regio Randstad, StatsCanada, US Census

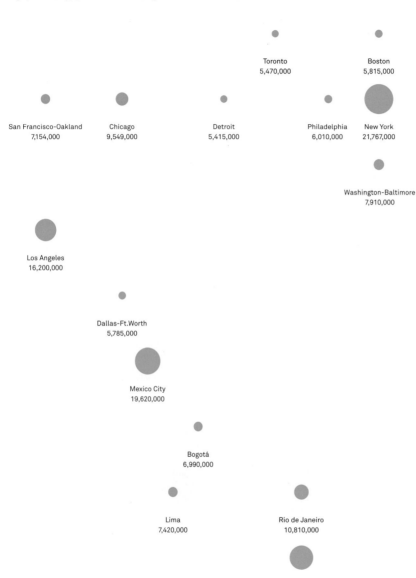

Toronto
5,470,000

Boston
5,815,000

London
13,945,000

San Francisco-Oakland
7,154,000

Chicago
9,549,000

Detroit
5,415,000

Philadelphia
6,010,000

New York
21,767,000

Paris
10,600,000

Washington-Baltimore
7,910,000

Los Angeles
16,200,000

Dallas-Ft.Worth
5,785,000

Mexico City
19,620,000

Bogotá
6,990,000

Lagos
10,030,000

Lima
7,420,000

Rio de Janeiro
10,810,000

Kinshasa
5,750,000

São Paulo
17,720,000

Santiago de Chile
6,061,000

Buenos Aires
13,390,000

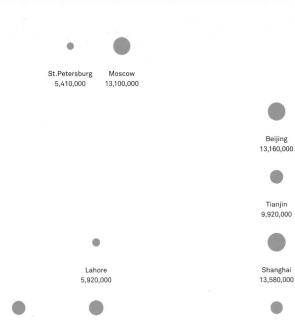
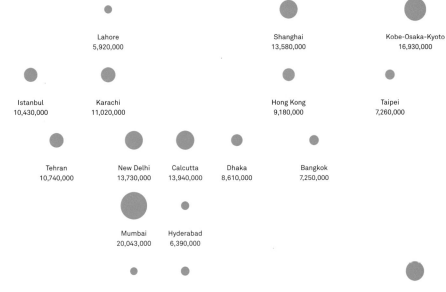

St.Petersburg
5,410,000

Moscow
13,100,000

Randstad Holland
6,600,000

Beijing
13,160,000

Seoul-Incheon
22,877,000

Tokyo-Yokohama
33,190,000

Rhine-Ruhr
11,100,000

Tianjin
9,920,000

Nagoya
8,837,000

Lahore
5,920,000

Shanghai
13,580,000

Kobe-Osaka-Kyoto
16,930,000

Istanbul
10,430,000

Karachi
11,020,000

Hong Kong
9,180,000

Taipei
7,260,000

Tehran
10,740,000

New Delhi
13,730,000

Calcutta
13,940,000

Dhaka
8,610,000

Bangkok
7,250,000

Cairo
14,000,000

Mumbai
20,043,000

Hyderabad
6,390,000

Manila
14,140,000

Bangalore
5,687,000

Chennai
6,700,000

Djakarta
13,330,000

Johannesburg
5,530,000

Container ship seaports [🚢 CNT]

The world's 25 largest seaports in terms of container capacity in the year 2000
marad.gov

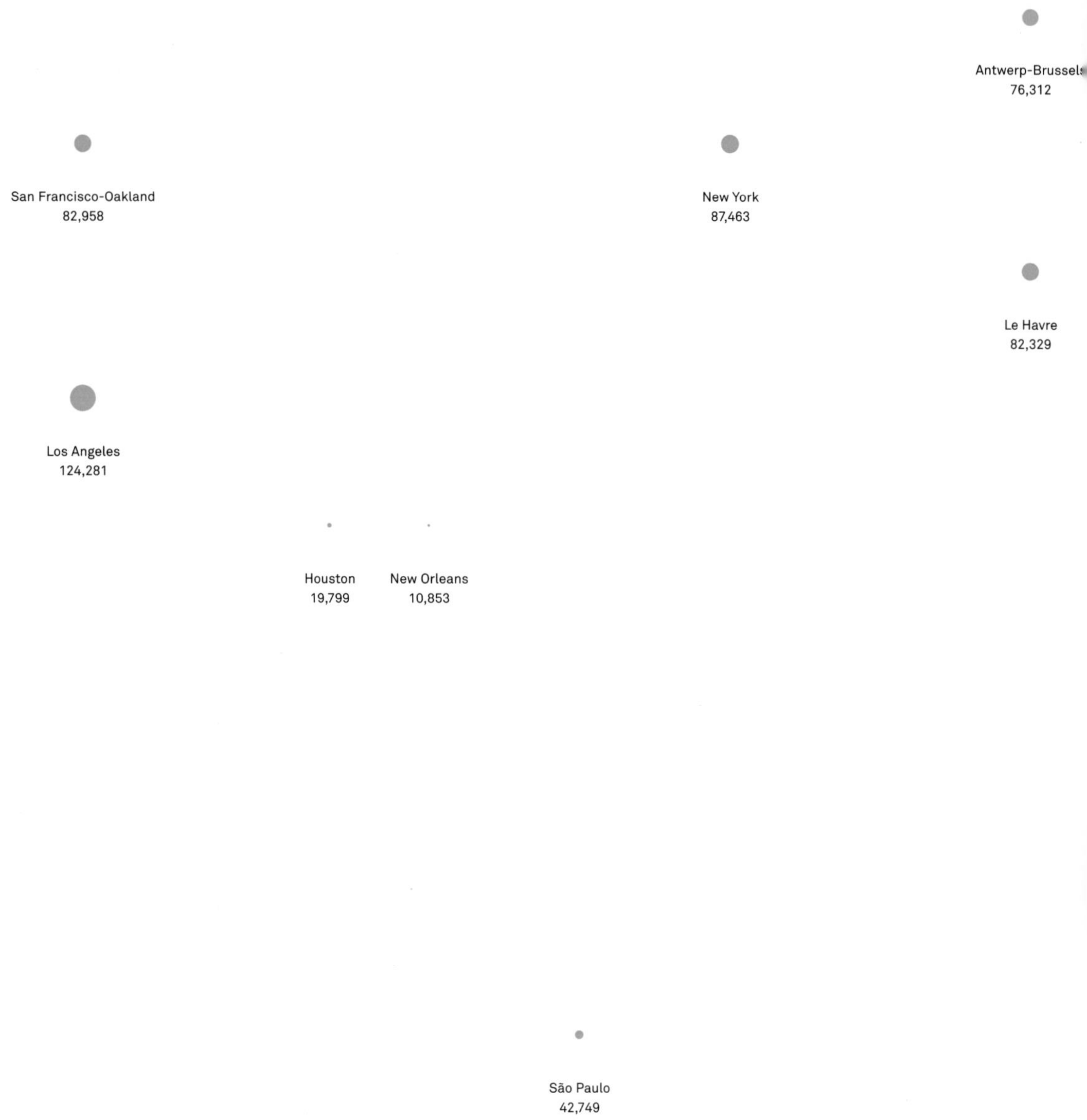

Antwerp-Brussels
76,312

San Francisco-Oakland
82,958

New York
87,463

Le Havre
82,329

Los Angeles
124,281

Houston
19,799

New Orleans
10,853

São Paulo
42,749

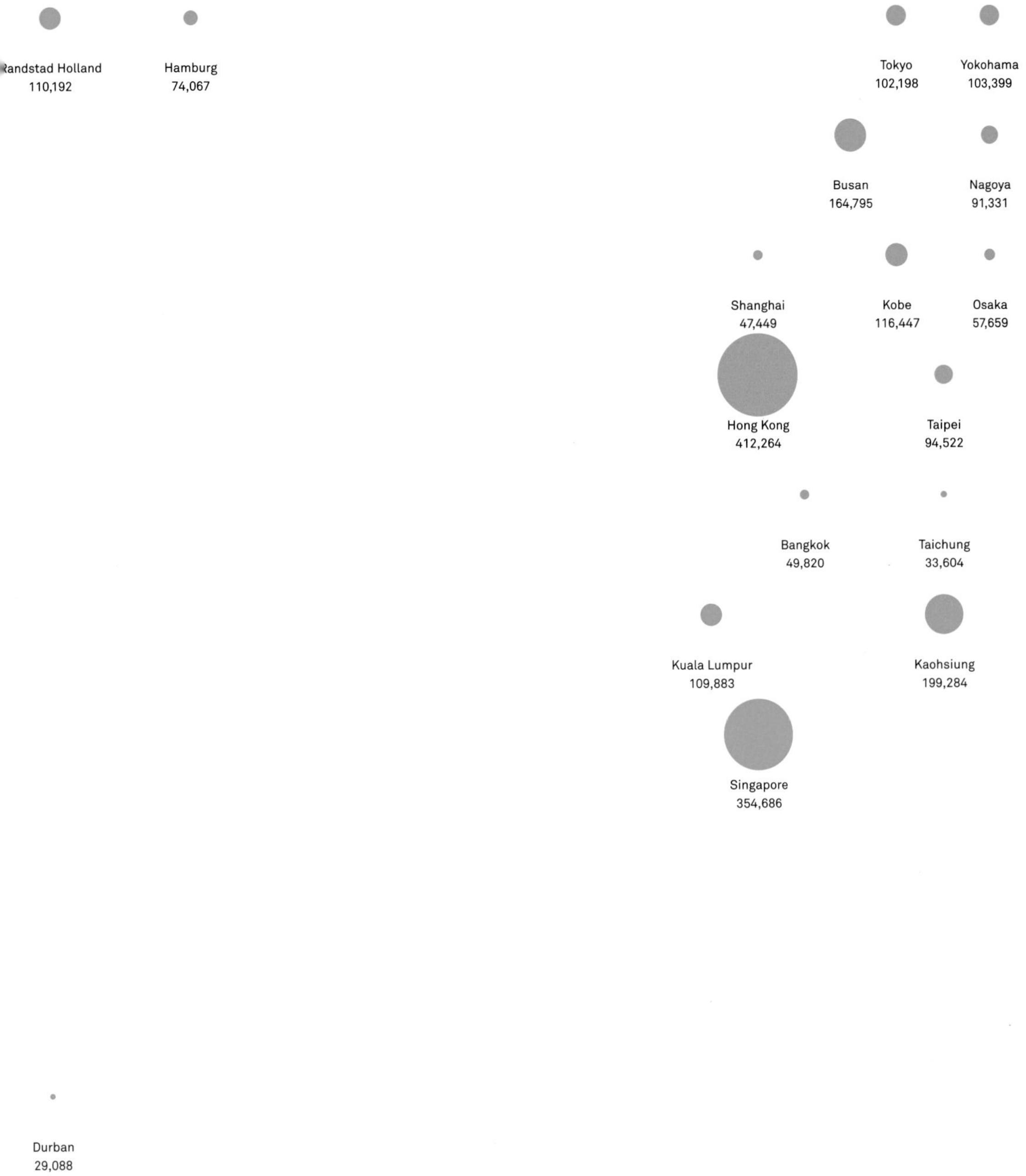

Randstad Holland
110,192

Hamburg
74,067

Tokyo
102,198

Yokohama
103,399

Busan
164,795

Nagoya
91,331

Shanghai
47,449

Kobe
116,447

Osaka
57,659

Hong Kong
412,264

Taipei
94,522

Bangkok
49,820

Taichung
33,604

Kuala Lumpur
109,883

Kaohsiung
199,284

Singapore
354,686

Durban
29,088

Oil tanker seaports [🛢OIL]

The world's 25 largest seaports in terms of oil tanker capacity in the year 2000

marad.gov

Antwerp-Brussel
34,071

San Francisco-Oakland
50,653

New York
65,965

Le Havre
53,308

Los Angeles
66,045

Houston
134,809

New Orleans
81,956

São Paulo
17,342

Randstad Holland
121,957

Hamburg
14,349

Tokyo
260

Yokohama
36,129

Busan
4,555

Nagoya
28,669

Shanghai
6,208

Kobe
9,012

Osaka
5,244

Hong Kong
26,774

Taipei
10,350

Bangkok
15,027

Taichung
25,561

Kuala Lumpur
10,480

Kaohsiung
48,032

Singapore
436,844

Durban
23,604

Dry-bulk seaports [🚢DRY]

The world's 25 largest seaports in terms of dry-bulk capacity in the year 2000

marad.gov

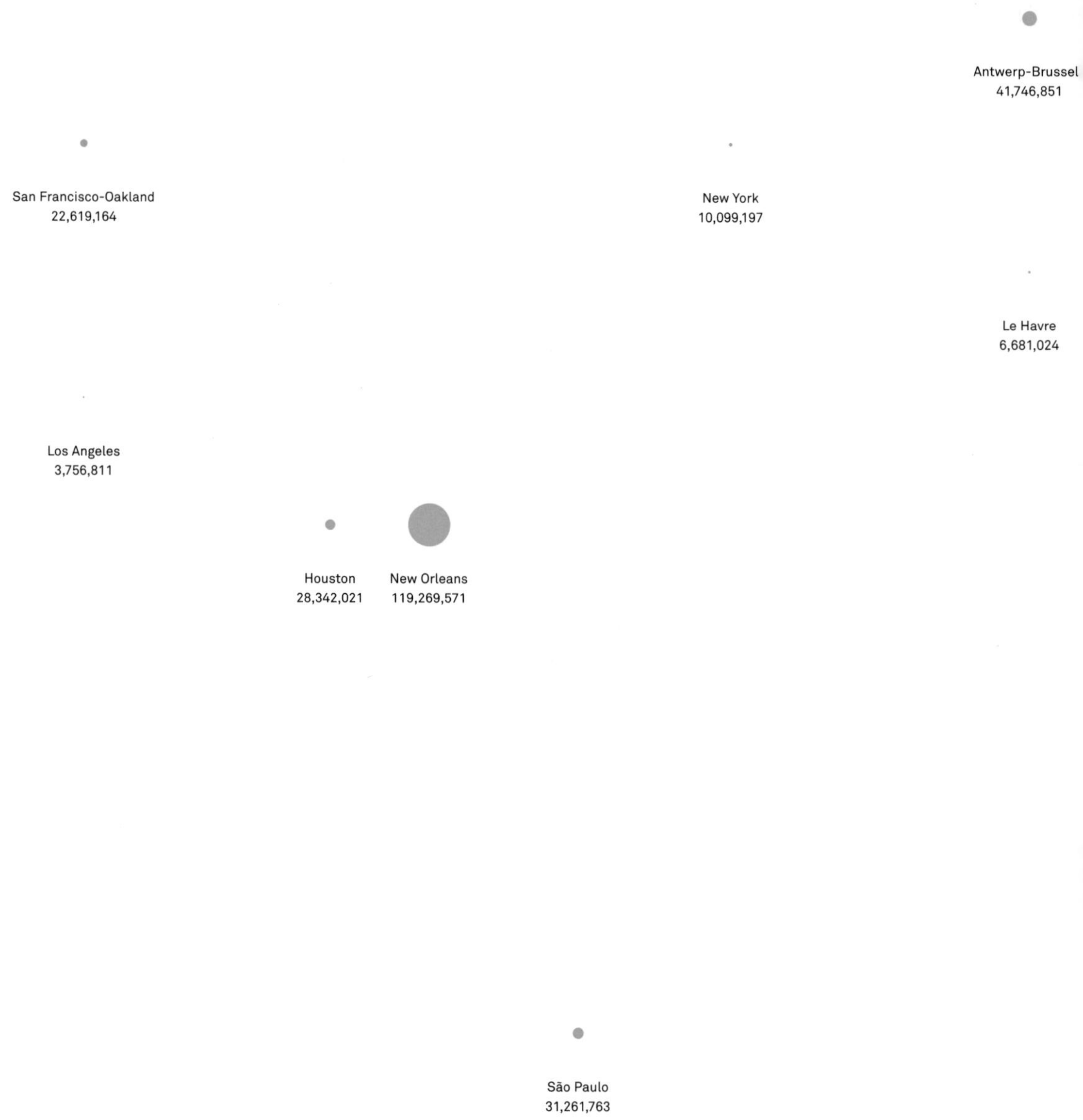

Antwerp-Brussel
41,746,851

San Francisco-Oakland
22,619,164

New York
10,099,197

Le Havre
6,681,024

Los Angeles
3,756,811

Houston
28,342,021

New Orleans
119,269,571

São Paulo
31,261,763

andstad Holland
73,729,965

Hamburg
32,753,024

Tokyo
769,992

Yokohama
17,725,119

Busan
51,190,873

Nagoya
51,990,836

Shanghai
4,415,656

Kobe
14,049,098

Osaka
17,638,437

Hong Kong
34,261,861

Taipei
13,544,786

Bangkok
20,056,938

Taichung
54,157,795

Kuala Lumpur
18,796,533

Kaohsiung
69,756,449

Singapore
242,708,835

Durban
27,353,729

Passenger airports [✈ PAX]

The world's 30 largest airports in terms of passengers transported in the year 2000 (arrivals, departures, transit

airports.org

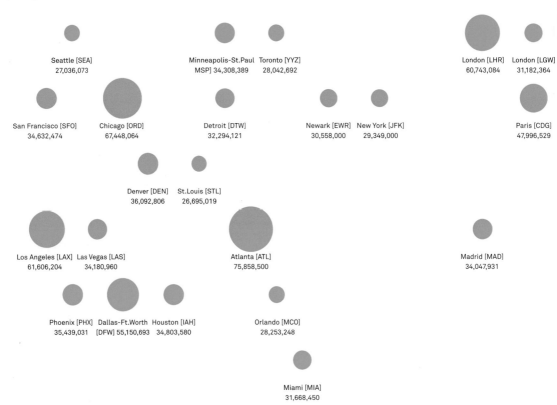

Seattle [SEA]
27,036,073

Minneapolis-St.Paul
MSP] 34,308,389

Toronto [YYZ]
28,042,692

London [LHR]
60,743,084

London [LGW]
31,182,364

San Francisco [SFO]
34,632,474

Chicago [ORD]
67,448,064

Detroit [DTW]
32,294,121

Newark [EWR]
30,558,000

New York [JFK]
29,349,000

Paris [CDG]
47,996,529

Denver [DEN]
36,092,806

St.Louis [STL]
26,695,019

Los Angeles [LAX]
61,606,204

Las Vegas [LAS]
34,180,960

Atlanta [ATL]
75,858,500

Madrid [MAD]
34,047,931

Phoenix [PHX]
35,439,031

Dallas-Ft.Worth
[DFW] 55,150,693

Houston [IAH]
34,803,580

Orlando [MCO]
28,253,248

Miami [MIA]
31,668,450

Amsterdam Holland [AMS]
39,531,123

Frankfurt [FRA]
48,559,980

Tokyo [HND]
58,692,688

Tokyo [NRT]
25,379,370

Rome [FCO]
25,565,727

Hong Kong [HKG]
32,546,029

Bangkok [BKK]
30,623,366

Singapore [SIN]
28,093,759

Cargo airports [✈ CRG]

The world's 30 largest airports in terms of cargo transported in the year 2000 (tonnes of cargo and mail)
airports.org

Anchorage [ANC]
1,873,750

London [LHR]
1,263,572

Antwerp-Brusse
583,685

San Francisco [SFO]
636,006

Chicago [ORD]
1,299,628

Indianapolis [IND]
1,115,272

Philadelphia [PHL]
536,270

New York [JFK]
1,430,727

Paris [CDG]
1,591,310

Oakland [OAK]
593,634

Louisville [SDF]
1,468,837

New York [EWR]
795,584

Los Angeles [LAX]
1,774,402

Memphis [MEM]
2,631,131

Atlanta [ATL]
739,927

Dallas-Ft.Worth Airport [DFW]
784,085

Miami [MIA]
1,639,760

242

dstad Holland [AMS]
1,234,161

Frankfurt [FRA]
1,613,179

Beijing [PEK]
591,195

Seoul [SEL]
598,620

Tokyo [NRT]
1,680,937

Incheon [ICN]
1,196,843

Tokyo [HND]
725,124

Kobe-Osaka [KIX]
871,161

Hong Kong [HKG]
2,100,276

Taipei [TPE]
1,189,874

Bangkok [BKK]
841,150

Dubai [DXB]
632,224

Singapore [SIN]
1,529,930

Flight movements []

The world's 30 largest airports in terms of flight movements in the year 2000 (number of takeoffs and landings)
airports.org

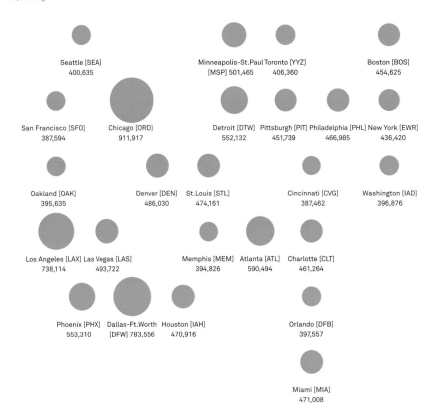

Seattle [SEA]
400,635

Minneapolis-St.Paul Toronto [YYZ]
[MSP] 501,465   406,360

Boston [BOS]
454,625

London [LHR]
463,568

San Francisco [SFO]
387,594

Chicago [ORD]
911,917

Detroit [DTW]
552,132

Pittsburgh [PIT]
451,739

Philadelphia [PHL]
466,985

New York [EWR]
436,420

Paris [CDG]
523,400

Oakland [OAK]
395,635

Denver [DEN]
486,030

St.Louis [STL]
474,161

Cincinnati [CVG]
387,462

Washington [IAD]
396,876

Los Angeles [LAX]
738,114

Las Vegas [LAS]
493,722

Memphis [MEM]
394,826

Atlanta [ATL]
590,494

Charlotte [CLT]
461,264

Phoenix [PHX]
553,310

Dallas-Ft.Worth
[DFW] 783,556

Houston [IAH]
470,916

Orlando [DFB]
397,557

Miami [MIA]
471,008

ndstad Holland [AMS]
432,101

Frankfurt [FRA]
456,452

Telecom ports [@TEL]

The world's 30 largest telecom ports in terms of megabits per second in the year 2000

telegeography.com

Seattle
58,917

London
855,187

San Francisco-Oakland
208,136

New York
1,498,345

Paris
225,518

Monterey
10,770

Sacramento
14,090

Washington-Baltimore
132,612

Los Angeles
112,270

Madrid
24,880

Dallas-Ft.Worth
15,460

Mexico City
21,660

Miami
119,124

Rio de Janeiro
9,810

São Paulo
43,165

Buenos Aires
22,857

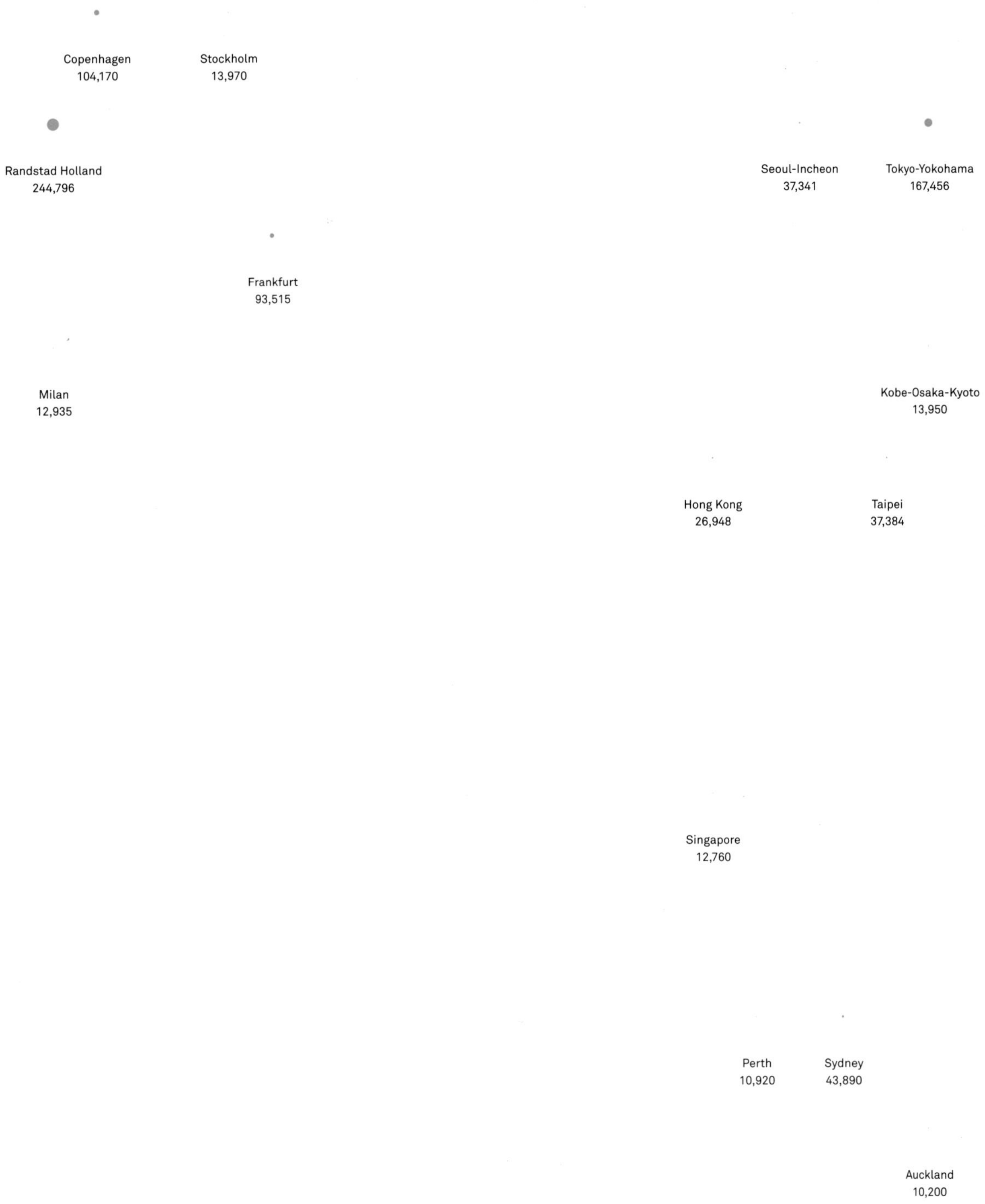

Copenhagen
104,170

Stockholm
13,970

Randstad Holland
244,796

Seoul-Incheon
37,341

Tokyo-Yokohama
167,456

Frankfurt
93,515

Milan
12,935

Kobe-Osaka-Kyoto
13,950

Hong Kong
26,948

Taipei
37,384

Singapore
12,760

Perth
10,920

Sydney
43,890

Auckland
10,200

Population

Number of inhabitants in the metropolitan area (c. 2000)
demographia.com, citypopulation.de, Eurostat, Regio Randstad, StatsCanada, US Census

Oslo
780,000

Anchorage
339,286

Seattle
2,712,000

Vancouver
2,118,000

Minneapolis-St.Paul
2,389,000

Toronto
5,470,000

Montreal
3,216,000

Boston
5,815,000

London
13,945,000

Antwerp-Brussels
3,725,000

San Francisco-Oakland
7,154,000

Chicago
9,549,000

Indianapolis
1,219,000

Detroit
5,415,000

Pittsburgh
1,753,000

Philadelphia
6,010,000

New York
21,767,000

Paris
10,600,000

Monterey
32,797

Sacramento
1,393,000

Denver
1,984,000

St.Louis
2,078,000

Louisville
864,000

Cincinnati
1,503,000

Washington-Baltimore
7,910,000

Le Havre
815,089

Los Angeles
17,263,000

Las Vegas
1,314,000

Memphis
972,000

Atlanta
3,500,000

Charlotte
759,000

Madrid
5,300,000

Barcelona
3,766,000

Phoenix
2,907,000

Dallas-Ft.Worth
5,785,000

Houston
5,176,000

New Orleans
1,009,000

Orlando
1,157,000

Lisbon
3,000,000

Mexico City
19,620,000

Miami
5,289,000

Tangier
497,147

Bogotá
6,990,000

Lagos
10,030,000

Lima
7,420,000

Rio de Janeiro
10,810,000

Kinshasa
5,750,000

São Paulo
17,720,000

Santiago de Chile
6,061,000

Buenos Aires
13,390,000

248

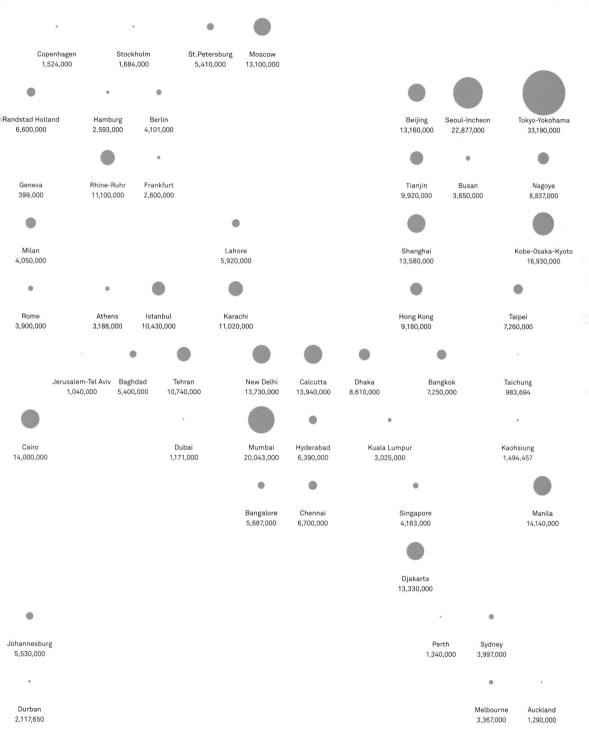

Copenhagen
1,524,000

Stockholm
1,684,000

St.Petersburg
5,410,000

Moscow
13,100,000

Beijing
13,160,000

Seoul-Incheon
22,877,000

Tokyo-Yokohama
33,190,000

Randstad Holland
6,600,000

Hamburg
2,593,000

Berlin
4,101,000

Geneva
399,000

Rhine-Ruhr
11,100,000

Frankfurt
2,600,000

Tianjin
9,920,000

Busan
3,650,000

Nagoya
8,837,000

Milan
4,050,000

Lahore
5,920,000

Shanghai
13,580,000

Kobe-Osaka-Kyoto
16,930,000

Rome
3,900,000

Athens
3,188,000

Istanbul
10,430,000

Karachi
11,020,000

Hong Kong
9,180,000

Taipei
7,260,000

Jerusalem-Tel Aviv
1,040,000

Baghdad
5,400,000

Tehran
10,740,000

New Delhi
13,730,000

Calcutta
13,940,000

Dhaka
8,610,000

Bangkok
7,250,000

Taichung
983,694

Cairo
14,000,000

Dubai
1,171,000

Mumbai
20,043,000

Hyderabad
6,390,000

Kuala Lumpur
3,025,000

Kaohsiung
1,494,457

Bangalore
5,687,000

Chennai
6,700,000

Singapore
4,163,000

Manila
14,140,000

Djakarta
13,330,000

Johannesburg
5,530,000

Perth
1,340,000

Sydney
3,997,000

Durban
2,117,650

Melbourne
3,367,000

Auckland
1,290,000

249

Core share (1965)

Percentage of the total number of inhabitants in the metropolitan area living in the core in the year 1965

demographia.com

Seattle
77.5%

Minneapolis-St.Paul
84.4%

Boston
18.9%

London
24.6%

Antwerp-Brussels
13.8%

San Francisco-Oakland
30.2%

Chicago
50.4%

Indianapolis
85.1%

Detroit
36.6%

Pittsburgh
44.2%

Philadelphia
48.3%

New York
49.5%

Paris
35.0%

Sacramento
65.1%

Denver
83.4%

St.Louis
61.2%

Cincinnati
62.0%

Washington-Baltimore
43.3%

Los Angeles
35.6%

Las Vegas
74.5%

Atlanta
65.3%

Madrid
95.1%

Barcelona
75.9%

Phoenix
49.1%

Dallas-Ft.Worth
63.2%

Houston
73.8%

New Orleans
86.4%

Orlando
71.2%

Mexico City
50.0%

Miami
21.7%

Bogotá
85.2%

Lagos
44.3%

Lima
14.8%

Rio de Janeiro
68.6%

São Paulo
81.2%

Santiago de Chile
9.7%

Buenos Aires
38.3%

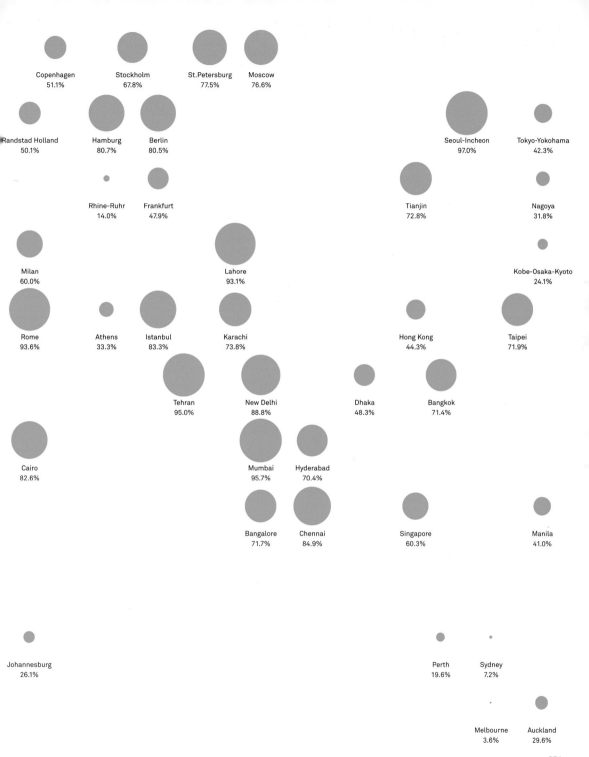

Copenhagen
51.1%

Stockholm
67.8%

St.Petersburg
77.5%

Moscow
76.6%

Randstad Holland
50.1%

Hamburg
80.7%

Berlin
80.5%

Seoul-Incheon
97.0%

Tokyo-Yokohama
42.3%

Rhine-Ruhr
14.0%

Frankfurt
47.9%

Tianjin
72.8%

Nagoya
31.8%

Milan
60.0%

Lahore
93.1%

Kobe-Osaka-Kyoto
24.1%

Rome
93.6%

Athens
33.3%

Istanbul
83.3%

Karachi
73.8%

Hong Kong
44.3%

Taipei
71.9%

Tehran
95.0%

New Delhi
88.8%

Dhaka
48.3%

Bangkok
71.4%

Cairo
82.6%

Mumbai
95.7%

Hyderabad
70.4%

Bangalore
71.7%

Chennai
84.9%

Singapore
60.3%

Manila
41.0%

Johannesburg
26.1%

Perth
19.6%

Sydney
7.2%

Melbourne
3.6%

Auckland
29.6%

Core share (c. 2000)

Percentage of the total number of inhabitants in the metropolitan area living in the core (c. 2000)

demographia.com

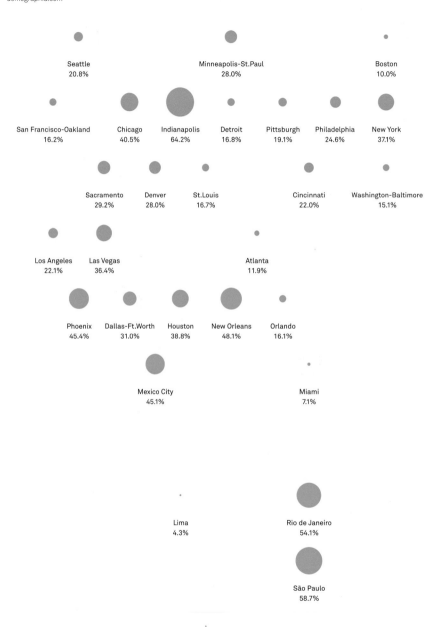

Seattle
20.8%

Minneapolis-St.Paul
28.0%

Boston
10.0%

London
19.8%

Antwerp-Brussels
7.9%

San Francisco-Oakland
16.2%

Chicago
40.5%

Indianapolis
64.2%

Detroit
16.8%

Pittsburgh
19.1%

Philadelphia
24.6%

New York
37.1%

Paris
22.0%

Sacramento
29.2%

Denver
28.0%

St.Louis
16.7%

Cincinnati
22.0%

Washington-Baltimore
15.1%

Los Angeles
22.1%

Las Vegas
36.4%

Atlanta
11.9%

Madrid
57.8%

Barcelona
39.9%

Phoenix
45.4%

Dallas-Ft.Worth
31.0%

Houston
38.8%

New Orleans
48.1%

Orlando
16.1%

Mexico City
45.1%

Miami
7.1%

Lima
4.3%

Rio de Janeiro
54.1%

São Paulo
58.7%

Santiago de Chile
3.3%

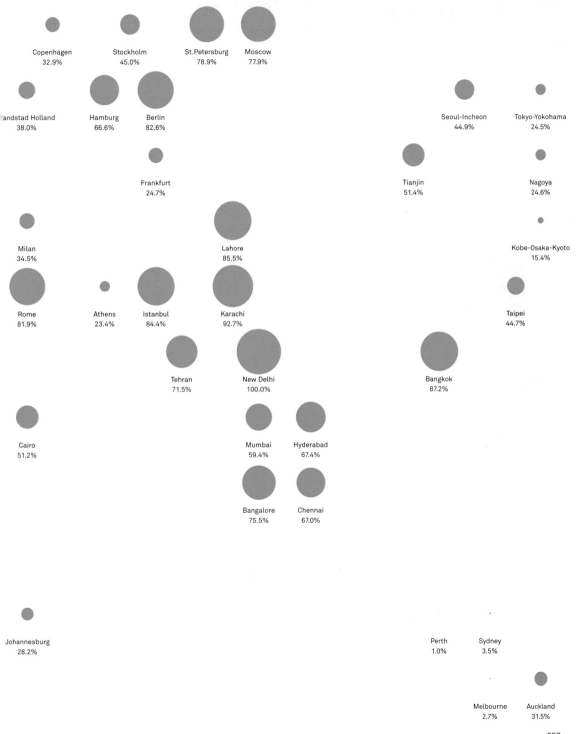

Copenhagen
32.9%

Stockholm
45.0%

St.Petersburg
78.9%

Moscow
77.9%

Randstad Holland
38.0%

Hamburg
66.6%

Berlin
82.6%

Seoul-Incheon
44.9%

Tokyo-Yokohama
24.5%

Frankfurt
24.7%

Tianjin
51.4%

Nagoya
24.6%

Milan
34.5%

Lahore
85.5%

Kobe-Osaka-Kyoto
15.4%

Rome
81.9%

Athens
23.4%

Istanbul
84.4%

Karachi
92.7%

Taipei
44.7%

Tehran
71.5%

New Delhi
100.0%

Bangkok
87.2%

Cairo
51.2%

Mumbai
59.4%

Hyderabad
67.4%

Bangalore
75.5%

Chennai
67.0%

Johannesburg
28.2%

Perth
1.0%

Sydney
3.5%

Melbourne
2.7%

Auckland
31.5%

253

Built-up area

Total built-up surface area of the metropolitan area in km² (c. 2000)

demographia.com

Oslo
298

Seattle
2,471

Vancouver
1,391

Minneapolis-St.Paul
2,315

Toronto
1,652

Montreal
1,738

Boston
5,144

London
1,186

Antwerp-Brussels
1,308

San Francisco-Oakland
2,038

Chicago
5,499

Indianapolis
1,432

Detroit

Pittsburgh
2,207

Philadelphia
4,659

New York
11,518

Paris
2,721

Sacramento
956

Denver
1,292

St.Louis
2,147

Louisville
1,013

Cincinnati
1,740

Washington-Baltimore
4,763

Los Angeles
5,457

Las Vegas
741

Memphis
1,063

Atlanta
5,084

Charlotte
1,126

Madrid
932

Barcelona
699

Phoenix
2,069

Dallas-Ft.Worth
3,644

Houston
3,354

New Orleans
513

Orlando
1,173

Lisbon
557

Mexico City
1,476

Miami
2,890

Bogotá
479

Rio de Janeiro
1,166

São Paulo
1,981

Santiago de Chile
974

Buenos Aires
2,771

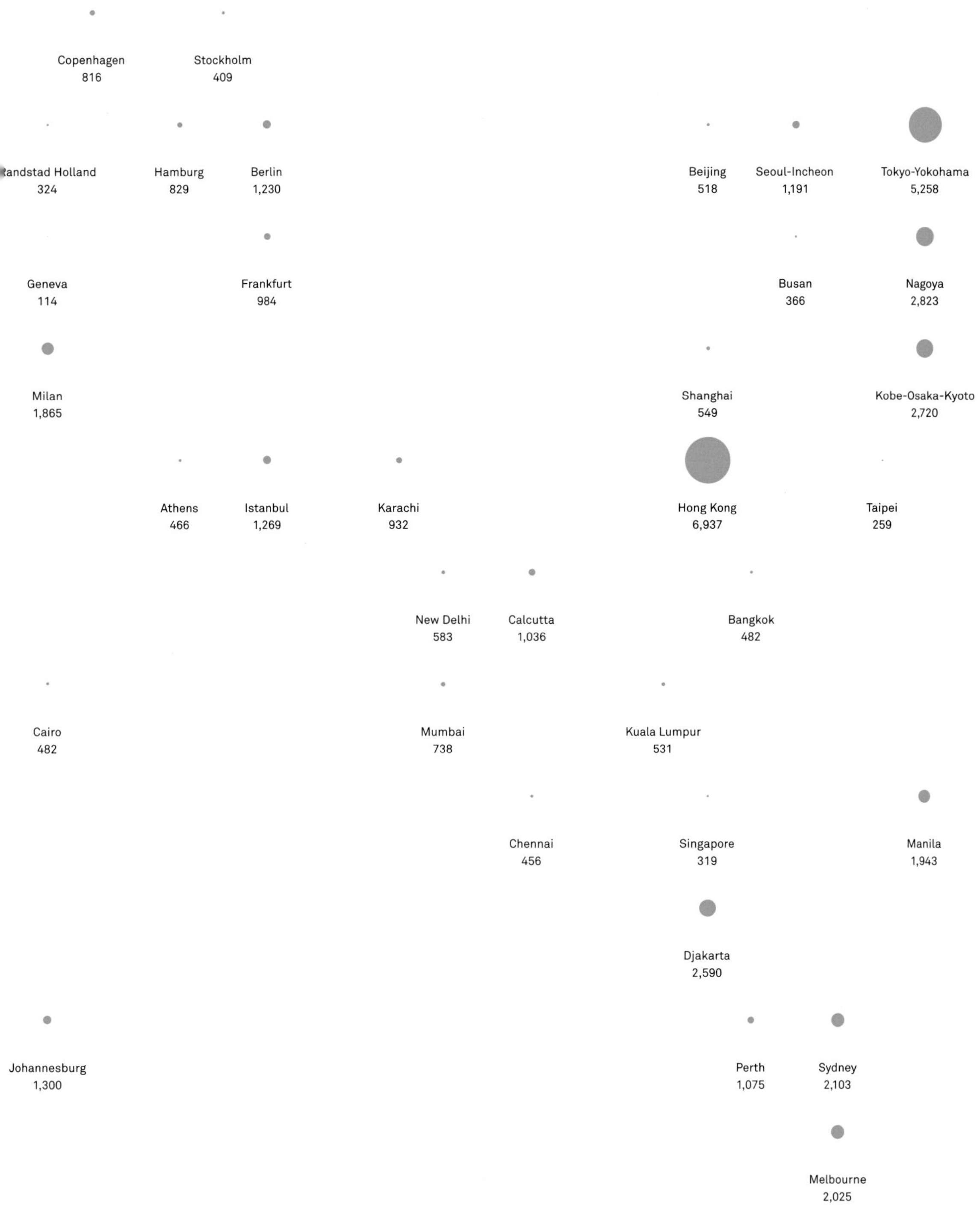

Copenhagen
816

Stockholm
409

Randstad Holland
324

Hamburg
829

Berlin
1,230

Beijing
518

Seoul-Incheon
1,191

Tokyo-Yokohama
5,258

Geneva
114

Frankfurt
984

Busan
366

Nagoya
2,823

Milan
1,865

Shanghai
549

Kobe-Osaka-Kyoto
2,720

Athens
466

Istanbul
1,269

Karachi
932

Hong Kong
6,937

Taipei
259

New Delhi
583

Calcutta
1,036

Bangkok
482

Cairo
482

Mumbai
738

Kuala Lumpur
531

Chennai
456

Singapore
319

Manila
1,943

Djakarta
2,590

Johannesburg
1,300

Perth
1,075

Sydney
2,103

Melbourne
2,025

Employment density

Average density of employment (employments/km²) in the metropolitan area in the year 1990, 1998 or 2001

demographia.com

Seattle 570	Vancouver 570	Minneapolis-St.Paul 565	Toronto 1,386	Montreal 786	Boston 424		London 5,059	Antwerp-Brussel 461

San Francisco-Oakland 1,547 • Chicago 704 • Indianapolis 455 • Detroit 634 • Pittsburgh 437 • Philadelphia 522 • New York 812 • Paris 1,878

Denver 761 • St.Louis 539 • Cincinnati 476 • Washington-Baltimore 732

Los Angeles 1,249 • Atlanta 289 • Charlotte 564

Phoenix 482 • Dallas-Ft.Worth 552 • Houston 530 • New Orleans 1,004 • Orlando 504

Miami 510

Copenhagen
1,172

Stockholm
1,220

Randstad Holland
988

Hamburg
1,183

Seoul-Incheon
5,980

Tokyo-Yokohama
4,393

Nagoya
1,417

Kobe-Osaka-Kyoto
2,757

Hong Kong
371

Bangkok
5,513

Singapore
4,818

Manila
1,399

Perth
437

Sydney
725

Melbourne
586

CBD area share

Percentage of total built-up surface area of the metropolitan area taken up by the central business district in the year 1990, 1998 or 2001 demographia.com

Seattle
0.4%

Vancouver
0.2%

Toronto
0.1%

Montreal
0.7%

Boston
0.2%

London
2.5%

Antwerp-Brussels
0.2%

San Francisco-Oakland
0.2%

Chicago
0.3%

Detroit
0.1%

New York
0.2%

Paris
1.1%

Denver
1.7%

Los Angeles
0.3%

Phoenix
0.2%

Houston
0.1%

Copenhagen
0.6%

Stockholm
1.0%

Randstad Holland
2.6%

Hamburg
0.6%

Frankfurt
0.2%

Seoul-Incheon
1.8%

Tokyo-Yokohama
4.2%

Nagoya
3.0%

Kobe-Osaka-Kyoto
4.4%

Hong Kong
0.2%

Bangkok
4.2%

Singapore
2.3%

Manila
1.9%

Perth
0.7%

Sydney
0.2%

Melbourne
0.1%

CBD employment share

Percentage of metropolitan employment in the central business district of the metropolitan area in the year 1990, 1998 or 2001 demographia.com

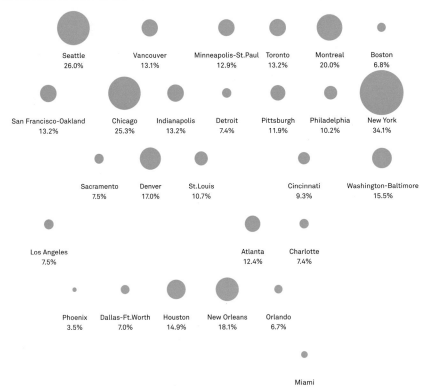

Seattle 26.0%	Vancouver 13.1%	Minneapolis-St.Paul 12.9%	Toronto 13.2%	Montreal 20.0%	Boston 6.8%		London 21.0%	Antwerp-Brussels 24.1%

San Francisco-Oakland 13.2% Chicago 25.3% Indianapolis 13.2% Detroit 7.4% Pittsburgh 11.9% Philadelphia 10.2% New York 34.1% Paris 22.8%

Sacramento 7.5% Denver 17.0% St.Louis 10.7% Cincinnati 9.3% Washington-Baltimore 15.5%

Los Angeles 7.5% Atlanta 12.4% Charlotte 7.4%

Phoenix 3.5% Dallas-Ft.Worth 7.0% Houston 14.9% New Orleans 18.1% Orlando 6.7%

Miami 5.1%

Copenhagen
12.8%

Stockholm
22.3%

Randstad Holland
25.0%

Hamburg
15.7%

Seoul-Incheon
17.2%

Tokyo-Yokohama
34.5%

Nagoya
31.3%

Kobe-Osaka-Kyoto
23.0%

Hong Kong
7.5%

Bangkok
10.2%

Singapore
18.2%

Manila
30.0%

Perth
21.3%

Sydney
11.5%

Melbourne
10.6%

CBD employment density

Average density of employment (employments/km²) in the central business district of the metropolitan area in the year 1990, 1998 or 2001 demographia.com

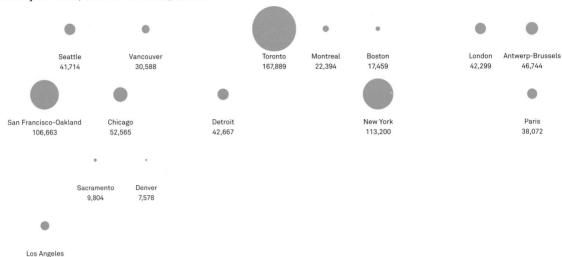

Seattle
41,714

Vancouver
30,588

Toronto
167,889

Montreal
22,394

Boston
17,459

London
42,299

Antwerp-Brussels
46,744

San Francisco-Oakland
106,663

Chicago
52,565

Detroit
42,667

New York
113,200

Paris
38,072

Sacramento
9,804

Denver
7,578

Los Angeles
33,480

Phoenix
9,043

Houston
67,933

Copenhagen
26,121

Stockholm
27,130

Randstad Holland
9,726

Hamburg
32,679

Seoul-Incheon
57,869

Tokyo-Yokohama
35,859

Nagoya
14,535

Kobe-Osaka-Kyoto
14,428

Hong Kong
12,648

Bangkok
13,266

Singapore
38,889

Manila
22,650

Perth
12,109

Sydney
42,834

Melbourne
54,907

Income per capita

Average per capita income of the metropolitan population in the year 2000 or 2002
asiaweek.com, bestplaces.net

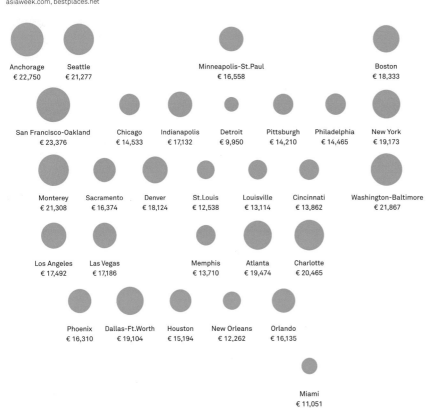

Anchorage
€ 22,750

Seattle
€ 21,277

Minneapolis-St.Paul
€ 16,558

Boston
€ 18,333

San Francisco-Oakland
€ 23,376

Chicago
€ 14,533

Indianapolis
€ 17,132

Detroit
€ 9,950

Pittsburgh
€ 14,210

Philadelphia
€ 14,465

New York
€ 19,173

Monterey
€ 21,308

Sacramento
€ 16,374

Denver
€ 18,124

St.Louis
€ 12,538

Louisville
€ 13,114

Cincinnati
€ 13,862

Washington-Baltimore
€ 21,867

Los Angeles
€ 17,492

Las Vegas
€ 17,186

Memphis
€ 13,710

Atlanta
€ 19,474

Charlotte
€ 20,465

Phoenix
€ 16,310

Dallas-Ft.Worth
€ 19,104

Houston
€ 15,194

New Orleans
€ 12,262

Orlando
€ 16,135

Miami
€ 11,051

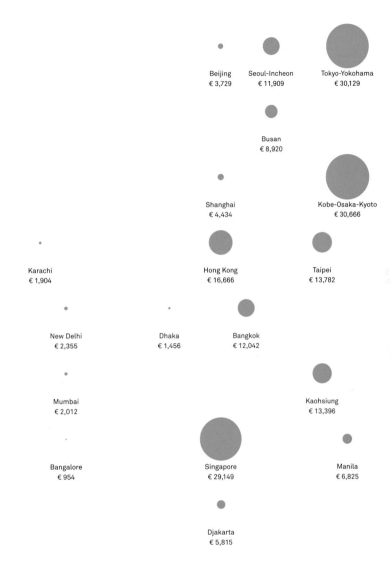

Beijing
€ 3,729

Seoul-Incheon
€ 11,909

Tokyo-Yokohama
€ 30,129

Busan
€ 8,920

Shanghai
€ 4,434

Kobe-Osaka-Kyoto
€ 30,666

Karachi
€ 1,904

Hong Kong
€ 16,666

Taipei
€ 13,782

New Delhi
€ 2,355

Dhaka
€ 1,456

Bangkok
€ 12,042

Mumbai
€ 2,012

Kaohsiung
€ 13,396

Bangalore
€ 954

Singapore
€ 29,149

Manila
€ 6,825

Djakarta
€ 5,815

Gross regional product per capita

Average gross regional product per capita of the metropolitan population in the year 1991

demographia.com

Seattle
€ 31,142

Minneapolis-St.Paul
€ 33,312

Boston
€ 32,241

London
€ 37,180

Antwerp-Brussels
€ 27,803

San Francisco-Oakland
€ 37,132

Chicago
€ 31,507

Detroit
€ 26,947

New York
€ 35,044

Paris
€ 25,874

Sacramento
€ 27,011

Denver
€ 32,622

Washington-Baltimore
€ 33,053

Los Angeles
€ 26,789

Las Vegas
€ 30,047

Atlanta
€ 32,849

Madrid
€ 22,660

Barcelona
€ 20,830

Dallas-Ft.Worth
€ 32,245

Houston
€ 31,839

Lisbon
€ 17,467

Miami
€ 22,182

Copenhagen
€ 41,944

Stockholm
€ 43,667

Randstad Holland
€ 31,212

Hamburg
€ 33,452

Berlin
€ 20,960

Tokyo-Yokohama
€ 35,052

Rhine-Ruhr
€ 27,419

Frankfurt
€ 35,268

Milan
€ 29,179

Kobe-Osaka-Kyoto
€ 20,039

Rome
€ 26,000

Unemployment rate

Percentage of working-age population that is unemployed in the year 1996, 2000 or 2002

asiaweek.com, bestplaces.net, Eurostat

Anchorage
4.2%

Seattle
3.4%

Minneapolis-St.Paul
2.2%

Boston
2.2%

London
6.7%

Antwerp-Brussels
7.4%

San Francisco-Oakland
2.1%

Chicago
4.1%

Indianapolis
2.4%

Detroit
3.1%

Pittsburgh
4.0%

Philadelphia
3.9%

New York
5.3%

Paris
8.1%

Monterey
9.2%

Sacramento
5.0%

Denver
2.2%

St.Louis
3.3%

Louisville
3.2%

Cincinnati
3.4%

Washington-Baltimore
2.3%

Le Havre
6.7%

Los Angeles
5.5%

Las Vegas
4.0%

Memphis
3.6%

Atlanta
2.8%

Charlotte
3.2%

Madrid
7.2%

Barcelona
5.2%

Phoenix
2.6%

Dallas-Ft.Worth
3.1%

Houston
4.2%

New Orleans
4.5%

Orlando
2.6%

Lisbon
3.5%

Miami
5.5%

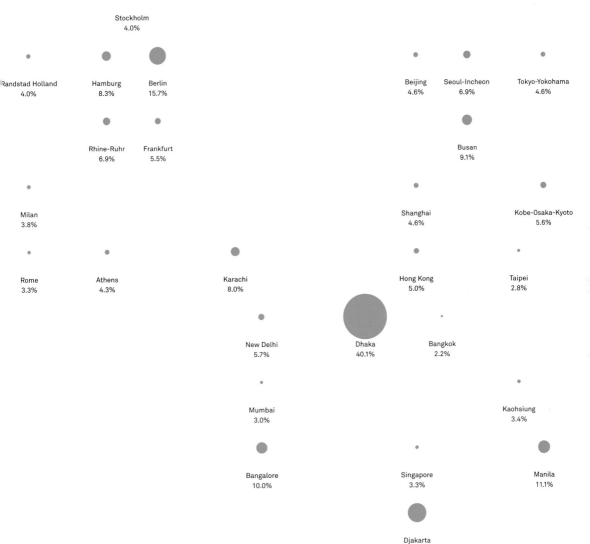

Stockholm
4.0%

Randstad Holland
4.0%

Hamburg
8.3%

Berlin
15.7%

Beijing
4.6%

Seoul-Incheon
6.9%

Tokyo-Yokohama
4.6%

Rhine-Ruhr
6.9%

Frankfurt
5.5%

Busan
9.1%

Milan
3.8%

Shanghai
4.6%

Kobe-Osaka-Kyoto
5.6%

Rome
3.3%

Athens
4.3%

Karachi
8.0%

Hong Kong
5.0%

Taipei
2.8%

New Delhi
5.7%

Dhaka
40.1%

Bangkok
2.2%

Mumbai
3.0%

Kaohsiung
3.4%

Bangalore
10.0%

Singapore
3.3%

Manila
11.1%

Djakarta
16.8%

Hospital beds

Hospital capacity in terms of average number of hospital beds in the metropolitan area available per 1,000 inhabitants in the year 1996 or 2000 asiaweek.com, Eurostat

Antwerp-Brussels
6

Paris
5

Le Havre
4

Lisbon
6

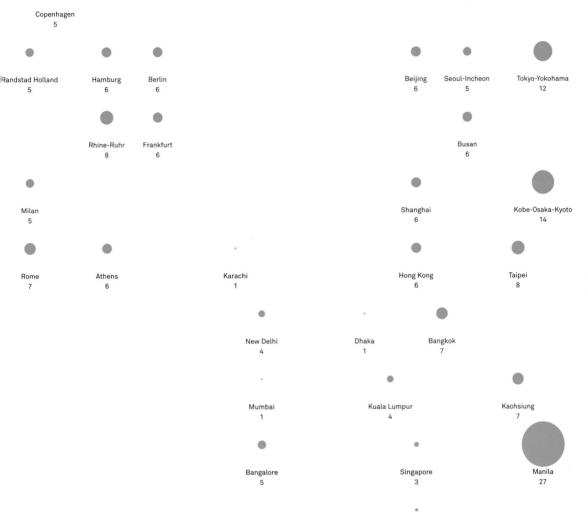

Copenhagen
5

Randstad Holland
5

Hamburg
6

Berlin
6

Rhine-Ruhr
8

Frankfurt
6

Milan
5

Rome
7

Athens
6

Karachi
1

New Delhi
4

Mumbai
1

Bangalore
5

Beijing
6

Seoul-Incheon
5

Tokyo-Yokohama
12

Busan
6

Shanghai
6

Kobe-Osaka-Kyoto
14

Hong Kong
6

Taipei
8

Dhaka
1

Bangkok
7

Kuala Lumpur
4

Kaohsiung
7

Singapore
3

Manila
27

Djakarta
2

Life expectancy

Average life expectancy for newborn babies in the metropolitan area in the year 1996 or 2000
asiaweek.com, Eurostat

Antwerp-Brussels
80

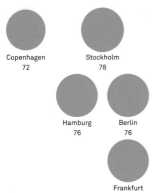

Copenhagen
72

Stockholm
78

Hamburg
76

Berlin
76

Frankfurt
75

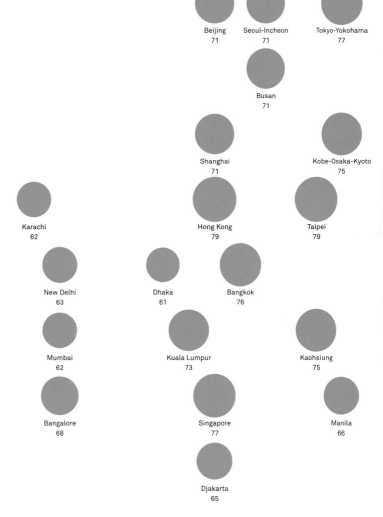

Beijing
71

Seoul-Incheon
71

Tokyo-Yokohama
77

Busan
71

Shanghai
71

Kobe-Osaka-Kyoto
75

Karachi
62

Hong Kong
79

Taipei
79

New Delhi
63

Dhaka
61

Bangkok
76

Mumbai
62

Kuala Lumpur
73

Kaohsiung
75

Bangalore
68

Singapore
77

Manila
66

Djakarta
65

Crime

Number of violent crimes and property crimes in the metropolitan area per 100,000 inhabitants in the year 1996, 2000 or 2002 asiaweek.com, bestplaces.net, Eurostat

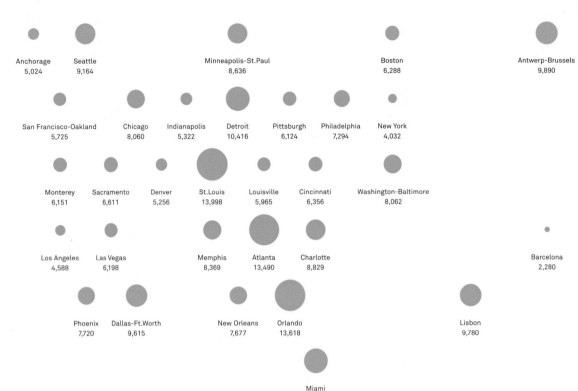

Anchorage 5,024	Seattle 9,164	Minneapolis-St.Paul 8,636	Boston 6,288	Antwerp-Brussels 9,890

San Francisco-Oakland 5,725 · Chicago 8,060 · Indianapolis 5,322 · Detroit 10,416 · Pittsburgh 6,124 · Philadelphia 7,294 · New York 4,032

Monterey 6,151 · Sacramento 6,611 · Denver 5,256 · St.Louis 13,998 · Louisville 5,965 · Cincinnati 6,356 · Washington-Baltimore 8,062

Los Angeles 4,588 · Las Vegas 6,198 · Memphis 8,369 · Atlanta 13,490 · Charlotte 8,829 · Barcelona 2,280

Phoenix 7,720 · Dallas-Ft.Worth 9,615 · New Orleans 7,677 · Orlando 13,618 · Lisbon 9,780

Miami 10,724

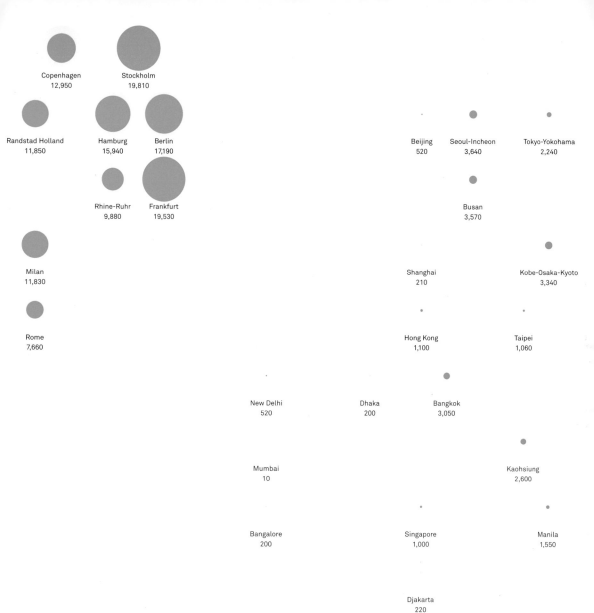

Copenhagen
12,950

Stockholm
19,810

Randstad Holland
11,850

Hamburg
15,940

Berlin
17,190

Rhine-Ruhr
9,880

Frankfurt
19,530

Milan
11,830

Rome
7,660

Beijing
520

Seoul-Incheon
3,640

Tokyo-Yokohama
2,240

Busan
3,570

Shanghai
210

Kobe-Osaka-Kyoto
3,340

Hong Kong
1,100

Taipei
1,060

New Delhi
520

Dhaka
200

Bangkok
3,050

Mumbai
10

Kaohsiung
2,600

Bangalore
200

Singapore
1,000

Manila
1,550

Djakarta
220

Metropolitan density

Population density in terms of number of inhabitants per km² of built-up area in the year 2000

demographia.com

Oslo
2,617

Seattle
1,098

Vancouver
1,523

Minneapolis-St.Paul
1,032

Toronto
3,311

Montreal
1,850

Boston
1,106

Antwerp-Brussels
1,900

San Francisco-Oakland
2,339

Chicago
1,629

Indianapolis
851

Detroit
1,195

Pittsburgh
794

Philadelphia
1,290

New York
1,760

Paris
3,545

Sacramento
1,457

Denver
1,536

St.Louis
968

Louisville
853

Cincinnati
864

Washington-Baltimore
1,560

Las Vegas
1,773

Memphis
914

Atlanta
688

Charlotte
674

Madrid
5,258

Barcelona
5,388

Phoenix
1,405

Dallas-Ft.Worth
1,375

Houston
1,140

New Orleans
1,967

Orlando
986

Lisbon
4,039

Mexico City
11,687

Miami
1,702

Bogotá
11,628

Rio de Janeiro
9,271

São Paulo
8,945

Santiago de Chile
5,069

Buenos Aires
4,042

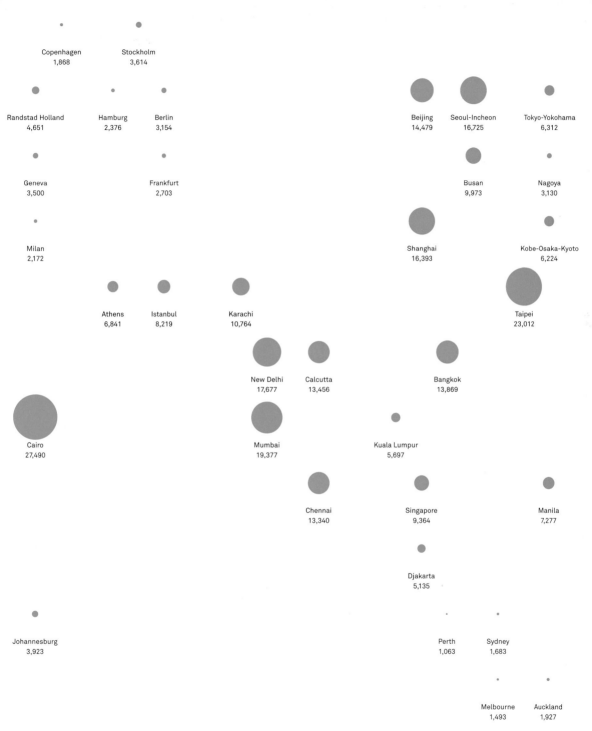

Copenhagen
1,868

Stockholm
3,614

Randstad Holland
4,651

Hamburg
2,376

Berlin
3,154

Beijing
14,479

Seoul-Incheon
16,725

Tokyo-Yokohama
6,312

Geneva
3,500

Frankfurt
2,703

Busan
9,973

Nagoya
3,130

Milan
2,172

Shanghai
16,393

Kobe-Osaka-Kyoto
6,224

Athens
6,841

Istanbul
8,219

Karachi
10,764

Taipei
23,012

New Delhi
17,677

Calcutta
13,456

Bangkok
13,869

Cairo
27,490

Mumbai
19,377

Kuala Lumpur
5,697

Chennai
13,340

Singapore
9,364

Manila
7,277

Djakarta
5,135

Johannesburg
3,923

Perth
1,063

Sydney
1,683

Melbourne
1,493

Auckland
1,927

Residential density

Population density in residential districts in terms of number of inhabitants per km² of residential area in the year 1985 demographia.com

Toronto
7,449

Montreal
6,652

Boston
3,151

London
4,172

San Francisco-Oakland
3,421

Chicago
3,300

Detroit
2,585

Philadelphia
3,302

Los Angeles
3,353

Barcelona
16,480

Houston
2,620

Mexico City
12,510

Bogotá
22,980

Lagos
41,752

Lima
17,514

Kinshasa
18,878

São Paulo
12,770

Santiago de Chile
14,199

Buenos Aires
7,762

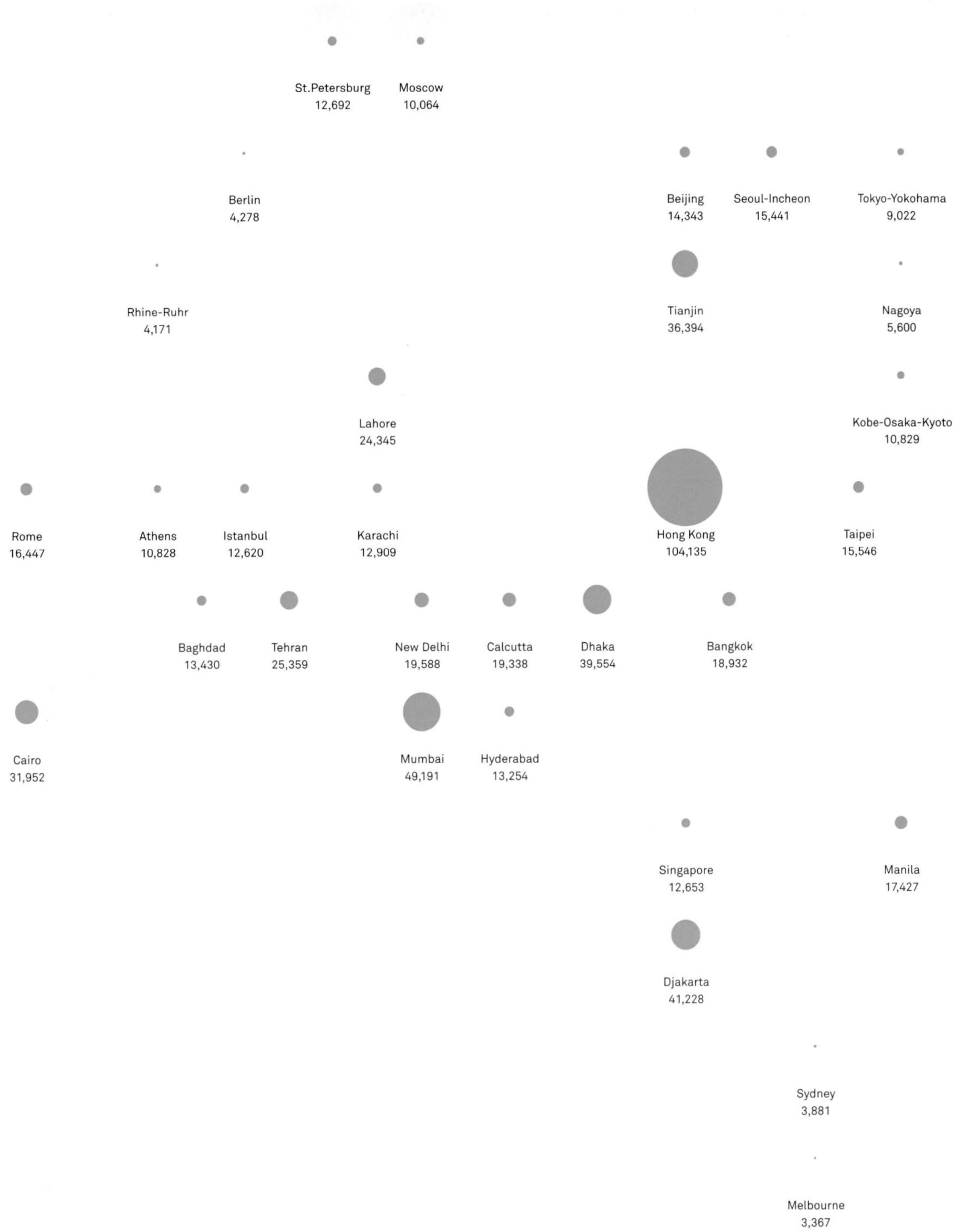

St.Petersburg
12,692

Moscow
10,064

Berlin
4,278

Beijing
14,343

Seoul-Incheon
15,441

Tokyo-Yokohama
9,022

Rhine-Ruhr
4,171

Tianjin
36,394

Nagoya
5,600

Lahore
24,345

Kobe-Osaka-Kyoto
10,829

Rome
16,447

Athens
10,828

Istanbul
12,620

Karachi
12,909

Hong Kong
104,135

Taipei
15,546

Baghdad
13,430

Tehran
25,359

New Delhi
19,588

Calcutta
19,338

Dhaka
39,554

Bangkok
18,932

Cairo
31,952

Mumbai
49,191

Hyderabad
13,254

Singapore
12,653

Manila
17,427

Djakarta
41,228

Sydney
3,881

Melbourne
3,367

Change in inhabitants (1970–1990

Increase or decrease in number of inhabitants in the metropolitan area in the year 1970–1990

demographia.com

Seattle
506,000

Vancouver
515,000

Minneapolis-St.Paul
379,000

Montreal
376,000

San Francisco-Oakland
642,000

Detroit
-274,000

Pittsburgh
-168,000

Philadelphia
201,000

Paris
1,416,000

Sacramento
455,000

Denver
471,000

St.Louis
64,000

Cincinnati
101,000

Washington-Baltimore
1,192,000

Los Angeles
3,051,000

Atlanta
985,000

Phoenix
1,143,000

Dallas-Ft.Worth
1,182,000

Houston
1,224,000

Miami
695,000

Seoul-Incheon
2,540,000

Tokyo-Yokohama
10,326,000

Hong Kong
1,586,000

Kuala Lumpur
1,572,000

Singapore
631,000

Manila
3,982,000

Djakarta
3,461,000

Perth
439,000

Sydney
731,000

Melbourne
519,000

Change in area (1970–1990)

Increase or decrease in built-up area in km² in the year 1970–1990

demographia.com

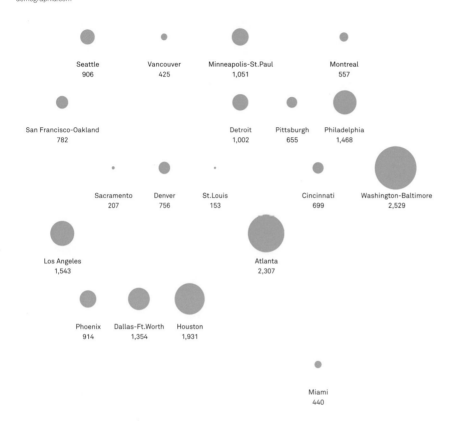

Seattle
906

Vancouver
425

Minneapolis-St.Paul
1,051

Montreal
557

San Francisco-Oakland
782

Detroit
1,002

Pittsburgh
655

Philadelphia
1,468

Paris
1,085

Sacramento
207

Denver
756

St.Louis
153

Cincinnati
699

Washington-Baltimore
2,529

Los Angeles
1,543

Atlanta
2,307

Phoenix
914

Dallas-Ft.Worth
1,354

Houston
1,931

Miami
440

Seoul-Incheon
88

Tokyo-Yokohama
2,664

Hong Kong
75

Kuala Lumpur
382

Singapore
153

Manila
185

Djakarta
213

Perth
498

Sydney
1,028

Melbourne
1,049

Change in density (1970–1990)

Increase or decrease in number of inhabitants in proportion to increase or decrease in urban built-up area (inhabitants/km²) in the year 1970–1990 demographia.com

Seattle
558

Vancouver
1,212

Minneapolis-St.Paul
361

Montreal
675

San Francisco-Oakland
821

Detroit
-273

Pittsburgh
-256

Philadelphia
137

Paris
1,308

Sacramento
2,198

Denver
623

St.Louis
418

Cincinnati
144

Washington-Baltimore
471

Los Angeles
1,977

Atlanta
427

Phoenix
1,251

Dallas-Ft.Worth
873

Houston
634

Miami
1,580

Seoul-Incheon
28,749

Tokyo-Yokohama
3,876

Hong Kong
21,147

Kuala Lumpur
4,115

Singapore
4,131

Manila
21,524

Djakarta
16,249

Perth
882

Sydney
711

Melbourne
495

Private vehicles

Market share of private vehicle traffic in total metropolitan traffic and transportation in the year 1991

publicpurpose.com

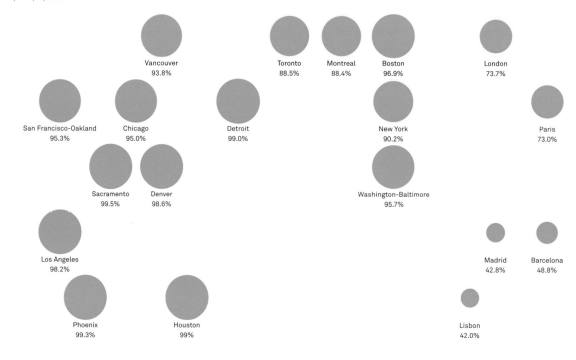

Vancouver
93.8%

Toronto
88.5%

Montreal
88.4%

Boston
96.9%

London
73.7%

San Francisco-Oakland
95.3%

Chicago
95.0%

Detroit
99.0%

New York
90.2%

Paris
73.0%

Sacramento
99.5%

Denver
98.6%

Washington-Baltimore
95.7%

Los Angeles
98.2%

Madrid
42.8%

Barcelona
48.8%

Phoenix
99.3%

Houston
99%

Lisbon
42.0%

Copenhagen
84.6%

Stockholm
46.0%

Randstad Holland
51.0%

Hamburg
60.0%

Berlin
54.0%

Rhine-Ruhr
71.0%

Frankfurt
65.0%

Seoul-Incheon
52.2%

Tokyo-Yokohama
51.0%

Hong Kong
38.9%

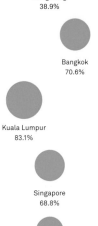

Bangkok
70.6%

Kuala Lumpur
83.1%

Singapore
68.8%

Manila
43.1%

Djakarta
62.7%

Perth
96.5%

Sydney
86.4%

Melbourne
93.4%

Commuting time

Average number of minutes an inhabitant needed to get to work in the metropolitan area in the year 1991, 1996, 2000 or 2002 asiaweek.com, bestplaces.net, demographia.com, Eurostat

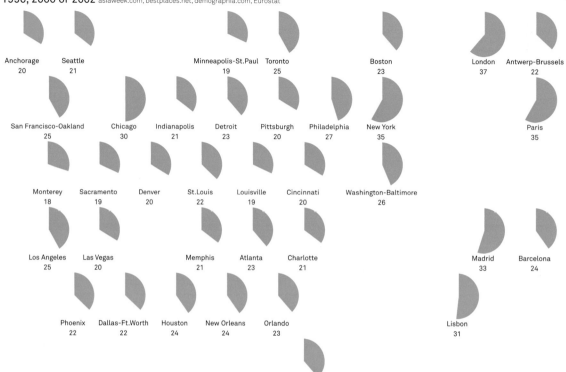

Anchorage
20

Seattle
21

Minneapolis-St.Paul
19

Toronto
25

Boston
23

London
37

Antwerp-Brussels
22

San Francisco-Oakland
25

Chicago
30

Indianapolis
21

Detroit
23

Pittsburgh
20

Philadelphia
27

New York
35

Paris
35

Monterey
18

Sacramento
19

Denver
20

St.Louis
22

Louisville
19

Cincinnati
20

Washington-Baltimore
26

Los Angeles
25

Las Vegas
20

Memphis
21

Atlanta
23

Charlotte
21

Madrid
33

Barcelona
24

Phoenix
22

Dallas-Ft.Worth
22

Houston
24

New Orleans
24

Orlando
23

Lisbon
31

Miami
23

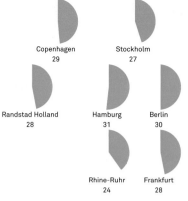

Copenhagen
29

Stockholm
27

Randstad Holland
28

Hamburg
31

Berlin
30

Rhine-Ruhr
24

Frankfurt
28

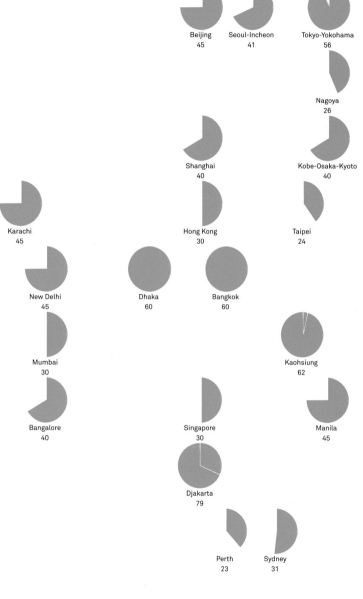

Beijing
45

Seoul-Incheon
41

Tokyo-Yokohama
56

Nagoya
26

Shanghai
40

Kobe-Osaka-Kyoto
40

Karachi
45

Hong Kong
30

Taipei
24

New Delhi
45

Dhaka
60

Bangkok
60

Mumbai
30

Kaohsiung
62

Bangalore
40

Singapore
30

Manila
45

Djakarta
79

Perth
23

Sydney
31

Road speed

Average speed on the metropolitan road network in km/hour in the year 1991

publicpurpose.com

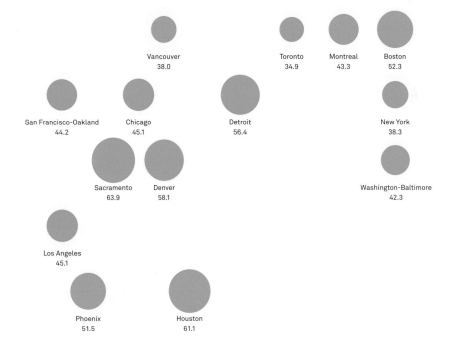

Vancouver
38.0

Toronto
34.9

Montreal
43.3

Boston
52.3

London
30.2

Antwerp-Brussels
37.8

San Francisco-Oakland
44.2

Chicago
45.1

Detroit
56.4

New York
38.3

Paris
25.7

Sacramento
63.9

Denver
58.1

Washington-Baltimore
42.3

Los Angeles
45.1

Phoenix
51.5

Houston
61.1

Copenhagen
34.0

Stockholm
26.7

Randstad Holland
34.9

Hamburg
29.9

Frankfurt
29.9

Seoul-Incheon
24.0

Tokyo-Yokohama
24.5

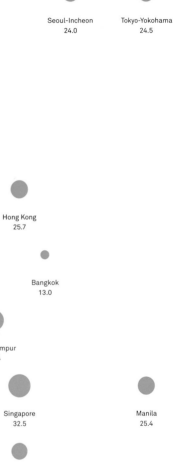

Hong Kong
25.7

Bangkok
13.0

Kuala Lumpur
29.4

Singapore
32.5

Manila
25.4

Djakarta
23.7

Perth
45.1

Sydney
37.0

Melbourne
45.1

Vehicle density

Average number of vehicle kilometres travelled per km² of metropolitan area in the year 1995

publicpurpose.com

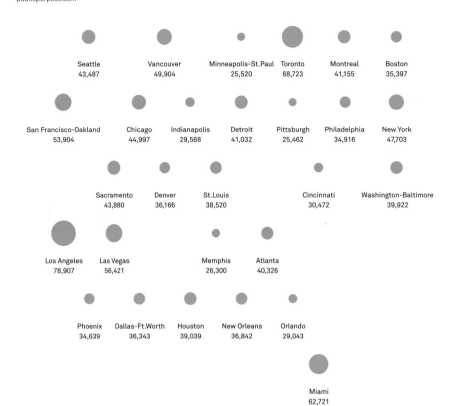

Seattle
43,487

Vancouver
49,904

Minneapolis-St.Paul
25,520

Toronto
68,723

Montreal
41,155

Boston
35,397

London
53,812

Antwerp-Brussels
110,913

San Francisco-Oakland
53,904

Chicago
44,997

Indianapolis
29,568

Detroit
41,032

Pittsburgh
25,462

Philadelphia
34,916

New York
47,703

Paris
51,821

Sacramento
43,880

Denver
36,166

St.Louis
38,520

Cincinnati
30,472

Washington-Baltimore
39,922

Los Angeles
78,907

Las Vegas
56,421

Memphis
26,300

Atlanta
40,326

Phoenix
34,639

Dallas-Ft.Worth
36,343

Houston
39,039

New Orleans
36,842

Orlando
29,043

Miami
62,721

Copenhagen
73,308

Stockholm
73,509

Randstad Holland
67,713

Hamburg
63,260

Frankfurt
84,744

Seoul-Incheon
141,864

Tokyo-Yokohama
73,795

Hong Kong
113,856

Bangkok
130,754

Kuala Lumpur
82,140

Singapore
85,564

Manila
48,907

Djakarta
74,810

Perth
25,804

Sydney
32,491

Melbourne
32,377

Passenger density

Average number of passenger kilometres travelled per kilometre of underground and light-rail network in the year 1990 demographia.com

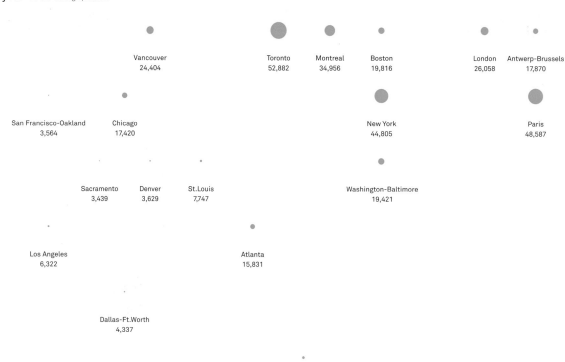

Vancouver
24,404

Toronto
52,882

Montreal
34,956

Boston
19,816

London
26,058

Antwerp-Brussels
17,870

San Francisco-Oakland
3,564

Chicago
17,420

New York
44,805

Paris
48,587

Sacramento
3,439

Denver
3,629

St.Louis
7,747

Washington-Baltimore
19,421

Los Angeles
6,322

Atlanta
15,831

Dallas-Ft.Worth
4,337

Miami
8,899

Stockholm
23,349

Randstad Holland
7,906

Hamburg
16,654

Seoul-Incheon
134,190

Tokyo-Yokohama
143,292

Frankfurt
10,429

Hong Kong
110,340

Singapore
58,520

Manila
133,444

Rail vehicle density

Average number of rail vehicle kilometres travelled per km² of metropolitan area in the year 1990

demographia.com

Seattle	Vancouver	Minneapolis-St.Paul	Toronto	Montreal	Boston	London	Antwerp-Brussels
74,763	168,506	26,857	252,709	327,717	79,089	942,892	756,371

San Francisco-Oakland	Chicago	Indianapolis	Detroit	Pittsburgh	Philadelphia	New York	Paris
131,649	117,737	13,734	32,246	43,355	70,679	238,081	527,163

Sacramento	Denver	St.Louis	Louisville	Cincinnati	Washington-Baltimore
27,684	63,966	32,722	29,900	28,636	72,701

Los Angeles	Las Vegas	Memphis	Atlanta	Charlotte
72,120	7,364	21,013	41,074	18,469

Phoenix	Dallas-Ft.Worth	Houston	New Orleans	Orlando
15,529	22,950	31,072	57,530	12,048

Miami
89,894

Copenhagen
623,976

Stockholm
1,139,158

Randstad Holland
473,939

Hamburg
455,121

Seoul-Incheon
4,490,766

Tokyo-Yokohama
1,021,163

Frankfurt
359,506

Hong Kong
6,795,116

Bangkok
2,652,288

Kuala Lumpur
469,872

Singapore
1,593,712

Manila
8,224,354

Djakarta
1,499,235

Perth
80,240

Sydney
254,345

Melbourne
119,749

Average January temperature

Average temperature in the metropolitan area in January in °C

weatherbase.com

Oslo
-6.7

Anchorage
-13.3

Seattle
2.2

Vancouver
0.6

Minneapolis-St.Paul
-15.6

Toronto
-9.4

Montreal
-13.9

Boston
-5.6

London
1.1

Antwerp-Brussels
0.6

San Francisco-Oakland
7.8

Chicago
-10.6

Indianapolis
-7.2

Detroit
-8.9

Pittsburgh
-6.7

Philadelphia
-4.4

New York
-3.3

Paris
1.1

Monterey
6.1

Sacramento
3.3

Denver
-8.9

St.Louis
-6.1

Louisville
-3.9

Cincinnati
-6.1

Washington-Baltimore
-4.4

Le Havre
1.1

Los Angeles
8.9

Las Vegas
1.1

Memphis
0.0

Atlanta
0.6

Charlotte
-0.6

Madrid
0.0

Barcelona
4.4

Phoenix
5.0

Dallas-Ft.Worth
1.1

Houston
5.0

New Orleans
6.1

Orlando
10.0

Lisbon
7.2

Mexico City
7.2

Miami
15.6

Tangier
8.3

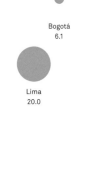

Bogotá
6.1

Lagos
26.1

Lima
20.0

Rio de Janeiro
23.3

Kinshasa
22.8

São Paulo
19.4

Santiago de Chile
12.2

Buenos Aires
17.8

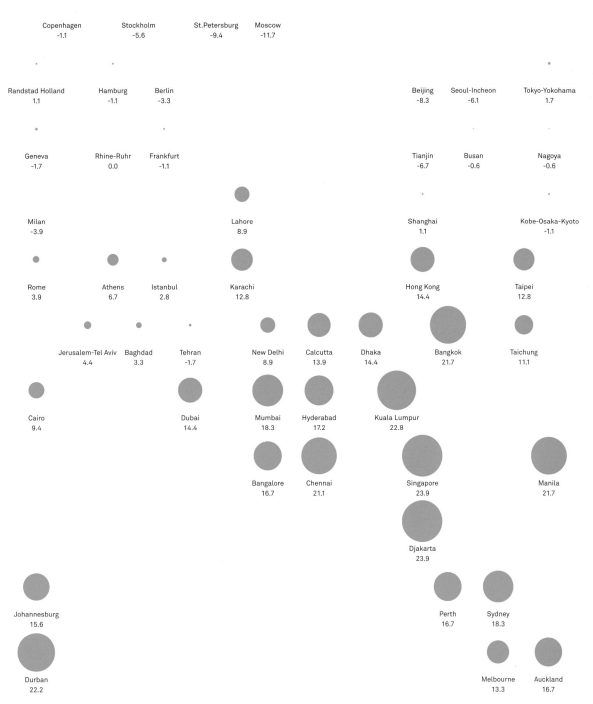

Copenhagen
-1.1

Stockholm
-5.6

St.Petersburg
-9.4

Moscow
-11.7

Randstad Holland
1.1

Hamburg
-1.1

Berlin
-3.3

Beijing
-8.3

Seoul-Incheon
-6.1

Tokyo-Yokohama
1.7

Geneva
-1.7

Rhine-Ruhr
0.0

Frankfurt
-1.1

Tianjin
-6.7

Busan
-0.6

Nagoya
-0.6

Milan
-3.9

Lahore
8.9

Shanghai
1.1

Kobe-Osaka-Kyoto
-1.1

Rome
3.9

Athens
6.7

Istanbul
2.8

Karachi
12.8

Hong Kong
14.4

Taipei
12.8

Jerusalem-Tel Aviv
4.4

Baghdad
3.3

Tehran
-1.7

New Delhi
8.9

Calcutta
13.9

Dhaka
14.4

Bangkok
21.7

Taichung
11.1

Cairo
9.4

Dubai
14.4

Mumbai
18.3

Hyderabad
17.2

Kuala Lumpur
22.8

Bangalore
16.7

Chennai
21.1

Singapore
23.9

Manila
21.7

Djakarta
23.9

Johannesburg
15.6

Perth
16.7

Sydney
18.3

Durban
22.2

Melbourne
13.3

Auckland
16.7

299

Average July temperature

Average temperature in the metropolitan area in July in °C

weatherbase.com

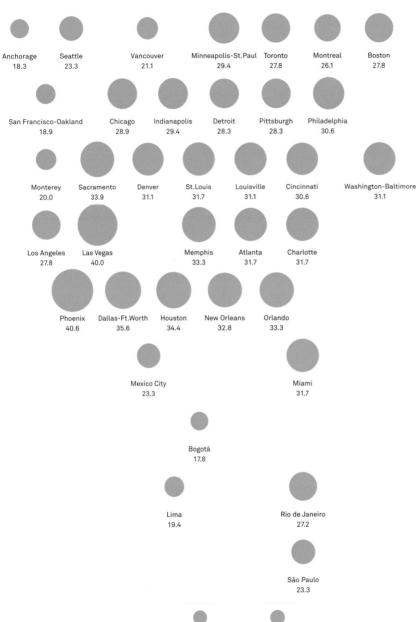

Anchorage
18.3

Seattle
23.3

Vancouver
21.1

Minneapolis-St.Paul
29.4

Toronto
27.8

Montreal
26.1

Boston
27.8

San Francisco-Oakland
18.9

Chicago
28.9

Indianapolis
29.4

Detroit
28.3

Pittsburgh
28.3

Philadelphia
30.6

Monterey
20.0

Sacramento
33.9

Denver
31.1

St.Louis
31.7

Louisville
31.1

Cincinnati
30.6

Washington-Baltimore
31.1

Los Angeles
27.8

Las Vegas
40.0

Memphis
33.3

Atlanta
31.7

Charlotte
31.7

Phoenix
40.6

Dallas-Ft.Worth
35.6

Houston
34.4

New Orleans
32.8

Orlando
33.3

Mexico City
23.3

Miami
31.7

Bogotá
17.8

Lima
19.4

Rio de Janeiro
27.2

São Paulo
23.3

Santiago de Chile
13.9

Buenos Aires
14.4

Oslo
21.7

London
21.7

Antwerp-Brussels
21.7

Paris
23.9

Le Havre
18.3

Madrid
32.2

Barcelona
27.2

Lisbon
27.8

Tangier
28.3

Lagos
26.1

Kinshasa
26.1

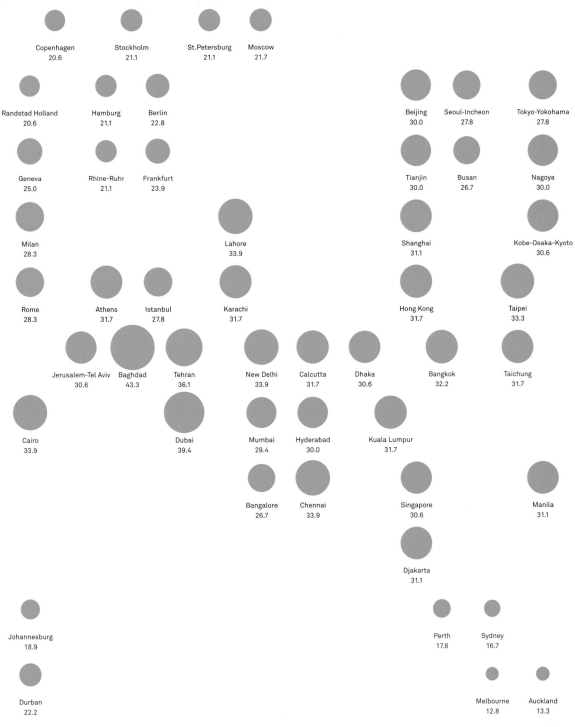

Copenhagen
20.6

Stockholm
21.1

St.Petersburg
21.1

Moscow
21.7

Randstad Holland
20.6

Hamburg
21.1

Berlin
22.8

Beijing
30.0

Seoul-Incheon
27.8

Tokyo-Yokohama
27.8

Geneva
25.0

Rhine-Ruhr
21.1

Frankfurt
23.9

Tianjin
30.0

Busan
26.7

Nagoya
30.0

Milan
28.3

Lahore
33.9

Shanghai
31.1

Kobe-Osaka-Kyoto
30.6

Rome
28.3

Athens
31.7

Istanbul
27.8

Karachi
31.7

Hong Kong
31.7

Taipei
33.3

Jerusalem-Tel Aviv
30.6

Baghdad
43.3

Tehran
36.1

New Delhi
33.9

Calcutta
31.7

Dhaka
30.6

Bangkok
32.2

Taichung
31.7

Cairo
33.9

Dubai
39.4

Mumbai
29.4

Hyderabad
30.0

Kuala Lumpur
31.7

Bangalore
26.7

Chennai
33.9

Singapore
30.6

Manila
31.1

Djakarta
31.1

Johannesburg
18.9

Perth
17.8

Sydney
16.7

Durban
22.2

Melbourne
12.8

Auckland
13.3

Pollution

Total pollution (NOX, CO and VOC) in tonnes in the metropolitan area in the year 1990

demographia.com

Toronto
869.1

Boston
324.7

London
552.1

Antwerp-Brussels
696.1

San Francisco-Oakland
382.6

Chicago
374.1

Detroit
379.2

New York
439.8

Paris
456.8

Monterey
257.4

Denver
354.1

Washington-Baltimore
310.4

Los Angeles
498.1

Phoenix
222.0

Houston
77.6

Copenhagen
371.0

Stockholm
1,339.4

Randstad Holland
257.5

Hamburg
297.3

Seoul-Incheon
1,392.3

Tokyo-Yokohama
216.2

Frankfurt
468.3

Hong Kong
1,070.7

Bangkok
1,664.5

Kuala Lumpur
728.2

Manila
1,741.7

Djakarta
1,422.0

Perth
245.1

Sydney
425.5

Melbourne
328.2

Metropolitan airports

Number of international civilian airports in the metropolitan area

Oslo

Anchorage Seattle Vancouver Minneapolis-St.Paul Toronto Montreal Boston London Antwerp-Brussels

San Francisco-Oakland Chicago Indianapolis Detroit Pittsburgh Philadelphia New York Paris

Monterey Sacramento Denver St.Louis Louisville Cincinnati Washington-Baltimore Le Havre

Los Angeles Las Vegas Memphis Atlanta Charlotte Madrid Barcelona

Phoenix Dallas-Ft.Worth Houston New Orleans Orlando Lisbon

Mexico City Miami Tangier

Bogotá Lagos

Lima Rio de Janeiro Kinshasa

São Paulo

Santiago de Chile Buenos Aires

Copenhagen

Stockholm

St.Petersburg

Moscow

Randstad Holland

Hamburg

Berlin

Beijing

Seoul-Incheon

Tokyo-Yokohama

Geneva

Rhine-Ruhr

Frankfurt

Tianjin

Busan

Nagoya

Milan

Lahore

Shanghai

Kobe-Osaka-Kyoto

Rome

Athens

Istanbul

Karachi

Hong Kong

Taipei

Jerusalem-Tel Aviv

Baghdad

Tehran

New Delhi

Calcutta

Dhaka

Bangkok

Taichung

Cairo

Dubai

Mumbai

Hyderabad

Kuala Lumpur

Kaohsiung

Bangalore

Chennai

Singapore

Manila

Djakarta

Johannesburg

Perth

Sydney

Durban

Melbourne

Auckland

305

Inhabitants per airport

Number of inhabitants per airport in the metropolitan area

Oslo
390,000

Anchorage
339,286

Seattle
452,000

Vancouver
353,000

Minneapolis-St.Paul
477,800

Toronto
607,778

Montreal
1,072,000

Boston
646,111

London
2,324,167

Antwerp-Brussels
1,241,667

San Francisco-Oakland
1,252,333

Chicago
1,061,000

Indianapolis
110,818

Detroit
451,250

Pittsburgh
250,429

Philadelphia
601,000

New York
3,109,571

Paris
1,514,286

Monterey
8,199

Sacramento
232,167

Denver
496,000

St.Louis
692,667

Louisville
288,000

Cincinnati
375,750

Washington-Baltimore
988,750

Le Havre
135,848

Los Angeles
2,157,875

Las Vegas
438,000

Memphis
972,000

Atlanta
875,000

Charlotte
189,750

Madrid
2,650,000

Barcelona
1,883,000

Phoenix
323,000

Dallas-Ft.Worth
964,167

Houston
647,000

New Orleans
201,800

Orlando
115,700

Lisbon
3,000,000

Mexico City
6,540,000

Miami
881,500

Tangier
124,287

Bogotá
6,990,000

Lagos
5,015,000

Lima
7,420,000

Rio de Janeiro
3,603,333

Kinshasa
1,916,667

São Paulo
5,906,667

Santiago de Chile
2,020,333

Buenos Aires
4,463,333

On-line sources

123World.com (2004)
  http://www.123world.com/stockexchanges
About.com (2002)
  http://geography.about.com
Adam Mickiewicz University (2002)
  http://hum.amu.edu.pl/`zbzw/glob/
  glob1.htm
Aircraft Charter World (2004)
  http://www.aircraft-charter-world.com
Airlines of the Web (2004)
  http://flyaow.com
Airports Council International (2004)
  http://www.airports.org
Aloe Front Page (2003)
  http://www.rev.net/~aloe
Asiaweek.com (2002)
  http://www.asiaweek.com
Brinkhoff, T. (2004)
  http://www.citypopulation.de
British Telecom Connected Earth (2004)
  http://www.connected-earth.com
Bureau of Transportation Statistics (2004)
  http://www.bts.gov
Business Week Online (2004)
  http://www.businessweek.com
CBS (2002)
  http://www.cbs.nl
CIA (2002)
  http://www.cia.gov
De Jong, T. M. (2003)
  http://www.bk.tudelft.nl/urbanism/
  TEAM/
Demographia Network / Wendell Cox
  Consulting (2002)
  http://www.demographia.com
ER Mapper Image Web Server (2003)
  http://www.earthetc.com
EuroMeteo (2002)
  http://www.eurometeo.com
Europa Technologies (2004)
  http://www.europa-tech.com/gallery.htm
European Commission Urban Audit (2004)
  http://europa.eu.int/comm/
  regional_policy/urban2/urban/audit/
  src/intro.html
Eurostat (2002)
  http://www.eurostat.com
Falling Rain Geonomics (2004)
  http://www.fallingrain.com/world/
Federal Aviation Administration (2004)
  http://www.fly.faa.gov/flyfaa/
  usmap.jsp
FltPlan Flight planning for General Aviation
  (2004)
  http://www.fltplan.com
Forbes Online (2004)
  http://www.forbes.com
Free Travel Tips (2004)
  http://www.freetraveltips.com/
  index.html
GaWC Loughborough University (2003)
  http://www.lboro.ac.uk/gawc/index.html
Geo Community (2002)
  http://www.geocomm.com

Geocover Stennis Space Centre (2004)
  https://zulu.ssc.nasa.gov
Geodan IT (2004)
  http://www.geodan.nl/nl/geodan/geodan/
  index.htm
Geohive Global Statistics (2004)
  http://www.geohive.com
Geography Network (2002)
  http://www.geographynetwork.com
Great Circle Mapper Flight Planning (2004)
  http://gc.kls2.com/faq.html
Greenwich Mean Time (2004)
  http://www.greenwichmeantime.com
Hoovers Business Information (2004)
  http://www.hoovers.com
Infomine (2002)
  http://www.infomine.com
International Airport Council (2002)
  http://www.airports.org
Korea Container Terminal Authority (2004)
  http://www.kca.or.kr
Map 4 Travel (2004)
  http://www.map4travel.com
Map24 (2004)
  http://www.map24.com
Mapquest (2004)
  http://www.mapquest.com
MARAD Marine Information (2002)
  http://www.marad.gov
Microsoft MSN Encarta
  http://encarta.msn.com
Nationmaster.com (2004)
  http://www.nationmaster.com/index.php
Perry-Castañeda Library Map Collection
  (2004)
  http://www.lib.utexas.edu/maps/
  map_sites/cities_sites.html
RESGI Central Michigan University (2004)
  http://webs.cmich.edu/resgi
Smithsonian Air and Space Museum (2004)
  http://www.nasm.si.edu
Sperling's Best Places (2002)
  http://www.bestplaces.net
Swiss Federal Institute of Technology library
  map collection (2004)
  http://www.maps.ethz.ch/
  map_catalogue-general2.html
Telegeography (2004)
  http://www.telegeography.com
The International Trade Data System – ITDS
  (2004)
  http://www.itds.treas.gov/
  scheduleK1.html#A
The Public Purpose / Wendell Cox
  Consultancy (2002)
  http://www.publicpurpose.com/
  index.html
United Nations (2002)
  http://www.un.org
United Nations Human Settlement
  Programme UN-HABITAT (2004),
  http://www.unchs.org
United Nations University (2004)
  http://www.inweh.unu.edu/inweh

United States Census Bureau (2004)
  http://www.census.gov
Weatherbase (2004)
  http://www.weatherbase.com
Whyfiles.org (2004)
  http://whyfiles.org/131fresh_water/
  2.html
World Bank (2002)
  http://www.worldbank.org
Worldstats.org (2002)
  http://www.worldstats.org
Yamakawa, T. Asia Broadband Programme
  (2002)
  http://www.oecd.org/dataoecd/15/29/
  1936546.ppt

Acknowledgements

This book is dedicated to Stefan Atzema, a fantastic friend and travelling companion during our many 'voyages of discovery' over the last seven years.
This atlas could not have come into being without the generous support of the Netherlands Architecture Fund, Rotterdam and the Van Eesteren-Fluck & Van Lohuizen Foundation, The Hague. Their trust and financial assistance were indispensable in producing this book.
In addition, the Faculty of Architecture at Delft University of Technology played an important part in creating this atlas. Both its staff and its resources were of great value, in particular Prof. Joost Schrijnen and Ali Guney MSc. Arch. of the Urban Architecture research group, who provided structure in the making of this atlas. My thanks and appreciation are also due to Prof. Dirk Frieling and Prof. Taeke de Jong for their professional knowledge and enthusiasm.
The Delft School of Design at the Faculty of Architecture, headed by Prof. Arie Graafland, was of immeasurable value. The academic climate was pleasant and instructive to work in, providing room for substantive cooperation, reflection and discussion.
Lastly, I would like to thank my publisher, designer Joost Grootens, my colleague Egbert Stolk and the drawing and data crew Suzanne van der Pluym, Annick van Tilburg, Sarah Jansen, Uli Budde, Menno Brood and Renata Alvares for their unstinting cooperation, expert insights and professional approach to thinking and working, which have resulted in this contemporary atlas of metropolitan areas.

Arjen van Susteren

Scientific Committee

Luuk Boelens, Professor of Spatial Planning at the University of Utrecht, The Netherlands
Willem Salet, Professor of Urban and Regional Planning at the University of Amsterdam, The Netherlands
Frank Werner, Professor of History and Theory of Architecture at Wuppertal University, Germany

Credits

Map drawing and data input by Arjen van Susteren, Renata Alvares, Menno Brouwer, Uli Budde, Sarah Jansen, Suzanne van der Pluym, Annick van Tilburg
Translation by Bookmakers, Nijmegen
Book and map design by Joost Grootens
Printed by Lecturis, Eindhoven

First edition: 2005
Second edition: 2007

© 2005, 2007 010 Publishers, Arjen van Susteren (Coolhaven Urban Engineers), Rotterdam
www.010publishers.nl
www.coolhavenue.com

ISBN 978-90-6450-548-5

Literature

Castells, M. (1997) The Power of Identity (Oxford) Blackwell Publishers

Chandler, T. (1987) Four Thousand Years of Urban Growth (Lewiston, N.Y) St. David's University Press

Clark, D. (1996) Urban World/Global City (London) Routledge

Cooper, A. (1989) Times Atlas of the Sea (London) Times Books

De Jong, T.M., Van der Voort, D.J.M. (2002) Ways to study (Delft) DUP-Science

James, H. (2001) The end of globalisation (Cambridge) Harvard Press

Kenworthy, J., Laube, F.B., Newman, P., Barter, P., Raad, T., Poboon, C., Guia, B. Jr. (1999) An International Sourcebook of Automobile Dependence in Cities 1960–1990 (Boulder) University Press of Colorado

Koolhaas, R. (2000) Mutations (Bordeaux) Arc en Rêve

Lerup, L. (2000) After the City (Cambridge) The MIT Press

McNeill, J.R., McNeill, William H. (2003) The Human Web (New York) W.W. Norton & Company

n/a (1973) SCIAM: Cities: their origin, growth & human impact (San Francisco) Scientific American

Noordhoff, W. (1981) De Grote Bosatlas 49th edition (Groningen) Wolters Noordhoff

Noordhoff, W. (2001) De Grote Bosatlas 52nd edition (Groningen) Wolters Noordhoff

Noordhoff, W. (2004) De Wereld Bosatlas (Groningen) Wolters Noordhoff

Rand McNally (2004) Atlas of the Road (Skokie) Rand McNally

Regio Randstad (2005) Randstad Holland in Europe/Randstad Monitor (Utrecht) Regio Randstad

Ruimtelijk Planbureau (2005) Atlas of Airports in Northwest Europe (The Hague) RPB

Sassen, S. (2001) The Global City, Princeton University Press

Sassen, S. ed. (2001) Global Networks, Linked Cities, Routledge

Times Atlas of the World (2000) (London) Times Books

Wallerstein, I. (1978) Europese wereldeconomie in de 16e eeuw (Nieuwkoop) Heureka

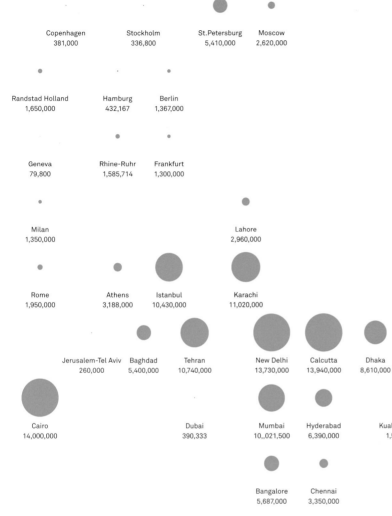

Copenhagen
381,000

Stockholm
336,800

St.Petersburg
5,410,000

Moscow
2,620,000

Randstad Holland
1,650,000

Hamburg
432,167

Berlin
1,367,000

Beijing
6,580,000

Seoul-Incheon
11,438,500

Tokyo-Yokohama
16,595,000

Geneva
79,800

Rhine-Ruhr
1,585,714

Frankfurt
1,300,000

Tianjin
9,920,000

Busan
912,500

Nagoya
8,837,000

Milan
1,350,000

Lahore
2,960,000

Shanghai
6,790,000

Kobe-Osaka-Kyoto
4,232,500

Rome
1,950,000

Athens
3,188,000

Istanbul
10,430,000

Karachi
11,020,000

Hong Kong
2,295,000

Taipei
3,630,000

Jerusalem-Tel Aviv
260,000

Baghdad
5,400,000

Tehran
10,740,000

New Delhi
13,730,000

Calcutta
13,940,000

Dhaka
8,610,000

Bangkok
3060,000

Taichung
491,847

Cairo
14,000,000

Dubai
390,333

Mumbai
10,,021,500

Hyderabad
6,390,000

Kuala Lumpur
1,512,500

Kaohsiung
1,494,457

Bangalore
5,687,000

Chennai
3,350,000

Singapore
832,600

Manila
7,070,000

Djakarta
6,665,000

Johannesburg
1,382,500

Perth
670,000

Sydney
1,332,333

Durban
705,883

Melbourne
1,122,333

Auckland
1,290,000